MEDIA DEFINITIONS
of COLD WAR REALITY

THE CARIBBEAN BASIN, 1953-1992

WALTER C. SODERLUND

Media Definitions of Cold War Reality: The Caribbean Basin, 1953-1992
Walter C. Soderlund

First published in 2001 by
Canadian Scholars' Press Inc.
180 Bloor Street West, Suite 1202
Toronto, Ontario
M5S 2V6

Canadian Scholars' Press gratefully acknowledges financial assistance for our publishing activities from the Ontario Arts Council, The Canada Council for the Arts, and the Government of Canada through the Book Publishing Industry Development Program.

Canadian Cataloguing in Publication Data

Soderlund, W. C. (Walter C.)
    Media definitions of Cold War reality : the Caribbean basin 1953 to 1992

Includes bibliographical references.
ISBN 1-55130-200-4

1. Cold War in mass media. 2. Caribbean Area – In mass media. 3. Carribbean Area – Politics and government – 1945-   . 4. Mass media – United States – History – 20th century. 5. Mass media – Canada – History – 20th century. 6. Mission media – Political aspects – Caribbian Area. 7. Mass media – United States – Influence. I. Title.

Marketing: Linda Palmer, Renée Knapp
Editing and proofreading: Lu Cormier
Production editor: Rebecka Sheffield
Interior design: Brad Horning
Cover design: Rebecka Sheffield

01   02   03   04   05   06   07   7   6   5   4   3   2   1

Printed and bound in Canada

 Canada Council for the Arts   **Conseil des Arts du Canada**

Contributors

E. Donald Briggs (Ph.D., University of London) is Professor Emeritus of Political Science at the University of Windsor, from which he retired in 1999. His major research interests lie in the area of international theory, especially with respect to foreign policy decision making. He is currently working on a research project dealing with problems of UN peace enforcement in Africa during the post–Cold War era.

Robert M. Krause retired from the Department of Political Science at the University of Windsor in 1966. During his career he specialized in teaching Canadian Politics and Public Administration. He developed the highly successful Public Management Internship Program at Windsor and continued to guide the program following his retirement. He is especially interested in problems of governance in small and micro-states.

Ralph C. Nelson is Professor Emeritus of Political Science at the University of Windsor where he taught Political Theory. Holding a Ph.D. in Philosophy from the University of Notre Dame, he is especially interested in democratic theory. In this context, he has followed events in Haiti closely since the end of the Duvalier dictatorship in 1986 and continues to monitor Haiti's uncertain path toward democratic development.

The late *Ian C. Pemberton* (Ph.D., University of Western Ontario) taught Diplomatic History at the University of Windsor until his retirement in 1996. He enjoyed a reputation as a brilliant lecturer, and for many years anchored the Department of History's contribution to

the University's International Relations Program. His research
interest focused on Canadian-American relations and American
diplomacy, especially around the time of the Spanish-American
War.

Richard G. Price, former Dean of Students and Professor of Political
Science at the University of Windsor retired in 1997. His major
research areas were political advertising, legislative behavior and
political leadership. Since his retirement he has remained active,
consulting on a number of areas related to continuing and distance
education, as well as fundraising.

Walter C. Soderlund (Ph. D., University of Michigan) began teaching
Political Science at the University of Windsor in 1968, and over
the years researched collaboratively with all of the contributors
included in this book. Skilled in content analysis, his research
and teaching interests include both American foreign policy and
mass media. The research included in this volume reflects the
convergence of these interests.

Stuart H. Surlin (Ph.D., Michigan State) was Professor of
Communication Studies at the University of Windsor and passed
away in 1995, midway through a brilliant career in research and
teaching. He was an expert in quantitative research methods and
data analysis and, following a Fulbright Fellowship to Jamaica,
developed a strong interest in the Caribbean, especially its culture
and mass media. This complemented his earlier interest in the role
of minorities in mass media.

Ronald H. Wagenberg, Professor Emeritus of Political Science at the
University of Windsor, retired in 1996 following a distinguished
career in teaching and public service spanning over thirty years.
Although the majority of his research and writing was in the area
of Canadian politics, he obtained his Ph.D. in International
Relations from the London School of Economics, and he maintains
a continuing interest in this area.

Acknowledgments

I should like to thank the various co-investigators and co-authors who have worked with me over the years as well as those organizations that provided the funds that permitted me to pursue the line of research dealing with media coverage of the Cold War as it played out in the Western Hemisphere.

A number of my colleagues, including Ralph Nelson, Ron Wagenberg, Don Briggs, Richard Price, Robert Krause and the late Stuart Surlin and Ian Pemberton, are listed as co-authors of various chapters. As well, Carmen Schmitt, a talented Chilean journalist, worked with me on a study that appears as part of chapter 5. Working with other people adds a social dimension to academic labor, and I consider all of these scholars friends as well as co-authors. In addition, I should like to recognize the efforts of the many research assistants who worked for me over the years, all of whom are acknowledged in the chapters they worked on. Walt Romanow, while not involved in Latin American and Caribbean research per se, contributed immeasurably to my understanding of mass media, and Ivelaw Griffith of Florida International University did much to make my 1997–98 sabbatical a successful enterprise.

The staff of the Word Processing Centre at the University of Windsor — Lucia Brown, Diane Dupuis, Claire Spekkens and Lorraine Cantin — toiled countless hours on multi-iterations of the papers and articles that now comprise this book. As well, Valerie Allard and Barbara Faria, secretaries in the Department of Political Science, offered me much needed help at various critical occasions. I would like to thank the various people at Canadian Scholars' Press who worked on the publication of this book: managing editor Ruth Bradley-St-Cyr, production editor Rebecka Sheffield, and copy editor Lu Cormier.

Much of the material that appears in the book was first presented at two sets of conferences: the Annual Meetings of the Speech Communication Association of Puerto Rico and the International/ Intercultural Communication Conferences sponsored by the School of Communication at the University of Miami. Both organizations are owed debts of gratitude for providing venues where this research could be critiqued by interested and knowledgeable scholars.

Finally, I owe thanks to the organizations that have funded the research upon which the book is based. Chief among these is the Social Sciences and Humanities Research Council of Canada (SSRHC), which under grant 410-91-0021 funded the research reported in chapters 1, 2, 3, 7, 11, 12 , 13 and 14. The Canadian Institute for International Peace and Security (CIIPS), during its brief existence, funded the research reported in chapters 4 and 8. The studies that comprise chapters 5, 6, 8 and 10 are the products of unfunded research. Of course neither of the organizations acknowledged bears any responsibility for the analysis done and conclusions reached.

Abbreviations

AP	Associated Press (United States)
AFP	Agence France Presse
ARENA	National Republican Alliance Party (El Salvador)
CEP	Provisional Electoral Council (Haiti)
CNG	National Council of Government (Haiti)
CIA	Central Intelligence Agency (United States)
CIIPS	Canadian Institute for International Peace and Security
CP	Canadian Press
FMLN	Faribundo Marti National Liberation Front (El Salvador)
FSLN	Sandinista National Liberation Front (Nicaragua)
GULP	Grenadian United Labour Party
IMF	International Monetary Fund
NATO	North Atlantic Treaty Organization
NORAD	North American Aerospace Defense Command
NNP	New National Party (Grenada)
OAS	Organization of American States
PD	percentage difference
PDC	Christian Democratic Party (El Salvador)
PDF	Panamanian Defense Force
PNC	People's National Congress (Guyana)
PPP	People's Progressive Party (Guyana)
PRG	People's Revolutionary Government (Grenada)

SSHRC	Social Sciences and Humanities Research Council (Canada)
UFCO	United Fruit Company
UN	United Nations
UNO	United Opposition Union (Nicaragua)
UPI	United Press International (United States)

Contents

Part I
The Initial Challenge:
British Guiana, Guatemala, Cuba
and the Dominican Republic

Part II
The Second Wave:
Nicaragua, El Salvador and Grenada

Part III
The End of the Cold War,
and Democratic Transitions:
Haiti, El Salvador, Nicaragua, Panama and Cuba

Introduction

It is not always possible to remember precisely when the idea for a book came into one's head. I had been working on North American media coverage of various dimensions of the Cold War since the early 1980s, and while this research was carried out as a series of discrete studies, at one time or another I did probably entertain the possibility of a book. It was, however, at the 1995 meeting of the Caribbean Studies Association in Curaçao that John Lent asked me why the various papers he had seen over the years had not been put together in the form of a book. John is a very persuasive individual and from that time on, the idea of a book on media coverage of the Cold War in the Caribbean Basin remained fixed among my priorities.

While I continued to serve as Head of the Department of Political Science at the University of Windsor until the summer of 1997, as well as being involved in other writing projects, not much was done on the idea before the fall of that year when my sabbatical leave at Florida International University began. With precious uninterrupted time on my hands, over that fall I thought through the organization of the book and, during the ensuing winter, I selected from among a variety of papers and journal articles the most appropriate pieces and began the process of editing. It was at this point that I sincerely wished that I had originally envisioned all the various research projects that now were to comprise the volume as a coherent whole, employing the same theoretical framework and research methods throughout to study the same matched set of media outlets. But research money and time available varied considerably over the years when the different studies were done. While there is underlying theoretical and methodological coherence to some sections of the book, no amount of editing (at least honest editing) could impose an overall homogeneity on a structure that lacked it at the outset.

This said, while the media studied, the topics examined and the methods used to study them varied, essentially what we have in the chapters that follow is a focus on North American media content (newspaper and television) dealing with a wide range of Cold War events that occurred in the Caribbean Basin. Moreover, that content is given meaning through the use of a number of key communication/ political science theories and concepts, serving either to underpin the studies (agenda setting, framing, image development and change, and democratic transitions) or as the subject of empirical tests (balance theory, media imperialism, demonstration elections, and the propaganda model of state-press relations).

While overall coherence of the volume may be somewhat wanting, the same cannot be said for its scope — a full forty-year period, covering almost the entire span of the Cold War, is included. While the Cold War has imprecise boundaries with respect to both its beginning and its end, scholars agree that it began with events in Europe between 1946 and 1948 and ended with events in the same part of the world between 1988 and 1992. While it cannot be said that the Western Hemisphere has been a main venue for the worldwide struggle between the U.S. and the U.S.S.R., the Caribbean Basin (especially Cuba) was the area in the hemisphere of primary contention. Of course, with respect to Central America and the Caribbean, U.S. policy had "been interventionary since the beginning of the republic, at least since the Monroe Doctrine in 1823" (Falk 1992, p. 132).

Part I of the book begins with a chapter dealing with events in then British Guiana and Guatemala, which introduced the Cold War to the Western Hemisphere in the early 1950s, and goes on to consider seminal events in Cuba and the Dominican Republic. In Part II, the new hemispheric challenge posed by the 1979 Nicaraguan Revolution including its impact on El Salvador and Grenada during the decade of the 1980s is examined. Treated here are the revolutionary period in Nicaragua itself, the early years of the insurgency in El Salvador, the 1983 U.S. invasion of Grenada, and the 1984 elections in all three countries. Part III is composed of chapters dealing with the related phenomena of the winding down of the Cold War and transitions to democracy, which during the late 1980s and early 1990s occurred everywhere in the hemisphere except Cuba. Included here are studies of the 1989/1990 elections in El Salvador and Nicaragua, elections in Haiti from 1987 to 1990, and the 1989 U.S. invasion of Panama. In addition there is a study of TV news coverage of Cuba during the transition from the Cold War to whatever has replaced it. In one form or another, press interpretations of virtually every major Cold War event that impacted Central America and the Caribbean are included. While most chapters focus on newspaper coverage, three chapters deal with television, the most powerful generator of "images of reality."

A special feature of the book is a comparison of how major political leaders involved in Cold War events were portrayed in Western media. In various chapters, data are presented dealing with the media images of leaders such as Cheddi Jagan, Jacobo Arbenz Guzmán and Francisco Caamaño Deño in the 1950s and 1960s; Roberto D'Aubuisson, Daniel Ortega and Maurice Bishop in the first half of the 1980s; Manuel Noriega and Jean-Bertrand Aristide in the late 1980s and early 1990s; plus Fidel Castro from the entire period 1953 to 1992. Based on the actual descriptive language found in reporting on these leaders, in the Conclusion differences in journalistic treatment afforded to leaders on the left, center and the right of the political spectrum are analyzed.

Editing one's own work, in some cases nearly fifteen years after a piece was first written, is an interesting and somewhat humbling experience. Sometimes, thankfully, I found that I was right — other times that I was wrong. I resisted rewriting that would make me and co-authors appear to be more wise than we were at the time of the original writing. I did not, however, resist taking the figurative blue pencil to text to clarify meaning, reduce the number of tables, eliminate repetition between chapters and add some references. In a number of cases, individual papers were combined to form single chapters.

Chapters were not written in the order in which they appear. By and large, chapters in Part II (with the exception of chapter 7) were written first, most of these without any funding, while two had support from CIIPS. With the aid of a substantial research grant from the Social Sciences and Humanities Research Council of Canada, chapters in Part III were for the most part written next, while those comprising Part I were the last to be completed.

While context is provided for every country and event included in the book, the actual studies are without exception data based and are not intended to argue a position one way or the other, either with respect to the Cold War itself or press performance in reporting it. Accordingly, research was designed to capture as accurately as possible how mass media outlets in the United States and Canada (and to a lesser extent Great Britain) reported on and interpreted various Cold War events and actors to their audiences. While I attempted to take a neutral stance with respect to the research, I realize that this is at best an uncertain enterprise. After all, I attended university in the United States during the late 1950s and served as an officer in the U.S. Air Force during the Cuban Missile Crisis. Aware of the effects of political socialization, I am reconciled to the fact that at times my own political leanings may be more obvious to readers than I would have hoped. In order to reduce possible subjectivity, all the studies were designed to include various intercoder crosschecks. In cases of leader profiles based on descriptive language, all words and phrases recorded, along with their panel codings of positive, negative or neutral/ambiguous interpretations, are included as appendices in the chapters within which they are presented.

The Cold War conditioned not only the formative period of my life, but it also extended over the major portion of my teaching and research career. In addition to suggesting one of the major lines of research that I have pursued, it has provided the context for much of my teaching in the areas of U.S. foreign policy, international relations in Latin America and the Caribbean, and comparative politics of Latin America and the Caribbean. Although the Cold War is over, in some obvious and many subtle ways it continues to intrude on United States relations with countries in the Caribbean Basin, a primary example being the saga of Elian Gonzalez over the winter and spring of 1999–2000. Thus, an understanding of what Americans were told regarding the Cold War and its various participants over the years is of more than historical interest. In retrospect, who won and who lost wanes in importance. It is the processes involved in how the various events unfolded and were interpreted that raise our interest. Of course, mass media continue to define the reality of the post–Cold War world, and an understanding of how this process works is vital to an informed citizenry forced to deal with a complex world.

Part I

The Initial Challenge: British Guiana, Guatemala, Cuba and the Dominican Republic

Chapter 1

The Arrival of the Cold War in the Western Hemisphere: British Guiana 1953 and Guatemala 1954[1]

WALTER C. SODERLUND AND E. DONALD BRIGGS

A s the world moved into the 1990s, the Cold War was in the process of passing into history. Over its forty-year duration countless battles were fought and lives lost by partisans on both sides of the ideological divide. Although, with the exception of Cuba, the Western Hemisphere was never at the center of the Cold War, attempts by the Soviet Union to extend its influence into the hemisphere and countermeasures taken by the United States to protect it from subversion, touched the societal, economic and political life of virtually every country and territory in the hemisphere (Alexander 1957; Parkinson 1974; Wesson 1982; Lowenthal 1987; Martz 1988). Again with the exception of Cuba, none were affected more profoundly and over a longer period of time than British Guiana (Guyana since its independence in 1966) and Guatemala, the places where, in the early 1950s, the Cold War made its initial landfall in the Western Hemisphere.

During this formative period of Cold War politics, perceived threats of communist subversion in British Guiana and Guatemala led to actions by Great Britain and the United States respectively. They not only dealt with the threats, but also placed both countries on paths toward long-term dictatorship and political repression (Ince 1974; Manley 1979; Jonas and Tobis 1974: Immerman 1982; Schlesinger and Kinzer 1983; Gleijeses 1991). It appears that in the 1990s, as the "Soviet threat" no longer drove United States policy toward the region, the situations in both countries improved. Free and fair elections were held in Guyana in 1992 (Griffith 1997b) and another election was held in 1997, although this one was surrounded with controversy (Bohning 1997). There appears to be progress in Guatemala as well, as that country is finally beginning to emerge from its seemingly interminable experience with civil wars, pitting guerrilla insurgents against repressive right-wing governments. But in spite of recent favorable developments, the fact that both countries suffered long and hard as a result of the intrusion of the Cold War into their political processes is beyond dispute.

In this chapter we try to reconstruct the press coverage of the 1953 "constitutional crisis" in British Guiana and the 1954 "exile invasion" in Guatemala in major newspapers in Great Britain and the United States, specifically *The Times* (London) and *The New York Times*. Both of these newspapers had, at the time, and continue to enjoy, reputations as leading newspapers of the world and serve as "newspapers of record" in their respective countries (Merrill 1995).

The primary focus here is the extent to which "communist framing" was employed in journalistic reporting and analysis of the two crises. Framing is defined as the "central organizing idea for making sense of relevant events and suggesting what is at issue" (Gamson 1989, p. 157), and has proven to be a useful concept in communications research (Entman 1991, 1993; and Iyengar 1991). In examining press framing, two factors that may have affected reporting need to be kept in mind. First, the actual situations prompting the crises in British Guiana and Guatemala were quite different, and responses to them by the British and American governments were radically different. Second, the United States and Great Britain were at different places in terms of accepting leadership in the post–World War II struggle against communism, and they had different press cultures. By examining press coverage of the two crises comparatively, we can identify systematic tendencies in British and American reporting that resulted in their framing as communist infiltration in the Western Hemisphere, thereby legitimizing the actions taken to deal with them.

Methods

All items dealing with British Guiana and Guatemala appearing in *The Times* and *The New York Times* in 1953 and 1954 respectively were read and coded. The resulting data set includes 226 items on British

Guiana and 487 items on Guatemala. Words and phrases linking the crises to the Cold War and communism in both headlines and text were coded.[2] As well, words and phrases used to describe Guyanese and Guatemalan political leaders, Cheddi Jagan and Jacobo Arbenz Guzmán, were recorded, collated and sent for evaluation to a panel of ten scholars working in the areas of political science and communications. Panelists adopted an American perspective and judged whether each word or phrase reflected positively or negatively on the two leaders. A descriptor with an agreement rate of less than 80% (that is, judged by more than two panelists to be neutral or ambiguous) was omitted from the analysis in Table 1.4.

Background to the Crises—British Guiana

The October 1953 Constitutional Crisis in British Guiana has to be seen not only as a part of the Cold War between the United States and the Soviet Union, but also in the context of the general struggle for political independence, which stirred the English-speaking Caribbean in the years following World War II (Tomasek 1959; McKitterick 1962). This juxtaposition of global forces was captured beautifully by Hinden, who, at the time of the crisis, wrote as follows: "All the ideological conflicts that rack democrats when freedom is used to foster totalitarianism, seemed to crystallize in this episode. British Guiana has become significant, not so much for itself, but because it is a microcosm of the world's malaise" (1954, p. 18). Important on the world scene or not, while Guyana eventually achieved independence in 1966, its independence had been delayed. Also, there is consensus among scholars that any hope Guyana may have had for the development of a pan-ethnic national identity and non-ethnically-based political institutions, was effectively destroyed by the intrusion of the Cold War into its politics (Newman 1964; Halperin 1965; Despres 1967; Glasgow 1970; Henfrey 1972; Premdas 1986; Singh 1988).

As is the case with societies virtually everywhere in the Caribbean, the imperial struggle between metropolitan powers (often resulting in the transfer of colonies from one jurisdiction to another), the imposition of centuries of non-democratic rule, and the creation of economies built on imported slave labor, have cast long-lasting shadows. This is especially true in the case of Guyana, where the transfer from Dutch to British rule in 1803, the end of slavery in the British Empire between

1834 and 1838 — leading to the importation of indentured labor from India and giving rise to two distinct ethnic-cultural groups (Premdas 1986, pp. 161–168) — combined with neglect of the development of democratic institutions, left the country in a weak and vulnerable situation with respect to the achievement of political independence (Hughes 1953).

As a part of Britain's overall policy of decolonization in the post-war period, a constitutional commission was sent to the colony in 1950 to assess the situation and develop a constitution that would lead to the eventual achievement of independence (Hinden 1954). The resulting Waddington Constitution, which came into force in 1953, provided for limited self-government based on elections (with no property or literacy qualifications) to a lower House of Assembly. An upper chamber was to be appointed and a British-appointed governor, having extensive reserve powers, was to preside over an Executive Council (Tomasek 1959; Glasgow 1970). While it did not provide for full self-government, the Waddington Constitution has been described as marking "a substantial step forward on the road to independence" (Newman 1964, p. 80).

The first elections under the new constitution were held in April 1953. The People's Progressive Party (PPP), the only mass-based political party in the colony, drawing its leadership from both the Afro-Guyanese and Indo-Guyanese ethnic groups, won eighteen of twenty-four seats in the House of Assembly and thus put forward six ministers to run the government and sit on the Executive Council. In an article written shortly following the election, Hughes commented that the "most encouraging development of the election was the disappearance of racial voting" (1954, p. 219).

Politics in the British colony did not go smoothly in the months between the formation of the government in May and the crisis that led to its dissolution in October. The PPP, led by Cheddi Jagan, challenged the legitimacy of continued colonial rule, while at the same time introduced controversial labor and land tenure legislation. As well, the party organized a strike on the sugar plantations (Sires 1954; Spinner 1984; Singh 1988). Although the governor had ample power under the constitution to block PPP-introduced legislation, the impending passage of a bill that would have transferred union representation in the sugar industry to a PPP-affiliated union (Singh 1988, pp. 23–24) lead the governor to claim "that the country was under the threat of communist subversion" (Jeffrey and Barber 1986, p. 22), and he called for additional British troops to be sent to the colony, suspended the constitution and dismissed the legislature as well as the PPP ministers. Arrests and detention of PPP leaders followed (Simms 1966, pp. 114–121; Spinner 1984, pp. 43–46).

In subsequent years the PPP split along racial/ethnic lines, with Linden Forbes Burnham, the leading Afro-Guyanese figure in the PPP, forming the People's National Congress (PNC) (Bradley 1963; Singh 1988). While both Jagan and Burnham were socialist as well as anti-colonialist, Jagan was seen as a "Marxist" and unacceptable, while Burnham, the "lesser of two evils," was seen as someone with whom it was at least possible to work (Manley 1979; Jeffrey and Barber 1986). Not until after the constitution was changed in 1964 to hold elections based on proportional representation (which permitted Burnham to form a coalition government) was Guyana granted political independence in 1966 (Schlesinger 1965; Hope 1985). As a consequence of Cold War anti-communist policies, Guyanese party politics was cast in terms of rival ethnicity (PPP-Indo-Guyanese vs. PNC-Afro-Guyanese), and in short order Burnham began to rig elections and created a dictatorship based on military/police support, which persisted into the early 1990s (Griffith 1991).

Background to the Crises—Guatemala

The 1954 crisis in Guatemala, which involved a United States–sponsored exile invasion and culminated in the overthrow of the Guatemalan government in a military coup d'etat, also has deep-reaching roots — roots in the Spanish conquest and the ensuing colonial system (which left the Indian population dominated by the Spanish/mestizo class); in foreign control of the economy (largely in the hands of the United Fruit Company); and in a long history of dictatorial political rule following political independence (MacLeod 1973; Woodward 1985; and Bulmer-Thomas 1987). The more immediate causes of the crisis can be found, on the one hand, in the conflict between the modernizing/democratic forces associated with the "four freedoms" popularized during World War II, which were felt not only in Guatemala but also virtually everywhere in the hemisphere (Szulc 1959); and, on the other hand, in the legacy of United States policy toward Central America, which, from the time of the Spanish-American

War through the early 1930s, can accurately be described as imperialistic (LaFeber 1983).

In October 1944 a popular revolution overthrew the long-time dictator Jorge Ubico y Castañeda, whose legacy to the country has been described as "a combination of political immaturity, an archaic social structure and economic backwardness" (Schneider 1959, p. 5). Under the presidency of Juan José Arévalo (1945-1951) a program of social, political and economic reforms was initiated. Although the scope of these reforms was wide-ranging, the pace of their implementation was slow, and, importantly, they did not include agrarian reform (Pike 1955, pp. 233-234). While communists were constitutionally barred from participating in government, due to a lack of political talent in the country, Arévalo came to depend on their political skills (Alexander 1954; Handy 1984).

A 1950 election in Guatemala was to be contested by two army officers, Col. Francisco Araña and Lt. Col. Jacobo Arbenz Guzmán. When Araña was assassinated in 1949, in circumstances that implicated Arbenz, the latter became heir apparent to Arévalo (Schneider 1959; Immerman 1982; Gleijeses 1991). Arbenz won the November 1950 election and was inaugurated on March 15, 1951, the date that is cited as marking the beginning of the communist revolution in Guatemala (James 1954, p. 54).

Assessments regarding the extent to which Arbenz and his government were under communist influence vary widely. Scholars writing at the time and soon after stress the connection (James 1954; Krehm 1954; Grant 1955; Taylor 1956; Alexander 1957; Schneider 1959). In contrast, scholars addressing the crisis in more recent times tend to minimize the importance of the communist connection, pointing instead to attempts by the United States to maintain the favored position of the United Fruit Company (UFCO) in the Guatemalan economy and its own dominant political and economic position in the hemisphere (Melville and Melville 1971; Jonas and Tobis 1974; Aybar de Soto 1978; Gordon 1983; Schlesinger and Kinzer 1983).

While at the time there was no firm evidence that Arbenz was a card-carrying communist, his government did legalize the Communist Party in 1951 and the Party subsequently won a handful of seats in Congress. More importantly, he had no trouble passing the American-imposed "duck test": If it looks like a duck, swims like a duck and quacks like a duck, even in the absence of a label, it probably is a duck

(Immerman 1982, p. 102). In August 1952 the Eisenhower Administration decided to oust Arbenz (Schlesinger and Kinzer 1983, p. 108). While the State Department, under John Foster Dulles, played a supporting role, primary responsibility for the removal of Arbenz was entrusted to Allen Dulles and the Central Intelligence Agency (CIA) (Wise and Ross 1964, p. 171).

The involvement of the Dulles brothers in the Guatemalan operation is clouded by their prior association with the law firm Sullivan and Cromwell, which represented the UFCO, at the time locked in a bitter dispute with the Guatemalan government over the right to expropriate UFCO lands as well as the amount of compensation to be paid for any lands expropriated. John Foster Dulles explicitly denied that the UFCO had anything to do with U.S. policy toward Guatemala, claiming that if the UFCO "gave a gold piece for every banana, the problem [of communist infiltration] would remain" (quoted in Immerman 1982, p. 82). Nonetheless, some scholars maintain that the UFCO's difficulties were at the heart of U.S. dissatisfaction with Arbenz (Jonas and Tobis 1974; Schlesinger and Kinzer 1983). While the motivation of the Dulles brothers and the extent of their influence on U.S. policy may be in question, what is beyond doubt is the extensive and effective lobbying and propaganda campaign carried out by the UFCO itself against the Guatemalan government (McCann 1976).

An assessment of press coverage of the Guatemalan crisis is complicated by the fact that contrary to the situation in Guyana, where the British government sent in troops, suspended the constitution and dissolved the Legislative Assembly, official American government involvement in efforts to remove the Arbenz government were covert (Forsythe 1992). Moreover, they were at a level of involvement where, at the time, "plausible denial" of overt sponsorship was possible. More recent research has established clearly that without United States initiative and support, the "exile invasion," which provoked the Guatemalan army to move against Arbenz, simply would not have occurred (Jonas and Tobis 1974; Immerman 1982; Schlesinger and Kinzer 1983; Gleijeses 1991).

The formal U.S. campaign against Arbenz opened in October 1953 with charges by the State Department that Guatemala was "openly playing the communist game" (quoted in Fenwick 1954, p. 597) and with the appointment of John E. Peurifoy, a veteran diplomat with Cold War experience in Greece, as U.S. Ambassador to Guatemala.

United States involvement in the overthrow of Arbenz was multifaceted and well coordinated, encompassing the recruitment, training and arming of an exile military force; diplomatic maneuvering in Guatemala and in neighboring Central American countries; attempts to secure the condemnation of Guatemala in the Organization of American States (OAS); conducting psychological warfare operations against the Guatemalan government; manipulating organizational jurisdiction of the crisis between the United Nations (UN) and OAS during the invasion phase; as well as negotiating a share of governmental power for the American-recruited and -supported commander of the exile forces, Col. Carlos Castillo Armas, following the army coup that deposed Arbenz.

Timing of the actual military operation, which was launched from neighboring Honduras, was almost assuredly influenced by the arrival in Guatemala of a shipment of Czechoslovakian arms on May 15, 1954. Just over a month later, on June 18, Castillo Armas led his CIA-backed "Liberation Army" of a few hundred men across the Honduran-Guatemalan border and engaged the Guatemalan army, which had little difficulty in halting his progress.

With the invasion sputtering, the CIA launched a propaganda/ psychological operations campaign against the Guatemalan government, and the crisis moved rapidly to a conclusion. The decisive factor that forced the removal of Arbenz was not the military attack of Castillo Armas, but the demand by his own armed forces that he step down. Apparently the army balked at Arbenz' plans to arm civilian militias (Schneider 1959, p. 576), and on June 27, in a radio address to the nation, Arbenz resigned the presidency (Gleijeses 1991, pp. 342–351). In the days that followed, Ambassador Peurifoy secured a position for Castillo Armas on the ruling junta, and, in a vote taken on July 8, the American-backed exile leader became the junta's choice as head of the new government.

From the perspective of the United States, the "communist crisis" in Guatemala may have ended with the removal of Arbenz, but we of course now know that as a consequence of the American "solution," Guatemala's problems were going to get far worse than anyone could have possibly imagined. Writing in 1983 with the benefit of hindsight, Harrison Salisbury remarked in his introduction to *Bitter Fruit*, that "Operation Success [code name for the American operation against Arbenz] should have been called Operation Disaster" (in Schlesinger and Kinzer 1983, p. xv), as the cycle of insurgency and repression that characterized Guatemalan life since the early 1950s resulted in an estimated 200,000 people killed or "disappeared" (Hegstrom 1998).

Findings

Given Guyana's status in 1953 as a colony, British politicians had primary responsibility for dealing with the crisis, and since their solution involved the dispatch of British troops, it is not surprising that *The Times* accounted for nearly 60% of total crisis coverage (131 of 226 stories).[3] In both newspapers, most of the coverage consisted of "hard news" (about 90%) and peaked at the time of the actual constitutional suspension in mid-October and continued through to the end of the year. Approximately half of the total stories carried Guyanese datelines, with about one-third filed from Great Britain and 10% from the United States.

Clearly, Guyana was seen as a British crisis, while the Guatemalan crisis was seen as primarily involving the United States. In contrast to Guyana, coverage of Guatemala was reasonably spread out during the year, especially in *The New York Times*, where 43% of stories ran before the beginning of the exile invasion on June 18. The Guatemalan crisis prompted over twice the volume of coverage garnered a year earlier by the one in British Guiana (487 stories), with, in this case, 72% of stories running in *The New York Times*. The ratio of hard news to opinion pieces varied only slightly from that seen with respect to Guyana — about 88% hard news. Approximately 60% of total stories were filed from Guatemala, with a large spread between *The New York Times* (70%) and *The Times* (36%). Somewhat paradoxically, *The Times* carried a much higher percentage of stories on Guatemala with U.S. datelines (43%) than did *The New York Times* (28%).

Data in Table 1.1 deal with the length of stories on the two crises appearing in *The New York Times* and *The Times*.[4] Differences between newspapers appear greater than do those between crises. Specifically, regardless of the crisis, *The Times* ran far more stories of five or less paragraphs, while *The New York Times* ran far more stories that were sixteen paragraphs or longer, with differences statistically significant ($p<.001$). Further, just as the Guatemalan crisis received a greater volume of coverage, so too were there fewer "short" stories and more "long" stories in the mix of coverage. Thus, overall, on two indicators

Table 1.1

Length of Item in British Guiana and Guatemala Crises

	British Guiana			Guatemala		
	NYT N=95	Times N=131	Total N=226	NYT N=351	Times N=136	Total N=487
Short (1-5)	50%	68%	61%	40%	74%	50%
Medium (6-15)	33	28	30	35	23	31
Long (16+)	17	4	9	25	3	19
	$X^2=13.161$ DF=2 Sig<.001			$X^2=53.665$ DF=2 Sig<.001		

of importance (volume and length), Guatemala clearly ranks ahead of Guyana as an item of press interest in the United States.

Data in Table 1.2, which focus on the source of material, indicate similarities and differences with respect to both crisis and newspaper. For both papers, overall the major source of information was local staff or special correspondents working directly for the newspaper. The lowest percentage was recorded for *New York Times'* coverage of Guyana (52%) and the highest was for that newspaper's coverage of Guatemala (78%). While figures in this range are not unexpected for newspapers of this stature, it is interesting that *Times'* correspondents covered Guatemala largely from the United States rather than from Guatemala itself. *The New York Times* relied on both American (Associated Press [AP] and United Press International [UPI]) and British (Reuters) wire services for coverage of both crises, while *The Times* relied exclusively on Reuters for its wire coverage, regardless of crisis.

Table 1.3 presents data that explore the relative amount of attention devoted to different dimensions of each crisis: actions of Great Britain compared with those of the PPP in the case of British Guiana; and United States and Guatemalan government action in the case of Guatemala. As well, differences in coverage of Cheddi Jagan and Jacobo Arbenz as political leaders are examined.

Given Britain's direct role in dealing with the Guyanese crisis, the fact that 65% of stories commented on its activities as opposed to only

Table 1.2

Source of Content in British Guiana and Guatemala Crises* (missing data omitted)

	British Guiana			Guatemala		
	NYT N=81	Times N=115	Total N=196	NYT N=341	Times N=133	Total N=474
Local Staff/Special Correspondent	52%	73%	64%	78%	77%	78%
American Wire Services	18	1	8	19	4	14
British Wire Services	26	23	24	1	13	5
Other	4	3	4	2	6	3

*Cell sizes too small to compute accurate statistics

Table 1.3

Relative Attention Paid to Initiatives in British Guiana and Guatemala

	British Guiana			Guatemala		
	NYT N=95	Times N=131	Total N=226	NYT N=351	Times N=136	Total N=487
British Initiatives	69%	62%	65%	–	–	–
PPP Initiatives	25	21	23	–	–	–
Cheddi Jagan*	55	31	41	–	–	–
American Initiatives	–	–	–	29%	31%	30%
Arbenz Government Initiatives	–	–	–	23	19	22
Jacobo Arbenz*	–	–	–	45	22	39

*Differences statistically significant (p<.001); all others not statistically significant

23% commenting on PPP initiatives is not surprising. Also, given the covert nature of American involvement in the Guatemalan crisis, that attention paid to the role of the United States government is so much lower (30%) than seen with respect to Britain's in British Guiana is understandable. On the other hand, there is virtually no difference between coverage of the initiatives of the Guatemalan government (22%) and the 23% given to those of the PPP in reporting on British Guiana.

On the leadership dimension, we see evidence of a decided emphasis on the "cult of personality" in American reporting. For both Cheddi Jagan and Jacobo Arbenz, coverage was over 20% higher in *The New York Times* than it was in *The Times*, with these differences being statistically significant (p<.001).

Data in Table 1.4 reflect the results of the panel judgments regarding the descriptors used with respect to Cheddi Jagan and Jacobo Arbenz Guzmán. (See the end of this chapter for the full list of descriptors and how they were coded.) The pattern is quite interesting. First, while "negativity" was the order of the day for both Jagan and Arbenz, Jagan's overall 94% negative descriptors place him in the company of Nicaragua's Anastasio Somoza Debayle and Panama's Manuel Noriega in the media's "hall of villains" (see chapters 4 and 13). While there are no sharp differences in the evaluation of the leaders between the two papers, it is apparent that *The New York Times* used descriptive words and phrases to refer to Jagan and especially to Arbenz considerably more often than did *The Times*. This is consistent with the greater attention paid to personalities in the American press and also means that of the two leaders, even though Jagan's portrayal was more negative, the negative image of Arbenz among the American

Table 1.4

**Descriptors Reflecting Positively or Negatively
on Cheddi Jagan and Jacobo Arbenz Guzmán**

Leader	NYT	Times	Total
Cheddi Jagan	N=37	N=13	N=50
Positive	5%	8%	6%
Negative	95	92	94
Jacobo Arbenz	N=104	N=20	N=124
Positive	19%	15%	19%
Negative	81	85	81

people would have received greater amplification. The number of his descriptors in *The New York Times* were nearly three times greater than the number of Jagan descriptors (Soderlund 1994).

The final table shows the comparative use of four "Cold War frames" (references to communism in headlines, in text, specific references to Jagan and Arbenz linked to communism and the actual word "communist" to describe the two leaders). First, it is necessary to point out that there is obvious multi-coding involved, so that individual percentages cannot be summed. This having been said, for the British Guiana crisis, on each indicator of communist salience, *The New York Times* far exceeds *The Times* in usage, with references to communism in story text and Cheddi Jagan's ties to communism present in over 50% of American press items. Indeed, differences between the two newspapers on all four indicators of communist framing are statistically significant ($p<.001$).

Data for the Guatemalan crisis are not as clear cut. While use of communist framing is far greater in *The New York Times*, differences between the two papers are not as dramatic as seen for Guyana, and

Table 1.5

Use of Cold War Frames for British Guiana and Guatemala (percentage of items in which frame occurs; due to multi-coding, figures do not add to 100%)

| Frame | British Guiana | | | | Guatemala | | | |
	NYT N=95	Times N=131	Total N=226	Sig	NYT N=351	Times N=136	Total N=487	Sig
"Red" Headline	22%	5%	12%	.001	23%	7%	19%	.001
"Red" Text	54	27	39	.001	71	45	63	.001
Jagan Linked to Communism	52	24	36	.001	–	–	–	–
Jagan Labeled "Communist"	19	4	10	.001	–	–	–	–
Arbenz Linked to Communism	–	–	–	–	17	10	15	.05
Arbenz Labeled "Communist"	–	–	–	–	.5	1.5	.5	NS

on only two indicators of communist salience are differences statistically significant (p<.001). Moreover, while the use of communist frames in headlines and references linking Arbenz and Jagan to communism are quite similar for both papers in both crises, somewhat curiously, communist framing in story texts is much higher overall for the Guatemalan than for the Guyanese crisis (63% to 39%), while neither paper actually labels Arbenz a communist to any extent.

Conclusion

Analysis of press coverage of the 1953 British Guiana and 1954 Guatemala crises points rather clearly to the greater extent that *The New York Times* framed these events in terms of "communist penetration" of the Western Hemisphere. While the Cold War dimension was not dismissed by *The Times*, neither did it dominate reportage in the way seen in the American newspaper. Even in coverage of British Guiana, which politically was not the primary responsibility of the United States and where *The New York Times* relied on Reuters for a quarter of its material, the greater American preoccupation with communist intrusion is apparent. One can only speculate that if *The Times* had its own reporters covering events from Guatemala rather than from the United States, a less communist-oriented perspective on that crisis in the British press might have been evident.

Explanations for the kinds of differences found in coverage of these two crises include at least three factors. The first is geographical and is based on the location of the crises in the Western Hemisphere. It encompasses the "special relationship" that the U.S. has maintained with countries in the region and brings into play the Monroe Doctrine with all that entails (Gill 1971; Maingot 1994). The second involves societal factors: one, the near anti-communist hysteria in the United States associated with the McCarthy period, which was at its height in the 1953–1954 period (Jonas and Tobis 1974); another, the switch in U.S. and British international positions following the end of World War II, resulting in American assumption of leadership of what was becoming referred to as the "free world"; and the greater British experience and sophistication in coping with third world anti-colonialism and nationalism. The third factor is the "propaganda model" of press-state relations as advanced by Herman and Chomsky. According to Herman and Chomsky, the American press serves as little more than a compliant spokesperson for the legitimization of government (in these cases, anti-communist) policy (1988, p. 289).

Of these, the last is the most interesting and also the most controversial. Clearly *The New York Times* framed both the Guyanese and Guatemalan crises in terms of communist penetration of the hemisphere to a significantly greater degree than did *The Times*. Equally clearly, this corresponded closely with the views of the American and British governments respectively (Bennett 1990). One can argue, therefore, that the evidence in these two cases does not challenge the Herman/Chomsky contention.

On the other hand, there is also evidence that at least the American government does not take for granted that the press will faithfully spout its line. In the Guatemalan case, for example, it has been claimed that Secretary of State John Foster Dulles, together with his brother Allen (CIA director) deliberately fed false information to the publisher of *The New York Times* about the paper's reporter on the Guatemalan beat, Sydney Gruson, in order to get him replaced. Gruson, the Dulles brothers feared, was too good a reporter and might see through the smoke screens and alert the American people to what was really going on in Guatemala (Schlesinger and Kinzer 1983, pp. xii–xiii).

Moreover, press manipulation is not a monopoly of governments, either. Thomas McCann has shown how the UFCO undertook a determined public relations campaign to convince journalists of the extent of "communist penetration" in Guatemala, notably by conducting carefully guided all-expenses-paid tours of the area for major newspaper, news magazine and electronic media reporters (McCann 1976, pp. 44–62).

However, as every student of statistics knows (but is nonetheless prone to forget), correlation between two factors does not prove the existence of a causal relationship. Thus, we would argue that while the Herman/Chomsky hypothesis is provocative (and even intriguing), it is also more an article of faith than a rational deduction from evidence. There is, in the first place, bound to be a considerable degree of congruence between government positions on events and media coverage of them, for no other reason than the public need to be informed of what their government's perspective on these events is. Secondly, it must be remembered that media personnel do not exist in a vacuum. They, and perhaps especially personnel of the elite, establishment media organs like *The New York Times* and *The Times,* are exposed to and must be presumed to share at least the generality of the prevailing political climate within their countries. Indeed, they must be held partially responsible for the creation of that climate.

At the same time, governments would not need to fear their media if the latter could be counted on always to see issues as the former saw them, and to act solely as positive conduits for the official line. The relationship among government, society, culture and the media is actually a complex and interdependent one in which factors do not retain a constant value over time or from one event to another occurring at the same time.

That American reporting of the crises was framed largely in terms of the Cold War should not come as any great surprise. As Rositzke has observed, beginning in 1948, the Cold War meant for the United States that

> The world was divided into two parts: "Communist" and "free." All countries were either good or bad....There was no serious dissent from this view for a decade. The White House, the secretaries of state, both parties in Congress, *the press and the reading public* all viewed the Communist threat through the same prism. Either the United States or the Soviet Union would win, for the conflict was a fight to the finish." (1977, pp. 13–14, emphasis added)

In the climate of paranoia existing in the United States at the time, far more pronounced than in Britain, it would have been extraordinary if *The New York Times* had not reflected government concerns and accepted the essential proposition that communism was an insidious and pervasive evil, which might manifest itself anywhere at any time, and certainly constituted a threat to U.S. security interests. Multidimensional as were both the Guyanese and Guatemalan crises, they were seen by America's premier newspaper largely in unidimensional terms, and thus may be said to fit the Cold War frame nearly perfectly.

Notes

1.   Material on British Guiana in this chapter was published previously in the article "Cheddi Jagan, the Cold War, and Press Images of the Constitutional Crisis in British Guiana, 1953," which appeared in *Indo*

Caribbean Review, 1 (1994). It is used in this chapter with permission.

2. Intercoder reliability for the Guyana data was calculated at 87%, while that for the Guatemala data at 84% (Holsti 1969, p. 140). The authors' thanks go to Livianna Tossutti, Joyce Zuk, Ann Hibbard and Patrick Dunn for their assistance in newspaper coding; to Richard Allicock for help in compiling the bibliography; and to Sukhiminder Osahan and Jim Kelly for assistance in computer analysis of the data.
3. By way of comparison, in 1992, the year in which Cheddi Jagan won the Presidency of Guyana, *The Times* ran a total of seven stories on Guyana (six of which focused on the election), while *The New York Times* ran a total of four stories (three of which dealt with the election).
4. Column inches of material were not calculated due to the high correlation between number of stories on a topic and overall space devoted to it (see Stevenson and Shaw 1984, p. 35).

Chapter 1 Descriptors

Cheddi Jagan

Words/Phrases Judged to Be Positive

Dark and handsome
Has great deal of support

Words/Phrases Judged to Be Negative

Moscow-trained
Leftist/leftist leader/leftist PM/left-leaning/head of leftist government
Visited East Berlin
Has extensive communist connections/linked to communism
A ringleader in communist agitation
Ousted PM/ousted premier/deposed premier/deposed colonial premier/
    deposed first minister/dismissed PM
Sidestepped question whether he was a communist
Openly preaches communism
A Marxist
Left-wing extremist
Communist propagandist
Not interested in working the constitution, but in wrecking it

Words/Phrased Judged to Be Neutral or Ambiguous

Premier/prime minister
PPP leader/PPP chief/legislative leader of the PPP
Thirty-five years old
Doctor/Dr.
Born in British Guiana
Of East Indian descent/origin/extraction/born of East Indian parents
Dentist/Indian dentist/East Indian dentist/trained in dentistry at
    Northwestern University

Husband (of Janet Jagan)
Chicago-educated

Jacobo Arbenz Guzmán
Words/Phrases Judged to Be Positive
Not a communist/no communist/denied he was a communist
Tough
Did not trust communists
Keeps his word
Has strengthened his position with the army
Firmly entrenched in power/in full control of the government
Listens to advice
Honor student
Enacted a popular agrarian reform law/pushed an ambitious program for improving the lot of the landless peasants/policies are alleviating poverty in Guatemala
Chief organizer of the revolt that overthrew dictator Jorge Ubico
Swept into power in a presidential election in 1950
Always counted on the support of the peasants
Idealistic and sincere

Words/Phrases Judged to Be Negative
Prisoner of the embrace he so long ago gave the communists/began a policy of close cooperation with the communists/feels he needs the communists to carry out his programs/turned to the communists for help/relied on communists/not of mind to act against communists/has allowed communists to hold important sub-cabinet posts/tolerant of communists/his and the communists' objectives are one and indistinguishable
Angry
Red-tinged/red-supported
His days are numbered
Waging a war of terror
Promoted socialist policies
His associates are affiliated with pro-Soviet organizations/his private secretary was at a communist meeting
Communist/pro-communist/influenced by communists/approves of communists/the communists' man/on the side of communism/communist-supported/communist-backed/dominated by the Communist Party/accused of strong communist sympathies/has an increasingly communistic attitude/the man thought like a communist, and talked like a communist and if not actually one, would do until one came along
A man on the left
Brooding
Humorless
An enigma
Shadowy figure
Ousted president

Whether he controls the communists or they control him is the key question
El Presidente Cumple
Told to break from the communists or resign
Walked a tightrope between his anti-communist army and his communist
    political allies
Traitor/will be tried as a traitor
Head of the only communist-dominated government in the Western
    Hemisphere
Intervened in the political affairs of a neighbor
To be arrested
To be charged with atrocities
Criminal #1 on the rebels' hit list of criminals
To be charged with the 1949 ambush slaying of Col. Francisco Araña
Must be punished
Holed up in a foreign embassy with a million dollars he obtained by fraud
    for the state bank
His legitimacy is questioned
Acted unconstitutionally
Has a fanatical lack of compromise
Ruthless
Unconditional servant of the Kremlin/Moscow directed and controlled
Repressive/killed citizens
Like a deflated balloon

Words/Phrased Judged to Be Neutral or Ambiguous
President/presidente
Citizen-president
Guatemalan chief
Army officer/a soldier/former infantry Lt. Col./Lt. Col./Captain
Forty/forty-one years old/born in 1913
Señor
Has remained silent on the crisis
Has not changed his mind on the internal situation
Preparing to leave Guatemala
Assumed personal command of the Army/is in personal charge of defense
    strategy
Imposed martial law
Rose from 2nd Lt. to Col. to presidency
Father was Swiss, mother was Guatemalan
Graduated from the Escuela Politechnica/Military Academy
Minister of war/minister of defense
Will be forced to fight
Rose to a high place in the Guatemalan government as a result of a military
    revolt in 1944
Has two years to serve
Reported en route to exile in Argentina
Former president

Chapter 2

Words and Images: Press Coverage of Fidel Castro in *The New York Times*, 1953–1992[1]

WALTER C. SODERLUND

Joseph Stalin, Winston Churchill, Franklin Delano Roosevelt, Charles DeGaulle and Fidel Castro are all world leaders of the twentieth century who have shaped the destinies of, and who are virtually synonymous with, the countries they led. By what processes are our perceptions of such major political leaders constructed, consolidated and indeed changed? Questions such as these first suggested a stream of research focusing on how the Western press used language (descriptive words and phrases) to construct mental images of leaders—projecting to readers such qualities as likable or detestable, strong or weak, friend or foe, trustworthy or untrustworthy (Corcoran 1984; Soderlund 1994). While it might be possible to test theories about why the press reacts to certain leaders in positive or negative ways (hegemony of dominant ideology, ownership profit, journalistic career rewards, government propaganda, complementarity of elite cultural/political values or simply accurate assessment), the focus of this chapter is an analysis of the actual images of Fidel Castro projected by the press, not establishing the motivations for that image projection.

Most of us find it extremely difficult to follow international events firsthand. Consequently, we rely on mass media for our information on, and perceptions of, the world that lies beyond the immediate range of our experience (Smith 1980; Parenti 1986; Thompson 1988). In shorthand terms, in the words of Todd Gitlin, media serve "to certify reality as reality" (Gitlin 1980, p. 2).

However, theories based on the concepts of gatekeeping (Bennett et al. 1985; Bennett 1983) and agenda setting (McCombs and Shaw 1972; Weaver 1984) have pointed out regarding the selection and programming of news that what we are likely to read in the newspapers and see on television contain systematic biases in terms of the kinds of news reported about specific countries and leaders. In their pioneering work on news flows, Galtung and Holmboe Ruge identified twelve factors that predicted which events would most likely be covered in the Western press:

- Frequency ("time-span needed for the event to unfold itself and acquire meaning")
- Threshold (intensity and increases in intensity — the bigger the event the more likely it will be reported)
- Unambiguity (clarity regarding what is occurring)
- Meaningfulness (cultural proximity and relevance)
- Consonance (predictability and demand — making for easy reception and registration of the event)
- Unexpectedness (unpredictability and scarcity)
- Continuity (the need to be defined as news for some time)
- Composition (the need for balance among international, national and local news)
- Reference to elite nations
- Reference to something negative
- Reference to elite persons
- Reference to persons in general (the ability to "personalize" the news)

Galtung and Holmboe Ruge argue that the factors are additive; "the higher the total score of an event, the higher the probability that it will become news, and even make the headlines" (1965, 71).

Rosengren prunes the list of news-triggering factors down to a crucial three: the importance of the event, the physical or cultural distance between the country where the event occurs and the country in which it is reported, and its degree of predictability in terms of *what*, *when* and *how* it will happen (1970). Gans, focusing specifically on what appears in the American press, lists the following as important determinants of news salience: American activities abroad, events abroad that have an effect on the United States, relations with communist countries, changes in heads of state, political conflict of a dramatic nature, and the excesses of dictators (Gans 1979). Again in the American context, Chang, Shoemaker and Brendlinger (1987), using techniques of factor analysis, report the relevance of an event to the U.S., normative deviance and potential for social change as the factors most likely to attract press attention. In studies of both the British and American press, Peterson (1980) and Riffe and Shaw (1982) see negativity as the most salient characteristic in news selection. Thus, the events and leaders that we will see and read about share common characteristics: The more negative an event or leader (bizarre, demonic, violent, repulsive, etc.), the greater the physical and cultural proximity to the U.S., and the more dramatic and personalized the event or leader might be, the more likely the press will pay serious attention.

Among Latin American and Caribbean leaders, none has been the object of more press attention than Fidel Castro. For more than forty years, since 1953 — when his raid on a military garrison in Santiago de Cuba on July 26 first brought him into public consciousness beyond the borders of Cuba — Fidel Castro has been a major political figure in his own country; since 1959, the dominant figure. Moreover, he has also been an important political actor in the Latin American/Caribbean region, and especially in the 1970s played a major role in the decolonization struggle in Africa. In addition, his involvement of Cuba in the post-World War II Cold War struggle between the U.S. and the Soviet Union brought the world probably the closest it has come to nuclear war during the Cuban Missile Crisis of October 1962 (Blight et al. 1987; Garthoff 1988).

Methods

In this chapter, the press images of Fidel Castro over the entire course of his long career are reconstructed and evaluated. For this investigation, four phases have been identified in the development of Castro's image: image construction — 1953 through 1958; image consolidation — 1959 through 1962; image consistency — 1963 through 1987; and image change — 1988 to 1992.

This formulation is based on the theoretical insights of Deutsch and Merritt, who argue that not only are "images" key components in our understanding of reality, but also once these images are formed, they tend to act as "screens" through which new information on the subject must pass (1965). In the initial image construction phase, we expected to find considerable range, ambiguity, and even contradiction in press images of Fidel Castro. In 1953, as the young student leader of a failed military operation against an American-supported dictator, his arrest, subsequent trial and conviction could be expected to produce press coverage both sympathetic and unsympathetic to Castro. Further, the dramatic events surrounding the landing of his invasion force in December 1956, and the following two years of guerrilla campaigns against Fulgencio Batista, captured the imagination of the American press (Ratliff 1987; Matthews 1969; Geyer 1991). Thus, during this initial image construction phase, we hypothesized an incomplete and ambiguous press image of Castro, featuring both positive and negative dimensions.

Between the triumph of the revolution in January 1959 and the resolution of the missile crisis in 1962, it was expected that a highly negative press image of Fidel Castro would become consolidated. Castro's ambiguous image no doubt began a process of sharp deterioration in 1959 as a consequence of the post-revolutionary violence carried out against Batista's army and police (Lewis 1960), along with what were perceived to be his "radical" domestic policies. Further, by 1961, following the unsuccessful and humiliating Bay of Pigs invasion and Cuban moves toward the Soviet Union, an essentially negative, Cold War–framed image of Castro would no doubt be in place (Blight and Kornbluh 1998). This negative image would be predictably strengthened by the discovery in Cuba in the fall of 1962 of Soviet strategic missiles, capable of delivering nuclear warheads against targets over a large portion of the southeast United States.

A key hypothesis underlying this image study is that once the essentially negative character of Castro's image had become "fixed" by the end of 1962, that image would remain relatively impervious to change.[2] Remaining static, the negative image would serve as a lens through which Castro's subsequent actions were interpreted. In order to test this hypothesis, press images of Castro appearing in *The New York Times* were studied in eleven key years between 1963 and 1987 (period three), during which important events involving Cuba to some significant extent, occurred:

- 1965 – the U.S. intervention in the Dominican Republic
- 1967 – the death of Ernesto "Che" Guevara in Bolivia

- 1970 — the election of Salvador Allende in Chile
- 1973 — the Pinochet coup and the death of Allende
- 1976 — the Cuban intervention in Angola
- 1977 — the Carter thaw
- 1979 — the Nicaraguan Revolution
- 1980 — the Mariel "boatlift" of Cubans to the United States
- 1983 — the murder of Maurice Bishop and the subsequent American invasion of Grenada
- 1985 — the inauguration of Radio Martí
- 1987 — the domestic "campaign of rectification of errors" and the defection of General Rafael del Pino

Beginning in 1988, and amplified by Mikhail Gorbachev's visit to Cuba in the spring of 1989, subtle changes with respect to Fidel Castro's press image were hypothesized to have occurred, and in period four all years between 1988 and 1992 were studied. While the essence of the new image was still seen to be negative, the character of the description was hypothesized as changing from one of "feared and formidable opponent" to one of being anachronistic and out of step with trends in world communism — that is, more of a "failed" than a "feared" figure. Again, we hypothesized that by the end of the trial of General Arnaldo Ochoa in the summer of 1989 (which resulted in his conviction and execution), this revised image would have overridden and replaced the old one, and that as Cold War–ending events in Eastern Europe and the Soviet Union itself continued to unfold, the new negative image of Castro would become consolidated.

For the year 1953, all items dealing with Cuba in *The New York Times* — the newspaper of record in the United States (Merrill 1983) — from July 26 onward, and for 1956 all items appearing in the month of December during which the Granma landing took place, were read and analyzed. Beginning with 1958 and continuing for each year through to the end of the project, the following sampling procedure was used: The month with the greatest number of Cuban entries in *The New York Times Index* was selected, plus five months chosen randomly, but in such a way that three months fell in the first half and three months in the second half of each year. In total, twenty-two years of press coverage of Fidel Castro were studied.

For each press item, all descriptors (words and phrases) used with respect to Fidel Castro were recorded. These descriptors were then divided into two broad categories: those commenting on his *personal character* (for example, "courageous," "dynamic," "unscrupulous") or his *political beliefs and policies* ("in close alliance with communists," "has growing sympathy among Cubans," "ruined the Cuban economy"). These descriptors were then evaluated as to whether, from an American perspective, they reflected positively or negatively on Castro. A panel of six political science and communication scholars was asked to judge the list of descriptors. At least five of the six (83%) had to agree on the likely impact of a descriptor on American readers before it was counted as either positive or negative. (See the full list of descriptors and how they were coded at the end of this chapter.) As well, variables such as dateline, source of content, placement in the newspaper and length of items were coded. Intercoder reliability on these latter variables was established at 92% (Holsti 1969).[3]

Findings

Over the twenty-two years of our sample, 1,212 items out of 3,416 (35%) originally examined contained codable references to Fidel Castro. In terms of the four time periods previously outlined, distribution of press items is as follows:

- Period one: 1953–1958, 160 items
- Period two: 1959–1962, 566 items
- Period three: 1963–1987, 333 items
- Period four: 1988–1992, 153 items

Forty-four percent of these items were filed from locations in the United States, while 37% were filed from locations in Cuba. Local staff members and special correspondents were responsible for 63% of content, American wire services, Associated Press (AP) and United Press International (UPI) were responsible for 16% while Reuters accounted for 3%. In total, 20% of items appeared on the front page of *The New York Times*, 56% as hard news on the inside pages, while editorials accounted for 6% and feature columns for 12% of total content. Short items (defined as five paragraphs or less) comprised 26% of content, medium items (defined as having between six and fifteen paragraphs) accounted for 38%, while long items (defined as sixteen paragraphs or longer) accounted for 36% of content.

Table 2.1

Major Castro Descriptors

Descriptor (#positive descriptor/*negative descriptor)	Total No. of Mentions
Political position held: PM/premier/head of state, etc.	540
Communist*	361
Señor/Mr.	330
Cuban leader	252
Doctor	195
Anti-American*	108
Danger to the hemisphere*	85
Totalitarian*	56
Linked to firing squads*	54
Dictator*	44
Cracking down on opponents*	42
Losing support among Cubans*	41
Number of years in power	38
Actual age	33
Wants good relations with U.S.#	33
Popular#	29
Powerful#	28
Opposed to reforming communism*	28
Destroyed Cuban economy*	28
Socialist*	28
Not a communist#	25
Young	25
Bearded	25
Anti-democratic*	23
Ideologue*	19
Willing to negotiate#	19
Leader of 26 July Movement	18
Tyrant*	17
National hero#	17

Table 2.1 (continued)

Descriptor (#positive descriptor/*negative descriptor)	Total No. of Mentions
Disagrees with U.S.S.R.	17
Played leading role in African and LA national liberation struggles	17
Dumped criminals and perverts in U.S.*	16
Can't tolerate criticism*	16
Lingers in power*	15
Expanding his role in Africa*	15
Involved in drug smuggling*	13
His days are numbered*	12
Head of Cuba's armed forces	12
Losing appeal in Latin America*	12
Hope in the U.S. that he will be overthrown*	12
His human rights record is improving#	12
Enjoys wide support#	11
Any description of his dress	11
Extraordinary leader#	11
Isolated*	11
Power-driven*	10
Brusque*	10
Subversive*	10
International outlaw*	10

A total of 294 distinct words and phrases used to describe Fidel Castro was coded. As shown in Table 2.1, in order of frequency of mention, forty-nine were used ten or more times. Of these most frequently used descriptors, over half (twenty-seven) were coded as reflecting negatively on Fidel Castro, nine were seen as positive, while the remaining thirteen were judged as either neutral or ambiguous.

Over the duration of the entire study, positive descriptors were used with respect to Fidel Castro 383 times, accounting for 21% of the total, while negative descriptors were used 1,444 times, accounting for 79% of all valenced descriptors. In total, 21% of press items contained at least one positive descriptor, while 61% contained at least one negative descriptor. While Fidel Castro was mentioned in only 497 headlines accompanying press items, 19% of those were positive, 42% were neutral or ambiguous, and 39% were negative toward the Cuban leader.

Interestingly, there is a considerable difference in how Castro's personal characteristics were described as opposed to the evaluation of his political role. First of all, with respect to the personal dimension there were only 169 references; of these, 63% were positive, while 37% were negative. It was Castro's political beliefs and policies that occasioned the bulk of press commentary (1,658 references) and this evaluation was decidedly negative, with 83% of political descriptors negative as opposed to 17% positive.

With respect to trends in Castro's press image over time, there is general confirmation of hypothesized developments, with some interesting departures as well. Data in Table 2.2 are arranged to show the percentage of negative personal, political, and total Castro descriptors by time period. As is evident, Castro emerged from period one (that of revolutionary warfare) enjoying roughly two-thirds positive descriptors as opposed to one-third negative ones. This pre-1959 image is far more positive in orientation than had been originally hypothesized. However, the absolute number of both positive and negative descriptors is quite small and it is uncertain how well fixed this positive Castro image would have been in the minds of the American public.

The press image of Fidel Castro does indeed turn strongly negative (80%) during period two — 1959 to 1962. Negative descriptors that were

Table 2.2

Percentage of Negative Castro Descriptors

	Personal Descriptors	Political Descriptors	Total Descriptors
Period One (1953–1958)	25%	40%	32%
Period Two (1959–1962)	42	85	80
Period Three (1963–1987)	28	80	76
Period Four (1988–1992)	48	87	86
All Periods (1953–1992)	37	83	79

highlighted in this period are "communist," "dictator," "linked to firing squads," "can't tolerate criticism," "losing favor among Cubans," "tyrant," "clear and present danger to the hemisphere" and "hope in the U.S. that he would be overthrown." Positive descriptors that were highlighted during the image consolidation period are "popular," "not a communist" and "national hero."

Overall, the data indicate that the twenty-five-year period three was indeed one of image consistency, as just over three-quarters (76%) of Castro descriptors remained negative. It is in the area of personal versus political descriptors that we see the gap in negative portrayal widening, with a considerable improvement recorded in the portrayal of Castro as a person. Negative descriptors highlighted in period three were "anti-American," "brusque," "socialist," "subversive," "expanding his role in Africa," "international outlaw," "dumping criminals and perverts in the U.S.," "losing appeal in Latin America" and "power-driven." Positive descriptors highlighted in this period of image consistency were "powerful," "wants good relations with the U.S.," "has international support," "willing to negotiate" and "extraordinary leader."

The transformation of Castro's image between periods three and four is both more substantive and more dramatic than was hypothesized. Negative descriptors account for 86% of the total, up a full 10% from period three, with negative personal descriptors increasing by 20%. As well, the character of these negative descriptors changed, as hypothesized, with "his days are numbered," "anti-democratic," "cracking down on opponents," "totalitarian," "isolated," "lingers in power," "ideologue," "involved in drug smuggling," "opposed to reforming communism" and "destroyed Cuba's economy" highlighted in period four. Only one positive descriptor, "his human rights record is improving," was prominent in the last period.

Conclusion

Fidel Castro's image, as reflected in the American press, clearly has undergone dramatic changes since he first achieved international recognition in 1953. A positive (if diffuse) image characterizes period one, with an abrupt shift to a strong negative evaluation evident in period two. This negative image remains remarkably consistent, softening only marginally during the twenty-five years of period three.

Changes in Castro's image in period four, beginning in 1988, are dramatic, as the percentage of negative descriptors exceeds even that recorded in the crisis period of 1959 to 1962. However, the analysis of specific descriptors used generally confirms the hypothesized transition from the "feared" to the "failed" in that negative image.

What is perhaps most interesting is the consistent difference evident between language used to describe "Castro the person" (always positive even if only marginally so in period four), and that used to describe "Castro the politician," which is consistently negative at 80% or greater during periods two, three and four. What has become evident is that as the Cold War was coming to an end, the personal characteristics of Fidel Castro were increasingly coming under scrutiny and that the evaluation of this dimension was deteriorating.

Notes

1. This chapter was originally published as an article under the same title in *Current World Leaders, 40*, 2 (April 1997): 73–91. It is published here with their permission.
2. A study of coverage of Cuba in nine newspapers and eight periodicals done in 1986 confirms the pervasiveness of the negative image of Cuba as well as Castro (McCaughan and Platt 1988). For details on how the study was performed, see Biancalana and O'Leary 1988.
3. Data for 1953 and 1956 were coded by the author. Elizabeth Ng, Ann Hibbard and LiviannaTossutti served as able research assistants on the remainder of the coding. Sukhiminder Osahan assisted with computer-related aspects of the study.

Chapter 2 Descriptors

Fidel Castro
Words/Phrases Judged to Be Positive
Withstood the most determined efforts of the best troops Batista sent against him

Chief power in Cuba/most powerful figure in Cuba/at peak of his power/ his rule is still strong/is in power/has strengthened his position/has substantial support/in control

Determined/tenacious

Courageous/brave/bold/daring

Popular/object of affection/has growing sympathy among Cubans/still adored/object of adulation/admired by the Cuban people/lionized/ esteemed

Dynamic/most dynamic figure in government

Remarkable/extraordinary
Master at guerrilla warfare/master tactician
Strapping/powerful/dominating/macho
Dedicated to the cause of Cuban democracy/fighter for democratic aim/
     has strong ideas on liberty, democracy and social justice/fighter against
     social injustice
Intelligent/brilliant/has a fertile mind/intellectual/well-read/scholarly
Ambitious
Clever/very clever
Not a communist/not under communist influence/thrown out communists/
     moving away from communists
Leader of successful rebellion/victorious rebel leader/victorious commander
As misunderstood as Abraham Lincoln or FDR/wrongfully interpreted
Honest/not corrupt/incorruptible
Sophisticated
Eloquent/articulate/great orator/good talker/speaks with verve
Not a socialist
His victory lifts Cuba's hope
A man of destiny
Idealist/man of high ideals
Wants good relations with the U.S./offers U.S. "respectful" ties/wants to
     improve relations with the U.S./sincerely wants to improve ties/relax
     tensions with the U.S.
Enjoys international support/enjoyed the support of the U.S. press
     throughout the period of the revolution/view that Castro was a fighter
     for freedom was widely shared in the U.S.
National hero/hero/hero for most Cubans/greatest hero Cuba has known/
     savior of Cuba
Larger than life/a living icon
Patriot/undoubtedly a patriot and national revolutionary
Spectacular leader/sensational leader
The boy means to do the right thing
Willing to negotiate differences/moderate/willing to conciliate/conciliatory/
     not rigid/softening his attitude
Sincere/dedicated
Confident that he is invulnerable/indestructible
Humane/tolerant
His human rights report card shows improvement/releasing political
     prisoners
Effective/exemplary politician
Appeared to be in good health/robust/looked fit
Made considerable progress in education, health, housing/helped
     campesinos
Confident/self-assured/has faith in himself
Relaxed
Free-wheeling and experimenting
Pragmatic

One of the most fascinating and influential political figures on the world stage today/most fantastic career of any leader in Latin America's independent history/leader of world stature/one of the personalities of the century/best-known man in the world today/one of the most extraordinary figures to appear on the Latin American scene/Latin American statesman/a liberator who has become not only a guide and ruler but a living institution/demonstrated leadership in the region/has given Cuba a global resonance/has taken a prominent place on the world stage

In a state of euphoria/euphoric

Has a magnetic personality/his appeal lies in his personality/mesmerizing personality

Charismatic

Liberator

Has to be given credit for making the leaders of the hemisphere aware of their common problems

Friendly/extremely friendly

Witty/amusing/has dry sense of humor

Praises/admires/lauds President Carter

Local boy who made good/one of Galicia's most famous progeny

Proud

Magnanimous in victory

Far-sighted/visionary

Political genius

[Rule is] legitimate

Shrewd observer of international economic trends/no dummy

Youthful liberator who felled the corrupt tyranny of Fulgencio Batista

Plays the leadership role with all the vigor of a quarter century ago

Charming/has rough charm

Cautious/careful/restrained

Individualistic/marches to his own drummer/independent

Impressive stage presence/has the capacity to stride center stage for hours/ used his hands like an Italian tenor delivering a Puccini aria/actor

A neuvo amigo

Amenable

Has helped blacks in Cuba

Liberated Cuban women

Intuitive

Words/Phrases Judged to Be Negative

Ruthless/brutal/merciless/unforgiving

Unscrupulous/corrupt

Communist/in close alliance with communists/communist-tinged/ communist-oriented/pro-communist/captive of communists/communist puppet/communist-stooge/communist-dominated/Marxist/Marxist-Leninist/[linked to communism]

Mad [crazy]

Authoritarian/betrayed an authoritarian streak/autocrat

Dictator/potential middle-class dictator/Red dictator/pro-communist dictator/one in a long line of dictators/exchanged a known dictator for an unknown dictator

Angry/furious/infuriated/piqued/annoyed/irked

Days are numbered/the beginning of the end will be crushed/will not last out the year

Made disastrous tactical mistakes

Burley

Fallen idol/falling star/in terminal decline/not seen as the awesome, towering giant he once seemed to be

Assassin/murderer/shot many Batista people/[linked to firing squads and executions]

A misfit/becoming more ridiculous

Does not give the impression of great talent for government/lacks ability to govern

Demagogue/insolent/raving demagogue

Cannot tolerate criticism/denounces/assails critics/equates all opposition with supporters of Batista/does not like to be opposed

Cannot logically argue that nobody wants an election/never submitted his regime to electoral judgment/does not hold elections/rejects elections

Attacks Cuba's press/virtually destroys any [press] organ whenever he attacks it

Traitor/traitor to all promises/traitor to the revolution

Needs to be chastened

Anti-American/has an anti-American attitude/has a consuming hatred of America/provokes and defies the U.S./raises the specter of anti-yankeeism to quell internal strife/ranting and raving about the U.S.

Brusque/impatient

Paranoid/suspicious

Nervous/looks to the future nervously/worried/

Brooding

Divorced from reality/illusionary/does not realize the world has changed

Betrayer of the Cuban revolution/betrayer of the Cuban people

Anti-democratic/not a democrat/autocrat/rejects elections

Losing appeal to Latin Americans/prestige in Latin America has dimmed substantially/image in Latin America is tarnished

Losing favor/losing support among Cubans/disenchantment with him in Cuba is widespread/enthusiasm for his government has eroded/target of unrest/fears a social explosion

Tyrant/great tyrant/stinking communist tyrant/his government a tyranny/despot/despotic

Insolent/impertinent

Liar/does not tell the truth

Capricious/impulsive/erratic/irrational/inconsistent/unpredictable

Consolidating personal power/determined to get rid of the last vestiges of internal opposition/tightening his hold on Cuba/cracking down on/

arrests opponents/expelled priests/purged the Communist Party/purged the army

A clear and present danger to the hemisphere/a threat to the hemisphere/ a threat to the Caribbean/exporter of revolution

Left-wing/leftist

Propagandist/darling of Soviet propagandists

Terrorist/runs a terrorist state

Forced to keep up his guard/kept off balance/caught off guard

Failed to deliver bread, much less freedom

Widespread hope in the United States that he would be overthrown/should be overthrown

I would rather have Castro against me than for me

Most formidable enemy of the U.S. ever to rise in Latin America

Could have completed the revolution without putting himself in the hands of the Russians and Chinese/revolution could have been saved without communism

Bully/bearded bully-boy/has become the bully

Cubans have chosen exile rather than live under his yoke

Socialist/declared Cuba a socialist state/symbol of socialism [linked to socialism]

Totalitarian/repressive/human rights violator/force alone keeps him in power/built a vice-like security apparatus

Inflexible

Obscure Latin American revolutionary

Self-centered/self-serving

Aggressive/militant/provocative

Eager to win membership in the Warsaw Pact

Desperate/reduced to a state of desperation

Megalomaniac/maintains an imperial self-image

Comrade

Evasive

Isolated

Doomed

Irritable

Fiery/firebrand

Arsonist

Has an overbearing personality

Subversive/linked to subversion/has not abandoned subversion

Rat/fink

Lingers on in power/anachronism/anachronistic/aging/a back-tired, cynical man whose generation is already passing from the scene/has been around for a long time/ last of the true believers/long-lasting dictator/fossil Marxist/Marxist museum piece/one of the few remaining communist leaders/ seems back in 1959/1960s/clinging to a crumbling ideology/ moving Cuba backwards

Sarcastic/cynical

His rhetoric is offensive/bloated

The scourge that has descended upon Cuba
His charisma has faded/personal luster has declined
Eager to be a spokesman for communist "liberation" organizations
Dreams of glory as a communist world historical figure/aspiring to be not only a Cuban leader but one of the towering figures of the worldwide communist movement
Expanding his role to Africa/pursuing a militant policy in Africa/extending his influence abroad/moving into Angola
An international outlaw/thief/bandit/criminal
Has increasing contacts with black revolutionary elements in the Caribbean/ has played the racial factor very cleverly
Adventurist
Up to something dirty
Power-driven/man who wanted power/centered all power in himself/ hungers/craves for power/fosters the cult of personality/craves for leadership/serves as the final arbiter over life and death
Opportunist
Suffered a humiliating setback/suffered a series of political, economic and psychological setbacks
Miscalculated/miscalculated badly/overreacted
[Rule is] illegitimate
Beating up on the little Bahamas/engaged in fierce mud-slinging against Spain
Has been dumping his criminals and perverts on American shores/sends us his criminals/opened the gates for the flood of Cubans to Key West to relieve the unemployment problem and rid his society of anti-revolutionary elements and other undesirables/using the U.S. as an escape valve for discontents/rid the country of malcontents
Offended some Latin American and Caribbean governments
A tricky demon
Excommunicated from the Catholic church
A grotesque joke
Exploiter
Despicable/detested
Foolish/a fool
Needs Soviet troops to remain in power
Ideologue/doctrinaire/hard-liner/orthodox/represents old thinking
Still sees himself as a leader of Marxist revolution
Involved in drug trafficking/defends Noriega on drug charges
Crabbed-caudillo
Rattled/disoriented
Radical/fiery, young maverick of the Marxist-Leninist world
Remote/distant
Destroyed the Cuban economy/an economic failure/bankrupted Cuba
Abusive
Scorns Gorbachev's model/rejects economic and political reforms/moving Cuba away from glasnost and perestroika

Polemicist
Strident
Stunned/shocked by events in Moscow/Soviet gods have failed him
Painted himself into his own corner
Eccentric/strange
Shielded by the Soviet Union's power
Almost started World War III/hotheaded/urged the Soviets to shower
    nuclear missiles on U.S. cities
Has been shrunk to his actual size/has lost his sting
Insists that communism has not failed in Cuba/socialism's last defender
Cunning
Beleaguered/increasingly beleaguered/circling the wagons
Some sort of Adolf Hitler/methods are exactly the same as Hitler's/
    compared to Stalin/Pol Pot/Ceausescu
Batista was just a little girl compared with Fidel
His role in actual fighting during the Cuban revolution had been small/
    given too much credit for success of revolution
Suspended Cuba's Christmas and New Year's celebrations
Fascistic
Failed to promote women to high-ranking government posts
Holds world opinion in contempt
A fossil with teeth
Stymied/doesn't know what to do
Mired in a distant, ugly past
Left wondering whom he can really trust
Doesn't understand anything

Words/Phrases Judged to Be Neutral or Ambiguous
Young/youthful
Leader of Orthodoxo Party/an Orthodoxo
Student/student leader/former student
[Actual age in years]
Cuba's leader for [number] of years
Agent of Prio Socarras/not linked to Prio
Restless
Lawyer/schooled in law
Leader/Cuban leader/chieftain/revolutionary leader/rebel leader/chief of
    revolt/leader of insurrection/leader of revolution
Weary/tired and sleepless/dazed/groggy
Señor/Mr.
Doctor/Dr.
Disaffected
Exiled
Jesuit-trained
Disappointed
Leader/commander of the 26 July Movement/began the revolt/Father of
    the Revolution

Symbol of the revolution/symbol of revolutionary opposition
Lacked support from anti-Batista politicians
Romantic/quixotic/given to periodic crusades
Bearded/the bearded one/wears a beard
Insulted
Maximum leader/jefe maximo
Six feet tall/tall/big
Low-voiced/soft-spoken
Has fair command of English/speaks some English
Son of wealthy sugar planter/son of a Spanish pick and shovel laborer who
    rose to be a rich sugar planter/son of a Galician immigrant
Head of nation's armed forces/commander in chief
Intense/tense
Ascetic/austere/has little time for personal life
As amusing as Adlai Stevenson
Believes that exceptional leaders influence history and even make it
Considers himself a leader of the Latin peoples in general and of Caribbean
    peoples in particular/cast himself as elder statesman and champion of
    regional unity
Premier/prime minister/president/president of state council/head of state
Green-uniformed/khaki-clad/dressed in fatigues/in full-dress military
    uniform/dressed in blue jeans and a blue shirt/[any description of his
    dress]
An unknown quantity
Impassioned high priest
Nationalist
Demonstrated that there can be no aristocracy in Cuba/believes in a no-
    class society
Has no intention or desire to run for president
Robin Hood
Defiant
Has achieved in two years what it has taken some socialist countries many
    years to accomplish/socialized everything in Cuba
A nationalist driven into the communist camp/forced into communist camp
Thrives on admiration and applause
Will stop at nothing to defend himself and his revolution
Hard/tough/means business
Uncompromising/uncompromising politically
Self-styled hemispheric oracle
Changed from insular leader to prophet of world revolution
Has special talent for turning bad situations into assets/made a brilliant
    recovery from a blunder/turns the tables
Oozes charisma like Lenin
The preacher/preaches socialist equality with the fervor of a Bible Belt
    evangelist
Seemed at pains to moderate his image

Has abandoned the barricades of revolution in favor of compromise and
    maneuver
Has a flair for self-publicity/publicity-hungry
Middle-aged/in middle age
Emotional/wept with emotion
Quiescent, Tito-like figure
An artful juggler
Vicarious avenger of the humiliation of the Spanish-American War
Wayward son of the Spanish Empire
Horatio Alger, once removed
Champion of struggles for national liberation/determined to play a leading
    role in the struggle of blacks in both Africa and Latin America for political
    power/committed to the liberation of Africa
Mixture of sweeping charm and evasiveness
Vulnerable
Will learn sad lessons in Africa
Indignant
Has a genuine devotion to "socialist internationalism"
Napoleon of the Caribbean
In a way has hypnotized the island of Cuba
Would not play the role of beggar/cannot occupy the role of obedient
    servant
Often not in agreement with Soviet policies, especially in the third world/at
    odds with Moscow's foreign policy
Came to recognize the tremendous cost of Soviet military assistance
Praised Maurice Bishop
Began to wonder about leading a communist revolution in the hemisphere
His usefulness to the U.S.S.R. seems to be diminishing
One of Gorbachev's prickliest allies/long a source of mingled pride and
    despair to the U.S.S.R./Kruschev's unsteady friend
Towering, theatrical, unreconstructed Cuban commander-in-chief
Suspicious of currents of change that are sweeping the world
Sportsman/baseball player
Predicted the U.S.S.R. might disintegrate
Adamant
Kind of like a sane drug
Had played the world leader
Had a poor relationship with his father
Implied the Russians were betraying him in 1991 and 1992 just like they had
    in 1962
Contradictory/enigmatic
El Caballo/the Horse
Took personal blame for the disarray in virtually every segment of the
    nation's economic life
Had severe doubts about putting Soviet missiles in Cuba
Believes he alone can set the terms for Cuban-American relations

Leader/chairman of the non-aligned third world nations
Stormy
Upstaged Gorbachev/eclipsed Gorbachev
Fidel is our Papa

Chapter 3

Press Framing of the 1965 U.S. Intervention in the Dominican Republic: A Test of the Propaganda Model

WALTER C. SODERLUND

D ue in large part to American fears of a second Cuban Revolution, the Dominican Republic first experienced the application of economic sanctions in 1960 to aid in the removal of the Trujillo dictatorship (Slater 1964; Wiarda 1965; Crassweller 1966). This was followed by a United States–led military intervention in 1965, undertaken to stabilize a civil war situation resulting from an attempt by junior military officers to restore a democratically elected president, Juan Bosch, to power (Wells 1963; Wilson 1966). The short-term impact of the U.S. intervention was to protect the high command of the Dominican military, which had been responsible for the removal of Bosch in a coup d'etat, on the grounds that the victory of the pro-Bosch forces would lead to a Cuban-style communist takeover of the island nation (Kurzman 1965; Szulc 1965; Center for Strategic Studies 1966; Martin 1966; Draper 1968).

Journalists reporting on the military operations from the Dominican Republic were at best unimpressed with official Washington charges of communist infiltration and subversion. Respected journalist Theodore Draper, writing less than a month following the U.S. military intervention, put the following spin on the operation: "Instead of supporting the forces 'committed to democracy and social justice,' the U.S. decided to support the forces that had overthrown them in 1963 and were determined to prevent them from returning in 1965" (1965, p. 13). The research reported in this chapter examines the way in which this intervention — the first overt commitment of American troops in a combat role in a Latin American political crisis since the proclamation of the Good Neighbor policy in the 1930s – was presented to the American people in the reporting of *The New York Times* during the year 1965. In doing so we will employ the concept of media "framing," defined as the "central organizing idea for making sense of relevant events and suggesting what is at issue" (Gamson 1989, p. 157; see also Entman 1991, 1993; and Iyengar 1991).

Given the critical tone of journalistic reporting of the intervention (not limited to Draper), it is clear that the official government line of an intervention needed to nip a communist insurgency in the bud, had not gone unchallenged. Thus, the extent to which the Herman and Chomsky "propaganda model" – positing the press as little more than a spokesperson for government policy – characterized crisis reporting (see chapter 1) needs to be examined. Specifically, to what extent were "official" versus "oppositional" views of the crisis expressed, and can *New York Times'* reporting of the crisis be seen as essentially serving a propaganda function?

Background

The Dominican Civil War, beginning in late April 1965, pitted pro-Bosch military forces (the "Constitutionalists") against the high command of the Dominican military (the "Loyalists").[1] By and large, hostilities between the two sides, as well as subsequent "peacekeeping" operations on the part of both U.S. and later OAS forces, were confined to the nation's capital. Three days into the Civil War, at a point where the Constitutionalist forces were near victory, U.S. forces were landed in the Dominican Republic to protect American citizens who were being evacuated and "to prevent a 'Communist takeover'" (Draper 1965, p. 16). This allowed the Loyalist side time to regroup and reorganize its military resources.

Much of the controversy that surrounds the U.S. action in the Dominican Republic centers around the question of communist control of the pro-Bosch Constitutionalist forces. The position of the U.S. government was that the threat of a communist takeover was a serious one (Martin 1966, pp. 673–676; U.S. Senate 1965, pp. 55–60), while U.S. journalists who accompanied the initial military landing were extremely skeptical about charges that the Constitutionalists were under communist control (Draper 1968, pp. 60–72; Kurzman 1965, pp.

157–161; Szulc 1965, pp. 51–56, 79–83). "Official" and "oppositional" points of view were clearly differentiated. The issue as framed by the U.S. government was one of communism versus anti-communism, while for journalists on the scene it was one of democratic restoration versus military dictatorship. The research question addressed in this chapter is, how well, in the face of significant journalistic hostility, did the U.S. government get its definition of reality reflected in *New York Times'* coverage of events occurring in the Dominican Republic?

Methods

There is little doubt that the press plays a crucial transmission and interpretation role in getting the American people "on side" with respect to foreign policy decisions. According to Bennett,

> The first important political observation about the American mass media is that to an important extent they regulate the content of pubic information and communication in the U.S political system. Mass mediated images of reality set the limits of who in the world we think we are as a people, and what in the world we think we are doing…. That is what the mass media do: translate the complex and multi-voiced reality of our times into another, symbolic realm of simpler images and fewer voices. (1988, p. 14)

Indeed, in the literature dealing with the role of the press in U.S. foreign policy, there is significant evidence that would lead us to hypothesize that the U.S. government would have done quite well in getting its representation of reality (a communist insurrection apprehended by American military action) across to the American people. Cohen identifies possible press roles as those of "advocate" or "critic" of government policy (1963, pp. 31–47), while Paletz and Entman point out that in the area of foreign policy (in contrast to domestic policy), there tends to be consensus among elites. "Elites concerned with foreign affairs tend to agree on goals, to disagree intermittently only on tactics" (1981, pp. 214). As mentioned, Herman and Chomsky, perhaps the most extreme critics of the press for following government leads, advance the "propaganda model" of state/press relations, charging the American media with serving as little more than a mouthpiece for government policy (1988, p. 289). Parenti seems to address the factors involved in the Dominican Republic directly, citing the following general patterns of omission and distortion in American press coverage: "(1) the way the media consistently suppress descriptions of the content of Third World struggles for national independence, economic justice, and revolutionary reform; (2) the way the media ignore U.S. sponsorship of reactionary repression and underplay the repression itself; (3) the way the media reduce Third World struggles to an encounter between U.S. virtue and Communist evil" (1986, p. 185).

For the research reported in this chapter, all news items dealing with the Dominican Republic appearing in *The New York Times* during 1965 were coded for descriptive words and phrases used with respect to (1) the two sides in the Civil War: Loyalist and Constitutional forces; and (2) the major leadership figures associated with each side: ex-President Joaquin Balaguer, Gen. Elias Wesin y Wesin and Gen. Antonio Imbert Barerra on the Loyalist side, and President Juan Bosch and Lt. Col. Francisco Caamaño Deño on the Constitutionalist side.[2] Particular attention was paid to language that would prompt readers to interpret the intervention as a response to a communist insurgency. Descriptive words and phrases were then collated and sent to a panel of six academics working in the areas of communication, political science and Latin American studies, along with instructions to adopt an American perspective and judge whether each descriptor would reflect positively or negatively on each side or individual. If at least five of the six agreed to a positive or negative evaluation (83%), the descriptor would be so coded. (See the full list of descriptors and how they were coded at the end of this chapter.)

Findings

A total of 646 stories were found to have codable descriptors with respect to either the two sides involved in the Civil War or their major political/military leaders. Roughly half of these stories appeared in the months of April and May, the time when major military operations and negotiations for a cease-fire were taking place. Of the 613 stories that had an identifiable dateline, 44% were filed from the Dominican Republic, 40% from the United States, while 15% were filed from other locations, primarily Puerto Rico and Cuba. Hard news, appearing either on the front page or elsewhere in the newspaper, accounted for 77% of content, with editorials, feature columns and letters to the editor accounting for 19%. Photos standing alone and editorial cartoons made up the balance of content. Journalists working directly for *The New York Times* were the source of 72% of content, while American wire services contributed 18%. Cold War language appeared in 39% of story texts overall, with specific mention of communism appearing in 33% of story texts and 8% of the headlines that accompanied them. Fidel Castro and/or the Cuban Revolution were mentioned in 11% of stories.[3]

Data in Table 3.1 show the balance of positive and negative descriptors used in referring to the two sides and their respective leaders. First among interesting findings is that the Loyalist forces and their leaders — the chief beneficiaries of the U.S. intervention — did not receive very much press attention. Only thirty-six evaluative descriptors were used to refer to the Loyalist forces in general, while less than twenty each were used with respect to Joaquin Balaguer, Antonio Imbert Barerra and Elias Wesin y Wesin. In contrast, evaluative descriptors were used in reference to the Constitutionalist forces 131 times, Juan Bosch sixty times and Francisco Caamaño Deño thirty-seven times. Press attention was clearly focused on the rebel Constitutionalists rather than the Loyalists.

Table 3.1
_____

**Percentage of Positive and Negative Descriptors
Attributed to Various Actors in the Dominican Civil War
(neutral and ambiguous descriptors omitted)**

	Positive	Negative
Loyalist Forces (N=36)	28%	72%
Joaquin Balaguer (N=19)	63	37
Elias Wesin y Wesin (N=15)	53	47
Antonio Imbert Barerra (N=19)	32	68
Constitutionalist Forces (N=131)	14%	86%
Juan Bosch (N=60)	52	48
Francisco Caamaño Deño (N=37)	46	54

Second, in general, the Constitutionalists and their leaders were treated more negatively than the Loyalists and their leaders. For the Constitutionalist forces, 86% of valenced descriptors were negative as opposed to 72% negative for the Loyalists, a 14% difference. Somewhat paradoxically, the major political figures associated with both sides (Balaguer and Bosch) ended up with positive evaluations, with Balaguer's 63% positive balance outstripping Bosch's positive balance of 52% by 11%. With respect to military leaders, leading Loyalist general, Wesin y Wesin, achieved a narrow positive balance of evaluative descriptors (53%), while the major military leader of the Constitutionalist forces, Lt. Col. Caamaño Deño, received a similar narrow, but negative balance (54%). Among Loyalist leaders, only General Imbert Barerra (a surviving assassin of Trujillo), who offered himself as a solution to the country's political difficulties over the summer of 1965, received a negative balance of evaluative descriptors (68%).

Significant for our analysis is that the location from which stories were filed appears to have contributed to the predominantly negative treatment of the Constitutionalists. The data in Table 3.2 clearly show that stories originating from the Dominican Republic were far less likely to focus on issues of communism than those filed either from the United States or from elsewhere in the Caribbean (many were filed from Cuba), with differences on all four communist indicators statistically significant, one (p<.01.), and three (p<.001). Obviously the Cold War implications of the Dominican intervention appeared more significant to those who wrote about the crisis from locations

Table 3.2

Percentage of Stories About the Dominican Republic Containing Communist Markers, by Dateline

	Dominican Republic N=272	US N=247	Other N=94	X^2 Sig
Cold War Frames	28%	40%	51%	.001
Communist Text	27	39	37	.01
Communist Headline	4	9	20	.001
Castro/Cuba	5	15	21	.001

other than on the ground in the Dominican Republic. Since well over half of the total content did not originate from the Dominican Republic, the views of journalists actually covering the crisis in the Dominican Republic did not predominate in the overall mix of coverage.

Conclusion

Based on this comprehensive examination of coverage in *The New York Times*, it seems fairly clear that as the Dominican intervention developed, to a significant degree the United States government succeeded in overcoming journalistic hostility with respect to its policy of keeping the Constitutionalist side from winning and restoring Juan Bosch to power. First, Cold War frames appeared in nearly 40% of press items, with specific references to communism appearing in fully one-third of content. Second, major press attention focused on the Constitutionalist forces, not on the Loyalist side. Thus, although forces representing both sides were evaluated negatively, the unsavory features of the Constitutionalists received greater press "amplification" than did those of the Loyalists (Soderlund 1994). While the evaluations of leaders of both sides (with the exception of Imbert Barerra) were more middle of the road, Balaguer and Wesin y Wesin both received more favorable treatment than did their Constitutionalist counterparts, Bosch and Caamaño Deño.

While it is impossible to explain fully the reasons why the U.S. government's interpretation of events prevailed in press coverage, Bennett's theory of "indexing" appears consistent with the pattern that emerged. Briefly, indexing suggests that American media follow closely official government voices in deciding what is news and what spin to put on that news. Specifically, "journalists may tend to support liberal or oppositional views in the news, but they give voice to those views only when parallel voices are being raised in circles of government power" (1990, p. 110). Applying Bennett's indexing theory to press reporting of the U.S. intervention in the Dominican Republic, what we see is that oppositional views coming from reporters in the field became diluted by contributions stressing "official versions of events" readily supplied to journalists covering the story from Washington (1990, p. 103).

Specifically, with respect to Herman and Chomsky's propaganda model, it is apparent that in the final mix, journalistic evaluation of the Dominican intervention is composed of two competing versions of events. Journalists reporting from the field, who were not buying into the government "communist insurrection" line regarding the situation, were not left without a voice, nor were Bosch or Caamaño Deño effectively demonized, as was, for example, General Manuel Noriega during the American invasion of Panama (see chapter 13). However, these oppositional journalistic voices did not prevail, as their version of events was significantly submerged in the chorus of "official" voices emanating from the American government in Washington. Thus the government did succeed in establishing the Cold War as the appropriate framework for interpreting the intervention, even faced with significant opposition from credible journalists seeking to present an alternative point of view. In the case of the Dominican intervention, the forces of officialdom more than held their own in establishing the dominant frame for popular interpretation of this seminal Cold War event in the Western Hemisphere.

Notes

1. The derivation of the Loyalist label is not clear. At best it appears that the generals were loyal to their own self-interest.
2. Thanks go to Livianna Tossutti who assisted in a major way with the coding and to Sukhiminder Osahan who did the computer analysis of the data.
3. These indicators cannot be added as in many stories there were two or more communist markers.

Chapter 3 Descriptors

Constitutional Forces
Words/Phrases Judged to Be Positive
Forces of liberation
Determined
Liberal and democratic
Progressive movement
A new Dominican social force
Young officers/lawyers/doctors/teachers/intellectuals
Middle class
Armed soldiers and civilians including women and teenagers
Contains moderate and democratic social reformers

Words/Phrases Judged to Be Negative
Disorganized
Ruffians
Linked to communism/communists included in ranks/communist junta/
  animated by communist elements/communist-dominated/communist
  conspirators/communists have decisive voice in policy/pro-communist/
  Marxist-Leninist revolutionaries
Leaders received training in Cuba
Killing individuals refusing to join them
Mobs of boys
Rampaging
Wild-eyed tigers
Revolutionaries/uniformed revolutionaries
Terrorized more than 600 Americans and other foreigners
Extreme left/left-wing extremists
Castroite/Castro-like
Communists, Trujillo fascists and adventurists dominated rebel commands
Critical of U.S.
Subversives
Have radical ideas
Obdurate
Now confined to a twenty-square-block section of the capital

Words/Phrases Judged to Be Neutral or Ambiguous
Pro-Bosch group
Rebels/rebel movement
Junta
Caamaño movement/Caamaño group
Bosch-Caamaño forces
Civilian commandos organized by a heterogeneous group of political parties
14th of June Group

Juan Bosch
Words/Phrases Judged to Be Positive
Liberal/true liberal/leader of liberal elements/regarded as a liberal
Leading contender for the presidency
Democrat
No communist/not a communist/to claim Bosch is a communist is ridiculous
First legally elected president in thirty-five years
Idol of the streets/exiled idol/people adore him
Inspirational leader of the rebels
Popularly elected
A very nice man
Last legally elected president
Strongly anti-communist
Respected leader

Reformist leader/non-communist social reformer
Father figure of Dominican politics

Words/Phrases Judged to Be Negative
Poor executive (during his term of office)
Extremist
Linked to communism/Castro/reluctant to reject communism/soft on
    communism
His government was becoming corrupt, disorderly and communist
Incompetent, poet-professor type
Do-gooder
Blamed the United States
Seemingly broken and embittered

Words/Phrases Judged to Be Neutral or Ambiguous
Former president/ousted president
Overthrown/toppled/deposed in a military coup in 1963
Exiled president/leader/in exile
Professor
Doctor/Dr.
Mr.
President
Gray eminence to the rebels
Leader of the left-of-center Dominican Revolutionary Party/leader of the
    DRP
Left-of-center reform advocate
Democratic socialist

Francisco Caamaño Deño
Words/Phrases Judged to Be Positive
Highly regarded for his abilities
Trained in the U.S.
Constitutional/legal president
Robust-appearing
Has a strong voice
Has an assured manner
Relaxed and confident
Confident and rested
Denies communist connection
Has resolute face
Determined leader
Has great popular support

Words/Phrases Judged to Be Negative
Son of an influential general under Trujillo
A killer by heritage

Linked to communism
Trembling with anger
Fidel Castro in the early stages
Cold to the OAS
Assails the U.S.

Words/Phrases Judged to Be Neutral or Ambiguous
High-ranking police officer
Army officer
Rebel/insurgent leader/commander/leading fight against junta
Colonel
President/interim/provisional/new president
Head of the rebel government
Thirty-two years old
Has dark thinning hair and a brown moustache
Leader of constitutional rebels
Wearing a green combat uniform and a pistol
Former rebel leader
May run for presidency or vice-presidency

Loyalist Forces
Words/Phrases Judged to Be Positive
U.S.-backed/created civilian-military junta
Emboldened by U.S. military support
Controls virtually all of the Dominican Republic

Words/Phrases Judged to Be Negative
Badly mauled
Anti-democratic
Unpopular
Brutal
Ultra-Nazi
Reactionary
Oligarchic associates
Obdurate
Accused of executions
Rump junta
Defiant
Dictatorship
"Guerrillacy" of the Pentagon

Words/Phrases Judged to Be Neutral or Ambiguous
Anti-Bosch military group/forces
Counter-revolutionary
Military rightists
Anti-Caamaño junta

Civilian-military junta
Imbert junta/troops loyal to Imbert
Anti-rebel junta/counterforce to the rebels
Government of National Reconstruction
Rightist successor to the Cabral government

Joaquin Balaguer
Words/Phrases Judged to Be Positive
Moderate
Has considerable oratorical powers
Popular in the Dominican Republic
Father figure of Dominican politics
Quite satisfactory to Washington
Known for his honesty and moderation
Leading contender for the presidency
Reformist
Has reputation for respectability
Scholarly
Urged peace in the Dominican Republic
Target of a communist assassination attempt

Words/Phrases Judged to Be Negative
Trujillo's old henchman
Originally served under the Trujillo dictatorship
Figurehead president in the 1960s
Played a front man's role under Trujillo
Docile

Words/Phrases Judged to Be Neutral or Ambiguous
Former president
Head of Reformist Party
Slight
Graying
Speaks softly
Doctor/Dr.
President from 1960 to 1962
Fifty-eight years old
Professional politician
Seeking support of rightists

Elias Wesin y Wesin
Words/Phrases Judged to Be Positive
Washington's man
Anti-communist
Public spirited
Incorruptible
Deeply religious

Strong

Words/Phrases Judged to Be Negative
Ultra-rightist
Swarthy
Agrees to resign and changes his mind
Symbol of a possible new military dictatorship
Forced out of the country

Words/Phrases Judged to Be Neutral or Ambiguous
Brig. general/general
Running Mr. Reid's military arm
Commander of the armed forces
Commander of Air Force elements
Head of armed forces chief training center
Short
Plump
Bushy-browed
Forty-one years old
Roman Catholic
Doesn't have much of a social life
Of Lebanese descent
Leading opponent of the rebels
Chief target of the rebels
Has right-wing political views
Appointed consul-general in Miami

Antonio Imbert Barerra
Words/Phrases Judged to Be Positive
One of two survivors of the conspiracy that assassinated Trujillo/the man
    who assassinated Rafael Trujillo
Chosen, groomed and put in by Washington
Urged by the U.S. to assume leadership of the junta

Words/Phrases Judged to Be Negative
Unpopular/not a popular national figure/has no popular support
Symbol of a new military dictatorship
The new Trujillo of the Dominican Republic
Hated
Cruel, corrupt and cynical
Military dictator
Uninspiring and unscrupulous
Criticizes the OAS

Words/Phrases Judged to Be Neutral or Ambiguous
President
Head of new junta/head of civilian-military junta

Right wing
Lackey of the American interventionists
Backed by a minority of the Dominican military

Part II

The Second Wave:
Nicaragua, El Salvador
and Grenada

Chapter 4

Images of the Nicaraguan Revolution, 1978–1980[1]

WALTER C. SODERLUND

In a seminal work on international press images, Merrill defines an image as "a composite of impressions, themes, opinions, and attitudes that form an overall or dominant 'representation.' It is a descriptive 'shortcut' or a consolidated characterization of the 'people' and the 'government' of a country" (1962, p. 203). The primary focus of the research in this chapter is on images of the Nicaraguan Revolution as portrayed in the leading newspapers of the United States, Great Britain and Canada during the crucial three-year period surrounding the success of that revolution in July 1979. This research reconstructs and evaluates the way in which the revolution and its various participants were presented to political elites and mass publics alike.

In a wide-ranging critique of modern media, Smith points out that for most people, most of the time, the press is the primary source of information regarding events that lie outside the range of their own experience.

> The journalist is sent somewhere, equipped with the right of ubiquitous trespass, to transpose some distant reality into the preconceptions of his own audience/society. The editor is the director of political reality, the reporter his myrmidon and in the relationship between the two of them and their audience lies a complete world structure, an image of reality shaped according to their mutual needs and aspirations (1980, p. 24).

It is also evident, based on poll data dealing with attitudes toward the press in both the United States and Canada, that at the time mass media enjoyed very high credibility with citizens. Data from the U.S. Gallup Poll indicated that major media outlets received believability scores ranging between 70% and 87% (*The New York Times* 1986), while an Environics poll in Canada reported that 60% of Canadians felt that media reporting was "fair and objective" (*The Citizen* 1988).

Moreover, there is a relationship between press coverage of international events and policy responses of other countries to these events. The press not only provides information to political elites, who may participate directly in foreign policy decision making (Cohen 1963), but also provides the raw materials for mass public opinion, which at minimum sets the parameters of acceptable policy options (McCombs and Shaw 1972; Semmel 1979; Munton 1983–84; Weaver 1984; Etheredge 1985; Taras and Gotlieb Taras 1987).

In the context of hemispheric relations it can be argued persuasively that the Nicaraguan Revolution was an event of considerable importance. It certainly set the tone for the Reagan Administration's foreign policy with respect to the entire Caribbean Basin area, a policy based on the view that Soviet-Cuban expansion was the major cause of problems in the region and that, as such, it required an American response (Nogee and Spanier 1988; North 1991). As a consequence, American policy toward the Faribundo Marti National Liberation Front (FMLN) in El Salvador, Maurice Bishop and the New Jewel Movement in Grenada, and Michael Manley in Jamaica, cannot be fully understood without an appreciation of what the administration believed had happened in Nicaragua. It is also possible to speculate that the altered American responses to popular agitation against long-time American clients Ferdinand Marcos in the Philippines and Jean-Claude Duvalier in Haiti in the mid-1980s were linked to "lessons learned" from a perceived earlier overcommitment to Anastasio Somoza in Nicaragua (Christian 1986, pp. 110–133).

In this context, how was the major political and social upheaval associated with the revolution in Nicaragua presented by the press to American, British and Canadian mass publics and decision makers, both prior to and following its success? Were the issues and images of the revolution contained in press reporting in the three countries essentially similar or dissimilar? To the extent that they were dissimilar, what was the nature of these differences? And how compatible was

American press coverage with the hostile policy toward the Sandinistas undertaken by the Reagan administration in 1981?

Methods

The New York Times, The Times/Sunday Times (London),[2] and *The Globe and Mail* (Toronto) were sampled for material on Nicaragua beginning in January 1978 and ending in December 1980 on the following basis: For each month, a random number from 1 to 6 was chosen, and, beginning with that day, every third day during the month was included in the sample. In 1978 this method produced a sample of 115 days; in 1979, 120 days; and in 1980, 116 days. The total sample over the three-year period consisted of 351 days.[3] Intercoder reliability was established at 83% (Holsti 1969, p. 140).

The New York Times enjoys the reputation of premier newspaper in the United States. Accordingly, it serves as the "newspaper of record" in that country, as does *The Times* in Great Britain (Cohen 1963, p. 134; Merrill 1968, p. 45; Underwood 1983, p. 63; and Barney and Nelson 1983, pp. 306–310). *The Globe and Mail*, while not ranking among the elite newspapers of the world, does fall within the group of secondary elite papers and is seen as the leading Canadian newspaper for coverage of international affairs (Soderlund et al. 1991).

For all press items dealing with Nicaragua found on sample days, the following variables were coded: date, type of content, source of content, dateline and length of item. In addition, thematic content,[4] headlines and descriptive words and phrases used with respect to Somoza and the Sandinistas were recorded. Finally, three of Cohen's roles of the press were operationalized: (1) the press as an instrument of government (i.e., a supporter of government policy); (2) the press as a critic of government policy (the watchdog role); and (3) the press as an advocate of policy of its own origination (1963, pp. 22–47). These roles of the press were examined with respect to both American policy and Nicaraguan policy under Somoza as well as the Sandinistas.

Images, as conceptualized by Fagen, are composed of two dimensions — the "cognitive" and the "evaluative." The cognitive dimension (measured by levels of information) can vary from low to high, while evaluation can be seen as negative or positive. By dichotomizing each dimension, it is possible to generate four types of image structure: low information/negative evaluation, low information/positive evaluation, high information/negative evaluation, and high information/positive evaluation (1966, pp. 70–76).

   From the variables coded for the study it is possible to examine both the "information supplying" and "evaluation supplying" roles of the press. Information supply is related to volume of coverage and, to a lesser extent, type and length of individual items. In addition, one can determine which specific substantive issue areas were most salient in press reporting on the Nicaraguan Revolution. Evaluative direction is determined by three measures. First, the actual words and phrases used to describe Somoza and the Sandinistas were recorded. These were then grouped into three categories (positive, neutral and negative), based on an American perspective of the meanings. Here we were especially interested in examining the use of the terms "leftist/left wing" as opposed to "communist/Marxist" to describe the Sandinistas. Finally, through an analysis of Cohen's roles of the press, we were able to assess the policy advice offered by the press in the three countries to various actors involved in the revolutionary process.

Findings

Over the three-year study period a total of 277 items dealing with Nicaragua appeared in the sample of the three newspapers. *The New York Times* accounted for 60% of total coverage, 22% appeared in the British papers, while 18% appeared in *The Globe and Mail*. Overall, just over two-thirds (68%) of the material appeared prior to the success of the revolution on July 19, 1979. Thus slightly less than one-third of total content dealt with Nicaragua under Sandinista rule. Post-

Table 4.1

Pre– and Post–Nicaraguan Revolution Coverage

	US	GB	Can	Total
	N=165	N=62	N=50	N=277
Pre-July 19	64%	76%	70%	68%
Post-July 19	36	24	30	32

X^2 =3.22, DF=2, NS

Figure   4.1

Comparative Volume of Nicaraguan Revolution Press Reports
January 1, 1978–July 18, 1979

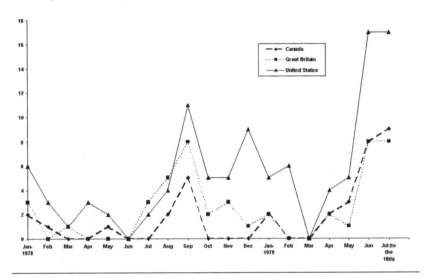

Figure   4.2

Comparative Volume of Nicaraguan Revolution Press Reports
July 19, 1979–December 31, 1980

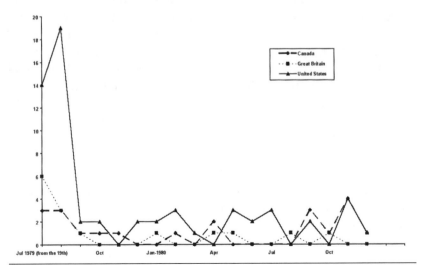

revolutionary coverage was especially sparse in Great Britain, accounting for only 24% of the content.

The month-by-month distribution of press items for pre- and post-revolutionary periods is displayed in Figures 4.1 and 4.2. Although the American newspaper maintained a consistently greater volume of coverage, all newspapers were clearly responding to the same set of stimuli in their coverage of Nicaragua. What was news in New York was also news in London and in Toronto.

The American and British papers relied primarily on local staff/ special correspondent generated material, supplemented by American (AP and UPI) and British (Reuters) wire service copy. *The Globe and Mail*, on the other hand, relied mainly on the American and British wire services. There was a dearth of Canadian-originated material.

With respect to datelines of material, only two countries are significant: Nicaragua and the United States. At least 50% of content in all three countries carried Nicaraguan datelines, with the total peaking at 75% in *The New York Times*. Somewhat curious is the fact that the highest percentage of American datelines (42%) appeared in the British press. This is because *The Daily Telegraph* (which replaced the non-publishing *Times* during the 1979 strike) covered the revolution largely through its New York bureau.[5] Less than 10% of material in *The Globe and Mail* carried American datelines, and *The New York Times* featured a number of pieces from Costa Rica and Mexico. (Data not shown in tabular form).

Data in Table 4.2 show the type of content that appeared in the newspapers of the three countries. Hard news (i.e., timely news reports appearing on the front page and inside pages) accounted for the majority of coverage: 79% in the United States, 91% in Great Britain and 84% in Canada. There were no front-page items on Nicaragua found in the Canadian sample. Analytical material (editorials and features) accounted for 14% of *The New York Times* content, but in Canada and Great Britain the percentages fell to 9 and 6 respectively. This appears to confirm the event-responsive stance of the press shown in Figures 4.1 and 4.2 above.

Items were coded "short" if they ran from one to five paragraphs, "medium" if they ran from six to fifteen paragraphs, and "long" if they ran sixteen paragraphs or longer.[6] On this indicator of importance, *The New York Times* ran the highest number of long items (21%), the British papers ran the highest number of short items (41%), while *The*

Table 4.2

Type of Content in Reporting on the Nicaraguan Revolution*

	US N=165	GB N=62	Can N=50	Total N=277
Front Page News	4%	14%	0	6%
Inside Page News	75	77	84%	77
Editorial	9	2	2	6
Features	5	7	4	5
Letters to the Editor	5	0	10	5
Other	2	0	0	1

*Cell sizes too small to accurately compute statistics

Table 4.3

Issue Area Coverage During the Pre– and Post–Nicaraguan Revolutionary Periods (due to multi-coding, columns do not add to 100%)

	Pre-Revolution				Post-Revolution			
	US N=105	GB N=47	Can N=35	Total N=187	US N=60	GB N=15	Can N=15	Total N=90
Military Action/ Defense	59%	68%	77%	65%	25%	20%	13%	22%
International Politics	55	64	54	57	65	60	87	68
Domestic Politics	51	53	66	55	43	80	67	53*
International Aid	9	2	11	8	43	27	7	34*
Economic Situation	6	6	11	7	23	27	40	27

*X² Significant at <.05

Globe and Mail ran the fewest both of short (26%) and long items (12%). (Data not shown in tabular form).

Data in Table 4.3 show the relative salience accorded major issue areas in terms of the percentage of total stories in which a given issue area appeared, broken down according to pre-revolution and post-revolution periods. While there are some statistically significant variations in issue coverage in the post-revolutionary period, on balance, data point to an underlying consistency in all three countries regarding what aspects of the revolution were deemed to be important.

During the period of the Sandinista challenge to the Somoza government, three issue areas dominated coverage: "Military actions" on the part of both the Sandinistas and the government led in press coverage in all three countries, but were especially salient in *The Globe and Mail*. In order of importance, coverage of "international politics" and "domestic politics" followed, with international politics receiving the most attention in the British papers and domestic politics in *The Globe*. Two less-dominant issue areas, "international aid" and the "economic situation" in Nicaragua, received minor attention on the part of the press in the period of revolutionary challenge.

During the eighteen months following the success of the revolution, the same five issue areas dominated press coverage, although the relative rankings were different and the prominence of issue areas among the three countries was more varied. "International politics" moved up to the number one issue area overall, and was the most salient in all papers except the British, where "domestic politics" occupied first place. "Domestic politics" occupied the number two position in *The Globe and Mail* and tied for second position in *The New York Times*. The variation in reporting on this issue area is statistically significant ($p<.05$). "International aid" was clearly most important to *The New York Times* and, somewhat curiously, least important to *The Globe and Mail*. Again, differences in reporting on this issue area are statistically significant ($p<.05$). As one would expect, in the post-revolutionary period, press attention to military activity decreased and reporting on the country's economic situation increased. This shift was particularly noticeable in *The Globe and Mail* reporting.

These differences aside, our investigation of the information-supplying role of the press confirms that while the amplification of the revolution (in terms of volume of coverage, length of items and percentage of analytical material) was greatest in *The New York Times*, the same issue areas tended to be reported in roughly similar patterns in the newspapers of all three countries. Thus, not only do the different newspapers appear to be responding to the same events, the basic information they supply to their readers concerning these events is also quite similar.

Table 4.4

**Positive and Negative Words and Phrases
Used to Describe Somoza and the Sandinistas**

	US	GB	Can	Total
Somoza	**N=56**	**N=25**	**N=30**	**N=111**
Positive	7%	4%	7%	6%
Negative	93	96	93	94
Sandinistas	**N=60**	**N=41**	**N=32**	**N=133**
Positive	17%	24%	38%	24%
Negative	83	76	62	76

Beginning with data in Table 4.4, which indicate the percentage of positive and negative descriptors referring to Somoza and the Sandinistas, we move from an examination of the information-supplying to the evaluation-supplying role of the press. In the case of Anastasio Somoza Debayle, the pattern is overwhelmingly negative (94%), with little difference evident among the newspapers of the three countries. (See the full list of descriptors and how they were coded at the end of this chapter.) For the Sandinistas, however, while negativity again dominates (76%), there are differences among the papers that indicate that the Sandinistas were portrayed differently in the three countries. While the overall evaluation of the Sandinistas was negative in each country, there is little question that they were portrayed most unfavorably in *The New York Times.* The British newspapers occupied a middle ground, while in *The Globe and Mail* nearly 40% of descriptors portrayed the Sandinistas in a favorable light.

Data in Table 4.5 focus attention on the use of two particular descriptors used in reference to the Sandinistas that appear to be relatively sensitive indicators of changing press perceptions of the revolutionary group: "leftist/left wing" versus "communist/Marxist." These data are of considerable interest. First, during the period of revolutionary challenge, *The New York Times* was least likely to refer to the Sandinistas as either "leftist/left wing" or "communist/Marxist." Both of these terms appear in the highest percentage of items carried in

Table 4.5

Percentage of Items Using the Terms "Leftist"/"Communist" in Pre– and Post–Nicaraguan Revolutionary Periods

	Pre-Revolution				Post-Revolution			
	US	GB	Can	Total	US	GB	Can	Total
	N=105	N=47	N=35	N=187	N=60	N=15	N=15	N=90
Leftist/Left Wing	17%	30%	31%	23%	10%	20%	0	10%
Communist/Marxist	3	11	20	8	15	40	7%	18

The Globe and Mail; "leftist/left wing" in 31% of items and "communist/ Marxist" in 20%. In all, up to July 19, 1979, the terms "leftist/left wing" and "communist/Marxist" were used in 23% and 8% of press items respectively.

In the period following the revolution, perhaps not surprisingly, we find the terms "communist/Marxist" were used more often to describe the Sandinistas than were the terms "leftist/left wing" (18% versus 10% of items). But it is surprising that the terms "communist/ Marxist" got the major play in the British newspapers, not the American. Again, somewhat paradoxically, while *The Globe and Mail* recorded the highest percentage use of these descriptors in the pre-revolutionary period, it posted the lowest percentage following the Sandinistas' accession to power.

In addition to the informational and evaluative material found within the text of a story, the headlines that accompany stories may often frame a particular actor in either a positive or negative light. Accordingly, data in Table 4.6 report the percentages of positive, neutral and negative headlines that can be tied to either Somoza or the Sandinistas. Data here reveal that during the active military phase of the revolution, not a single headline that was favorable to Somoza appeared in any of the papers, while nearly 15% were negative. For the challenging Sandinistas, while fully 95% of headlines were neutral or did not apply, the balance was evenly split: 3% positive and 2% negative. Following the success of the revolution, for the most part Somoza dropped out of the picture. For the Sandinistas, however, the

Table 4.6
_____

Percentage of Positive, Neutral, and Negative Headlines in the Pre- and Post-Nicaraguan Revolutionary Periods

	Pre-Revolution				Post-Revolution			
	US	GB	Can	Total	US	GB	Can	Total
	N=105	N=47	N=35	N=187	N=60	N=15	N=15	N=90
Somoza								
Positive	0	0	0	0	0	0	0	0
Neutral	87%	82%	89%	86%	93%	100%	100%	96%
Negative	13	18	11	14	7	0	0	4
Sandinistas								
Positive	3%	4%	3%	3%	10%	7%	13%	10%
Neutral	95	94	94	95	78	60	80	76
Negative	2	2	3	2	12	33	7	14

headline pattern is reasonably consistent with internal descriptor data previously discussed. *The New York Times* was basically balanced in its headlines (10% positive versus 12% negative), while the British newspapers especially took the Sandinistas to task (7% positive versus 33% negative). *The Globe and Mail*, which had shown the greatest support for the Sandinistas in its use of descriptive language, also recorded the only favorable headline balance (13% positive versus 7% negative).

Data in Table 4.7 indicate the respective "roles of the press" performance of newspapers in relation to both American policy toward Nicaragua and Nicaraguan policy under Somoza as well as Sandinista rule. Two findings emerge from this analysis. First, none of Cohen's roles of the press were pursued especially vigorously. To the extent that they were, the watchdog role appears to be the most prominent, especially with respect to Nicaraguan policy under Somoza and American policy generally. In the case of the Sandinistas, *The Globe and Mail* again stands alone as a supporter of Sandinista policy, while criticism of Sandinista policy was highest in the British press. In *The*

Table 4.7

Roles of the Press Regarding U.S., Somoza and Sandinista Policy

	US N=165	GB N=62	Can N=50
United States Policy			
Supporter	1%	0	0
Critic	10	5%	0
Advocate	1	0	0
Somoza Policy			
Supporter	0	0	0
Critic	10%	5%	8%
Advocate	0	0	0
Sandinista Policy			
Supporter	1%	0	6%
Critic	2	5%	0
Advocate	0	0	0

New York Times, while there was little support in evidence for Sandinista policies, neither was there much criticism of them through 1980.

Conclusion

In terms of Fagen's four-cell conceptualization of an image composed of informational and evaluative dimensions, Table 4.8 displays the major differences between American, British and Canadian press representations of the Nicaraguan Revolution. Reporting on the revolution was primarily event oriented, with military activities associated with Somoza's downfall receiving primary attention in all newspapers prior to July 19, 1979. International politics became the chief area of press attention following the success of the revolution, with domestic political concerns important during both periods. That the same set of events should elicit similar patterns of reporting, while certainly not an astounding finding, is interesting, given that

Table 4.8

Comparative Press Images of the Nicaraguan Revolution

Evaluation	Amount of Information	
	Low	High
Positive		
	Canada	
Negative		United States
	Great Britain	

newspapers in the three countries relied on quite different sets of sources for their material.

Regarding the positive or negative evaluations, in all countries the "dominant representation" of participants in the revolution was negative. In terms of textual language, the words and phrases used to describe Somoza and the Sandinistas were negative, overwhelmingly so in the case of Somoza. While all newspapers were uniformly negative with respect to Somoza, *The Globe and Mail* stood out from the others in offering the most positive descriptors of the Sandinistas. This finding is especially curious since at least 41% of *Globe and Mail* items originated with American wire services. Since 75% of Canadian material was datelined in Nicaragua, a plausible explanation for this apparent anomaly is that material originating in Nicaragua was more likely to be favorable to the Sandinistas than that originating in the United States (see chapter 3).

In the area of headlines, the British newspapers were most negative with respect to both Somoza and the Sandinistas. Only in *The Globe and Mail* were the Sandinistas given a favorable balance of headlines after they had taken power. In *The New York Times* the percentage of anti-Somoza headlines prior to the success of the revolution was nearly identical to the percentage of anti-Sandinista headlines following July 19, 1979. It is also interesting to note that in *The New York Times* positive headlines regarding the Sandinistas nearly equaled the number of negative ones.

With respect to policy evaluation, all newspapers assumed the role of critic, being especially critical of policies pursued by Somoza and the United States. These data show that at least until the end of 1980, the press did not offer much in the way of criticism of Sandinista policies, and, indeed, the revolutionary government was modestly supported by *The Globe and Mail*.

Turning to the use of the key terms "leftist/left wing" versus "communist/Marxist" to describe the Sandinistas, the data do point to a shift in the presentation of the Sandinistas concomitant with the success of the revolution. While this is most apparent in the British newspapers, it is evident in *The New York Times* as well. Thus, important changes in press representations of the revolution had already occurred prior to Ronald Reagan's assumption of presidential power in January 1981, which led to the initiation of hostile changes in United States policy toward Nicaragua in the first year of the Reagan presidency.

In terms of possible constraints on Reagan's Central American policy, we find American press portrayals of the Sandinistas largely ineffective. While lacking in specificity, their portrayal is congruent with the administration's characterization of them as communist enemies of the United States. For Reagan, there was certainly no positive press image of the Sandinistas to have to overcome.

Canadian foreign policy toward the region, while for the most part (with the notable exception of Cuba) congruent with American policy (Lemco 1986b), diverged greatest from the Americans in the policy toward the revolutionary Sandinista government of Nicaragua (Baranyi 1985; Haglund 1987). While it would be imprudent to suggest a cause-and-effect relationship, the data are certainly congruent with the press as the setter of appropriate parameters for policy. With respect to Nicaragua, this meant a Canadian policy that was much more sympathetic to the Sandinista government than that followed by the Reagan administration in the United States.

Notes

1. This chapter was originally published under the title "The Nicaraguan Revolution in the Canadian and American Press" in *Mass Comm Review*, Vol. 20, Nos. 1 & 2 (1993). It is published here with permission.
2. Due to a labor dispute at *The Times*, *The Daily Telegraph* was used as a replacement from December 1978 to January 1980.
3. The author wishes to thank Elizabeth Burton, Ann Boyd, Iris Kohler and Anne Mander for assistance in newspaper coding and Robert Burge for his assistance on various computer-related aspects of the study.

4. Since the period of the study extended over three years and consequently specific issues would be expected to change over time, we employed the general issue area categories used by Stevenson and Shaw in their seventeen-nation study of news (1984, p. 27).
5. A similar situation was evident in British coverage of events in Guatemala in 1954 (see chapter 1).
6. Column inches of material were not recorded due to the high correlation between measures based on number of items on and space devoted to a topic (Merrill 1962; Stevenson and Shaw 1984).

Chapter 4 Descriptors

Somoza/Somocistas
Words/Phrases Judged to Be Positive
Fights for what he believes in

Words/Phrases Judged to Be Negative
Dictator/dictatorship/right-wing dictatorship/dynastic dictatorship/
    murderous dictatorship/corrupt dictatorship/deposed dictatorship
Authoritarian/authoritarian right-wing regime
Dynastic right-wing regime/family dynasty/dynasty
Despots and tyrants/tyranny/tyrant/tyrannical
Abominable
Sanguinary
Desperate
Corrupt
Repressive
Bankrupt
Failed caudillo
Autocrat
Cruel
Intransigent
Embattled
Beleaguered/beleaguered strongman
Vile
Hitler
Stupefyingly rich
Hated
Dead like a dog on the corner
Rules with an iron hand
Political cadaver

Words/Phrases Judged to Be Neutral or Ambiguous
President/former president
General

Mr. Somoza
Deposed/deposed ruler
Nicaraguan leader
Fifty-three years old
Exiled

Sandinistas

Words/Phrases Judged to Be Positive

Not communist
Social democrats
Broadly-based popular revolution
Friendly
Moderate
Not financed by Cuba

Words/Phrases Judged to Be Negative

Leftist/left wing/leftist rebels/obscure leftists/leftist guerrillas/leftist
    dominated/left supported
Marxist/Marxist oriented/Marxist-Leninist/Marxist dominated/hardline
    Marxists/Cuban-trained Marxists
Communists/red-blooded communists/communist-inclined
Revolutionaries/Marxist revolutionaries/revolutionary movement
Terrorist movement
Ultra-left/radical left
Guerrillas
Armed insurgents
Radical regime
Pro-Castro/pro-Cuban/friends of Cuba
Cannot control own forces
Subversives
Linked to PLO
Leading the nation to communism
Cuban-style communism
Backed by foreigners

Words/Phrases Judged to Be Neutral or Ambiguous

Government of Nicaragua
Rebels
Nationalists
The boys/youths
Opposition
Vanguard of the people
Revolutionary junta/revolutionary government
Ruling junta
Own form of socialism
Non-aligned
Marxist-Christian

Chapter 5

El Salvador: A Comparison of Canadian and American Press Reporting, 1981 and 1983[1]

WALTER C. SODERLUND

N either the colonial nor the post-colonial history of El Salvador can be described as particularly trouble free with respect to social problems. Dominance relationships of Peninsulares (Europeans) over Indians (Natives) were ingrained in the social fabric of New Spain during the colonial period. The achievement of independence in the 1820s did little to change this reality, as a Creole (new world–born European) elite in large measure replaced the Spanish-born ruling class, leaving the oppressive colonial social structure intact (Lambert 1967).

Rather than ameliorating over time, problems for the Indian/ mestizo peasantry in El Salvador actually intensified during the late nineteenth century when "liberal" reforms, especially in the area of landholding, were implemented. These reforms were directed at communal forms of landholding (i.e., those lands held by Indian communities) in favor of a system that combined individual land ownership with export-oriented agriculture. Following extensive usurpation of Indian lands, El Salvador experienced bloody revolts during the last three decades of the nineteenth century (North 1981).

In 1932, partly as a result of the disastrous economic effects of the Great Depression, and, as some have argued, spurred by communist organization, a revolt broke out in El Salvador (Anderson 1971). The government reacted swiftly and with great repression, and, in what became known as "la matanza" — the massacre — killed an estimated 30,000 peasants within a few weeks (North 1981, pp. 35–39).

Since the 1930s military government was the rule rather than the exception in El Salvador (Rodriguez 1965). Although in the 1950s some economic growth did occur, the reality of El Salvador continued to be that of a small country, beset with severe overpopulation, where a domestic oligarchy known as the "fourteen families" controlled the vast majority of all that was worthy of controlling, from land to commerce (LaFeber 1983, pp. 69–72).

Social tension in El Salvador escalated in 1968 following the so-called "Soccer War" with neighboring Honduras, when a large number of Salvadorans living in Honduras illegally were forced back to their native soil (North 1981; LaFeber 1983). By the late 1970s El Salvador was engulfed in a full-scale civil war with the Faribundo Marti National Liberation Front (FMLN), named after one of the slain leaders of the 1931 insurrection, challenging the incumbent government for control of the country. The government, the oligarchy and the military fought back fiercely, using both legitimate force and illegal government and paramilitary violence against the guerrillas as well as their presumed civilian supporters (North 1981).

Following the Sandinista victory in Nicaragua over the National Guard of Anastasio Somoza in 1979 (see chapter 4), the civil war in El Salvador intensified and became increasingly internationalized. The United States, always a supporter of the Salvadoran government, dramatically increased its level of aid, while at the same time it leveled charges that Cuba and Nicaragua were supporting the Salvadoran guerrillas and that the hemisphere was being threatened anew by communist infiltration.

This was the situation in El Salvador in the fall of 1981, the first period of press coverage studied in this chapter. Two years later, in the fall of 1983, the feared "regionalization" of the conflict had indeed taken place, as the United States was not only continuing to support the Salvadoran government, but was also (through the CIA), financing and directing a counterrevolutionary movement (the Contras) against the Nicaraguan government. In addition, the United States was building radar installations and combat airstrips in Honduras in order to be better able to project its military power into the region (LaFeber, 1983, pp. 293–299). This then was the general state of affairs in El Salvador and surrounding countries during the second period of press coverage examined in this chapter.

Methods

Material in this chapter deals not as much with the reality of what was happening in El Salvador during the early 1980s as it does with how this reality was presented to North American readers by leading Canadian and American newspapers. Research has demonstrated that the press plays an important role in transmitting information that lies beyond the personal experience of its readers (McCombs and Shaw 1972; Weaver 1984). Indeed it is difficult for even those of us with a professional interest and personal contacts in the region to know but a fraction of what is transpiring there. For the general public, the attentive public, and even experts in the field, the press serves as a major provider of information. This chapter is intended to probe, in a systematic and structured way, the "pictures of reality" about El Salvador that were transmitted to their readers by four leading North American newspapers at a two-year interval in the early 1980s.

The major national newspapers in Canada and the United States, *The Globe and Mail* (Toronto) and *The New York Times*, as well as the major newspapers serving each nation's capital city, *The Citizen* (Ottawa) and *The Washington Post,* were selected for study.[2] Beginning on dates randomly selected in the first week of October and continuing until the end of the second week of December, in 1981 twenty-seven issues and in 1983 twenty-five issues of each newspaper were selected on an every-three-day basis. Each of these issues was read in its entirety for material on El Salvador. While the 1981 and 1983 studies differed somewhat in purpose and design, data presented in this chapter were collected and coded according to the same criteria. Therefore, with the exception of some specific differences with respect to issue coverage, which are noted in Table 5.5, the data are directly comparable.[3]

Six dimensions of press coverage were analyzed:

1. Volume of coverage — based on the number of items per issue;
2. Type of content — front page news, inside page news, editorials, feature columns and editorial cartoons;
3. Source of content — local staff and special correspondents, Canadian and American wire services and freelance writers;
4. Coverage of the roles played by various international actors in the conflict;
5. The changing nature of issue coverage from 1981 to 1983;

6. The comparative use of Cold War terminology — language such as "communist," "Marxist-Leninist," "Soviet-backed" and "Cuban-backed" — in press reporting.[4]

Findings

Data in Table 5.1 show the volume of coverage as measured by the number of items per issue. As is readily evident, the events in El Salvador proved to be of far greater interest to newspapers in the United States than to those in Canada, accounting for approximately two-thirds of total coverage in each period. Given the prominent American role in the conflict, this is hardly surprising. It is also apparent, however, that in neither country were events in El Salvador considered to be an especially "hot" news item. In the United States only about one item per newspaper issue concerning El Salvador appeared in both 1981 and 1983, with totals in both years slightly higher for *The New York Times*. In Canada, approximately one item appeared in every two newspaper issues, with the overall volume decreasing slightly from 1981 to 1983.[5] However, when we examine individual Canadian newspapers, there is not a uniform trend, but rather an apparent shift in attention. Whereas in 1981, *The Globe and Mail* and *The Citizen* exhibited virtually identical levels of interest in El Salvador, by 1983 *The Citizen*'s interest had increased, while that of *The Globe and Mail* had decreased.

Table 5.1

Volume of Press Reporting About Events in El Salvador

Items Per Issue	1981			1983		
	G&M	Cit	Total	G&M	Cit	Total
Canada	N=14	N13	N=27	N=8	N=15	N=23
	.52	.48	.50	.32	.60	.46
	NYT	Post	Total	NYT	Post	Total
United States	N=33	N=22	N=55	N=30	N=19	N=49
	1.2	.81	1.0	1.2	.76	.98

Table 5.2

Type of Newspaper Content About El Salvador (percentage of items)

	Can		US	
	1981	1983	1981	1983
	N=27	N=23	N=55	N=49
Front Page News	0	0	11%	21%
Inside Page News	93%	91%	69	61
Editorials	0	0	2	2
Features	7	9	18	16

Data in Table 5.2 indicate the type of newspaper content in which material on El Salvador was reported. The most important finding is the great amount of similarity between the press in Canada and the United States, as well as stability within each country across the two time periods. There is a predominance of "hard news" reporting — over 90% of the items in Canadian papers and over 80% in American papers in both 1981 and 1982. While no Salvadoran story merited front page placement in the Canadian press, just over 10% and 20% of American reporting in 1981 and 1983 respectively was seen to be sufficiently important to be placed on the front page. In-depth analytical pieces in the form of editorials and feature columns comprised less than 10% of Canadian material and under 20% of American material. Again, we see great stability in these percentages over the two time periods.

Interpretations of events often reflect national biases of reporters; thus, where news comes from is a factor that is not without significance. This is especially true of international news appearing in Canadian newspapers, which past research has shown to be predominantly American in origin (Scanlon 1974; Scanlon and Farrell 1983). As is clear from data in Table 5.3, with respect to the ongoing conflict in El Salvador, American sources predominated, accounting for 46% of total content in 1981 and 57% in 1983. Further, as reported by the Royal Commission on Newspapers, the Canadian wire service Canadian

Table 5.3

Source of Content About El Salvador
(missing data omitted)

	Can		US	
	1981	1983	1981	1983
	N=24	N=21	N=51	N=49
Local Staff/Special Correspondent	21%	14%	51%	74%
Canadian Wire Service	8	10	0	0
American Wire Services	34	48	27	18
European Wire Services	25	19	6	2
American Freelancers	12	9	16	6

Press (CP) gets much of its international news directly from the Associated Press (AP) wire (Canada 1981). If this is in fact the case here, the percentages of content reported coming from American sources may actually be understated. The use of European wire services (chiefly Reuters) is quite high in Canada, although the percentage was somewhat lower in 1983 than it had been in 1981. Likewise, material originating from local staff/special correspondents in Canadian papers declined between 1981 and 1983. *The Globe and Mail* and *The Citizen* demonstrated considerable differences in their use of sources. *The Globe* featured a mix of American, Canadian and European material, while *The Citizen* exhibited a far greater dependence on American sources, with about two-thirds of its material judged to be American originated. (Data not shown in tabular form).

Whereas in Canada, American wire services were the single largest source of material, in the United States local staff and special correspondents were the major source of material for both newspapers, with American wire services and American freelancers also significant contributors. Non-American voices were relatively hard to find in American newspapers, as Reuters provided only 6% of total material in 1981 and 2% in 1983. A not unexpected, yet interesting finding is that absolutely no Canadian-originated material appeared in either American paper.

Table 5.4

Percentage of Stories Dealing with the Role of International Actors in El Salvador (due to multi-coding, columns do not add to 100%)

	Can		US	
	1981	1983	1981	1983
	N=27	N=23	N=55	N=49
Role of U.S.	52%	52%	73%	80%
Role of Canada	7	0	0	0
Role of Cuba	19	0	37	4

Data in Table 5.4 focus on coverage dealing with the role of international actors in the Salvadoran conflict. Here we see evidence of both stability and change with respect to the activities of these actors. Stability is seen in the roles of the United States and Canada. The American role was seen as paramount in both Canadian newspapers (mentioned in over 50% of items in 1981 and 1983), as well as in the American newspapers, where about 70% of items in 1981 and 80% in 1983 focused on American actions. Likewise, there was a consistency in reporting on the Canadian role in the conflict, such commentary appearing in only 7% of Canadian newspaper items in 1981 and then disappearing entirely in 1983. Canadian activities dealing with El Salvador occasioned not a single mention in the American press in either year.

On the other hand, with respect to the role of Cuba in the conflict, we see evidence of considerable volatility. In 1981 the Cuban role was mentioned in just under 20% of Canadian items (mainly in *The Citizen*) and in 37% of American press items. In 1983, the Cuban dimension had dropped entirely from Canadian press reports of the conflict, while in the United States it was mentioned in less than 5% of items. This of course represents a major shift in the framework within which the crisis was being interpreted for readers. Whatever the motivation, by the autumn of 1983, newspapers in both countries virtually ceased to mention Cuba in their reporting on El Salvador.

Table 5.5 examines the leading issues pertaining to coverage on El Salvador in the two years studied. With the exception of "U.S. aid"

Table 5.5

Percentage of Stories Dealing with Major Issues in El Salvador
(due to multi-coding, columns do not add to 100%)

	Can		US	
	1981	1983	1981	1983
	N=27	N=23	N=55	N=49
Human Rights Violations	11%	52%	15%	65%
Guerrilla Military Action	37	30	26	18
Government Military Action	41	22	20	14
Domestic Political Conditions	15	17	31	35
1982 Election	26	**	20	**
1984 Election	*	4	*	6
Kissinger Commission	*	9	*	10
U.S. Aid	*	13	*	49
U.S. Policy-Making Process	*	4	*	35

*Not coded in 1981
**Not coded in 1983

and "U.S. policy-making processes," which were not coded in 1981, all other issues were subject to the same coding rules, making the percentage figures directly comparable.

Trends in issue reporting follow a remarkably consistent pattern. Issues that interested newspapers of a country in 1981 in terms of paramount coverage ("guerrilla activity" in Canada and "domestic political conditions" in the United States) continued to do so in 1983. As well, trends in story play (more or less coverage devoted to an issue) were identical in both countries. There were also changes in issue attention. In 1981 "human rights violations" largely on the part of the Salvadoran government appeared in 11% and 15% of the total of Canadian and American items respectively. By 1983, interest in this issue had skyrocketed to where it was mentioned in fully 50% of Canadian items and a remarkable 65% of American items. Both "guerrilla" and "government military activities" had more salience to the Canadian press in 1981 and 1983, but these issues generated less interest in the latter year. "Domestic political conditions" in El Salvador were of greater interest to the American newspapers. As with "human rights violations," interest in domestic politics increased, but not nearly to the same extent.

The elections held in El Salvador in 1982 and 1984 present an interesting comparison. First, there was considerably more press interest on the part of both Canadian and American newspapers in the 1982 constituent assembly election than evidenced for the 1984 presidential election. Since both elections were scheduled to take place during the spring following the periods of study, timing of the elections was definitely not the factor accounting for the lessened interest in the 1984 event. Also, since interest in "domestic political conditions" increased slightly from 1981 to 1983, it appears that it was the 1984 election itself that occasioned less interest. The "Kissinger Commission," which was traveling in Central America during the 1983 study period, "U.S. aid" and the "U.S. policy-making process" (neither of which were coded in 1981) were, as might be expected, more heavily covered in American newspapers than in Canadian ones.

The extent to which events in El Salvador were interpreted in a Cold War framework is shown in Table 5.6. When first designing the study, it was hypothesized that such Cold War frames (operationalized by the use of language such as "communist," "Marxist-Leninist,"

Table 5.6

Percentage of Items Using "Cold War" Language
About Events in El Salvador

Items Per Issue	1981			1983		
	G&M	Cit	Total	G&M	Cit	Total
Canada	N=14	N13	N=27	N=8	N=15	N=23
	21%	62%	41%	13%	27%	22%
	NYT	Post	Total	NYT	Post	Total
United States	N=33	N=22	N=55	N=30	N=19	N=49
	42%	55%	47%	47%	42%	45%

"Soviet-backed," "Cuban-backed," etc.) would be more prevalent in American newspapers. The 1981 data were inconclusive on this question—between 40% and 50% of news items in both countries' newspapers used this kind of language. However, in 1983 the hypothesis does indeed appear confirmed, as American newspapers used Cold War terminology 23% more often than did their Canadian counterparts.

The biggest change in the use of Cold War language was found in *The Citizen*, which in 1981 actually led the two American papers, with such language found in 62% of its items. *The Globe and Mail* used Cold War language less than any other paper in both 1981 and 1983, while *The New York Times* and *The Washington Post* were reasonably consistent in their use of Cold War language over the two-year period.

Conclusion

First, when examined as a whole, it is obvious that American press interest in the Salvadoran conflict was far greater than was Canadian interest, since nearly twice as many items appeared in the American papers. Also, American papers were far more likely to put Salvadoran material on the front page, another indicator of press interest in an event. At the same time, given the importance of the conflict in hemispheric relations, the overall level of coverage for both countries can at best be characterized as barely adequate.

Second, most of the newspaper reporting on El Salvador fell into the category of hard-news reporting. Human rights abuses, guerrilla raids, government military retaliation and the effects of these on the political life of the country were the major substantive issues that attracted press attention. Reporting on human rights abuses and domestic political conditions increased from 1981 to 1983, while reporting on the strictly military dimensions of the conflict decreased. The percentage of editorials and features (reporting that tends to place events in a broader context) was disappointingly low, especially in Canadian newspapers.

With regard to the role of international actors involved in the conflict, the United States was seen as the dominant outside influence, with its perceived importance increasing from 1981 to 1983. Concomitantly, the role of America's primary antagonist in the region, Cuba—while even in 1981 never approaching the level of press interest accorded to the United States — by 1983 had virtually disappeared from the press' frame of reference. Along with declining press interest in Cuban involvement, the manner in which the 1982 and 1984 elections were covered is a puzzle. While the 1982 election generated considerable press interest in the fall of 1981, the 1984 election did not occasion analogous levels of press attention in the fall of 1983. We might speculate that the interest in the 1982 election was at least in part prompted by the perception that it really might offer a solution to the civil war. By 1983, it can be argued that cynicism had set in as it became apparent that in spite of the outcome of the election, the underlying bases of the conflict would remain unchanged.

Finally, the data in this chapter confirm the fears expressed by analysts of Canadian media that much of the information on world events presented to Canadians is filtered through American perceptual lenses. In this context, it is significant that *The Globe and Mail,* which relied on American-originated material to a far lesser extend than did *The Citizen,* also provided a less Cold War–oriented picture of the conflict, including less emphasis on Cuban involvement, to its readers. Overall, between 1981 and 1983 we see a decrease in the use of Cold War language in both Canadian newspapers, while the use of this type of language remained relatively unchanged in the American newspapers.

Notes

1.   Material in this chapter appeared previously in the article "El Salvador's Civil War as Seen in North and South American Press," co-authored with Carmen Schmitt and appearing in *Journalism Quarterly* 63 (Summer, 1986) and in the chapter "Reporting of Events in Central America by Canadian and American Newspapers: October–December, 1983," in W.C. Soderlund and Stuart H. Surlin, eds. *Media in Latin America and the Caribbean: Domestic and International Perspectives* (Windsor, Ontario: Ontario Cooperative Program in Latin American and Caribbean Studies, 1985). Material is published here with the permission of both publishers.
2.   *The New York Times, The Washington Post* and *The Globe and Mail* were all listed among the world's fifty greatest newspapers (Merrill and Fisher 1980). While *The Citizen* did not make this list, it was nevertheless the only English-language daily published in Ottawa and after *The Globe and Mail* was the newspaper most widely read by members of Parliament (Dewitt and Kirton 1983).
3.   The 1981 study involved a comparison of eight newspapers, two each in Argentina, Chile, Canada and the United States and was done in

collaboration with Carmen Schmitt, who coded the Latin American
newspapers (Soderlund and Schmitt 1986). The 1983 study compared
coverage of Central America in three American and three Canadian
newspapers (Soderlund 1985).

4. Since Schmitt coded the Latin American newspapers in Chile while
Soderlund coded the North American papers in Canada, no intercoder
reliability tests were run on the 1981 data. However, in a post-test of
intracoder reliability for the data reported in this chapter, a percentage
agreement of 96% was found. The 1983 data were gathered as a project
in a graduate seminar on research methods. An intercoder agreement
rate of 82% was achieved (Holsti 1969, p. 140).

5. In contrast, *The Globe and Mail* carried 4.1 items per issue on Grenada
during the American invasion of the island, which also occurred in the
autumn of 1983 (Cuthbert and Surlin 1985). The author sampled coverage
of the Grenada invasion in *The New York Times* during the same period,
with the average number of stories per issue at 9.9. Thus, in reporting
on that event as well, the ratio of American to Canadian stories was
approximately 2 to 1.

Chapter 6

The Press as a Predictor of Cold War Crises: Grenada 1983[1]

WALTER C. SODERLUND

Despite the ongoing violence in El Salvador and Nicaragua, prior to the December 1989 invasion of Panama (see chapter 13), during the 1980s the United States had engaged in but one operation in the Caribbean Basin involving the overt commitment of its armed forces. That occurred in October 1983, when, along with Eastern Caribbean allies, the United States invaded the island of Grenada following the murder of its prime minister, Maurice Bishop. While there is no doubt that the world's press responded very quickly to the crisis once it had begun and that coverage tended to be voluminous (Cuthbert 1985; also see chapter 7), the intent of the research reported in this chapter is to assess the extent to which the elite press in Great Britain and the United States had focused the attention of their readers on the Grenadian situation prior to the initiation of the crisis.

Scholars engaged in the study of crises have tended to emphasize a similar set of characteristics as necessary for an event to be so defined. Herman defines a crisis as "a situation that (1) threatens the high-priority goals of the decision-making unit, (2) restricts the amount of time available for response before the situation is transformed; and (3) surprises the members of the decision-making unit" (1969, p. 29). Young's definition is more general in that a crisis is seen as "a set of rapidly unfolding events which raises the impact of destabilizing forces in the general international system or any of its subsystems substantially above 'normal'...levels and increases the likelihood of violence occurring in the system" (1967, p. 19). Brecher lists "four necessary and sufficient conditions" in order for an event to qualify as a crisis: "(1) a change in [the decision-making unit's] internal or external environment which generates (2) a threat to basic values with a (3) simultaneous or subsequent high probability of involvement in military hostility and the awareness of (4) a finite time for their response to the external value threat" (1977, pp. 43-44). Finally, Bell defines a crisis as "a tract of time during which the conflicts within the international relationship rise sharply above the normal level, threatening damaging change or transformation of that relationship" (1982, p. 2).

A threat to basic values, an escalation in the preexisting level of violence, combined with surprise and a need to make a quick response, appear to be the consensus components of a "crisis" as defined above. While on objective criteria it would be hard to make a case for tiny Grenada as constituting a threat to the basic values of the United States, it may have posed such a threat in the "psychological environment" of the decision makers involved (Sprout and Sprout 1957; Brecher et al. 1969). All other elements necessary to constitute a crisis appear to have been present.

The crucial period leading up to the crisis was quite condensed. The arrest and detention of Maurice Bishop took place on October 15, his execution occurred on October 19, and the American military invasion began on October 25 (Adkin 1989, pp. 28-81). Thus, less than a week elapsed between the first indication that a change in the status quo might be occurring (the initiation of the crisis) and a major escalation of violence (Bishop's murder). Moreover, the military response on the part of the United States was underway almost immediately.

While press attention to the island increased dramatically once the crisis had begun and the level of violence escalated, what concerns us in this chapter is the question, How extensive and perspicacious was the elite press coverage of Grenada in the period immediately preceding the events that initiated the crisis? In order to answer this question, press coverage of Grenada in the respective "newspapers of record" in the United States and Great Britain — *The New York Times* and *The Times* (London) — was examined during the six months preceding the initiation of the crisis. In addition to counting the actual number of newspaper items dealing with Grenada (as gleaned from the respective indexes of the newspapers), each item was also examined in detail to determine what issues were discussed and to assess whether the likelihood of possible military operations was explored to any extent.

Background

The United States military invasion of Grenada clearly was a product of the Cold War. Prior to its independence in 1974, Grenada had been a British colony. Upon achieving independence, it adopted a parliamentary system of government based on the Westminster model. It kept the Queen of England as the titular head of state and joined the Commonwealth of Nations. The island nation's first prime minister, Sir Eric Gairy, became eccentric, autocratic and corrupt (DaBreo 1979). Elections were manipulated and political opponents were intimidated (some killed) by Gairy's "Mongoose Gang," a personal secret police force. In this political climate, opposition took extra-legal forms, and in 1979, while Gairy was off the island, Maurice Bishop, a London-trained lawyer and leader of the opposition New Jewel Movement (for Joint Endeavor for Welfare, Education and Liberation) led a successful and virtually bloodless coup d'etat against Gairy (DeBreo 1979).

Bishop assumed the position of prime minister in the People's Revolutionary Government (PRG) and instituted domestic reforms in areas such as education, health and housing, which sought to narrow the gap between the "haves" and "have nots" on the island. At the same time, the press was censored, opponents were imprisoned and elections were not held. Moreover, on the international scene, Bishop moved Grenada to the left, supporting the U.S.S.R. in the United Nations on its Afghanistan policy, and aligned the country with Fidelista Cuba and Sandinista Nicaragua in the hemispheric subsystem (Nylen 1988).

The Carter Administration, which had seen Gairy as somewhat of an embarrassment, adopted a "wait and see" attitude toward Bishop (Pastor 1990). However, when Ronald Reagan came to power in January 1981, the entire framework for analyzing events in the Caribbean Basin shifted from societal poverty and human rights abuses to an almost exclusive emphasis on the Cold War. According to Nogee and Spanier, "Since, unlike his predecessor, President Reagan saw the U.S.-Soviet conflict as central, all issues were judged in that light. Third World issues were not approached in terms of their own merits but were seen in an east-west context" (1988, pp. 101–103). With respect to Grenada, the Reagan Administration perceived the chief problem facing the region to be Soviet and Cuban expansionism. The primary locations of this expansionism were in El Salvador (which was seen as being under attack) and Nicaragua and Grenada (where it was claimed that "communist regimes" had been allowed to come to power during the "Carter Watch").

In 1982, the concern of the United States with Grenada was heightened by the construction of a new airport with a runway variously described as 9,000 to 10,000 feet. The project was justified by the Bishop government as necessary for the development of the nation's tourism industry (similar developments had already been undertaken in Barbados and St. Lucia), while the Reagan administration saw it as hard evidence of a new Soviet-Cuban military foothold in the hemisphere (Nylen 1988). This view was etched in the minds of Americans when, during a major foreign policy speech in March 1983, the president showed satellite photos of the runway and referred to Grenada as a threat to United States security interests (Brown 1985).

Findings

The six months prior to the initiation of the crisis leading up to the American invasion begins in April, the month following President Reagan's speech. What kind of quantitative and qualitative assessments can be made of press coverage of Grenada during this critical pre-crisis period?

As is evident from Figure 6.1, there were a total of fifteen items on Grenada in the newspapers of record in the United States and Great Britain, eight appearing in *The New York Times* and seven in *The Times*. An average of approximately 1.3 items per month in the immediate pre-crisis environment can hardly be described as either impressive or likely to catch the reading public's attention. Moreover, only a quarter of these (four items) appeared in the three months immediately preceding Bishop's arrest, indicating no pattern of growing press concern with the situation in Grenada.

When we move from a discussion of quantity to quality of the pre-crisis reporting on Grenada in the two newspapers, the assessment is hardly more encouraging. In Great Britain two of the seven items on Grenada were feature stories by Paul Flather in *The Times Higher*

Figure 6.1

Press Reporting During the Six Months Prior to the Crisis in Grenada

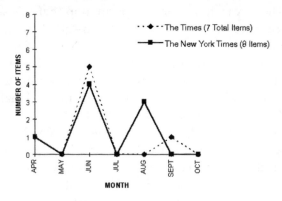

Education Supplement dealing with education policy on the island (1983a; 1983b). The first article dealt with a new adult education program, while the latter focused on problems found in the primary school system. Both articles were favorably oriented toward the revolution (which is described as "Marxist" in one article), and close ties between Grenada and Cuba were highlighted in both pieces. Since there was no reference to the United States in either article, the dimension of Grenadian-American relations was simply not dealt with. Neither was there any hint of internal divisions within the PRG.

The major event that occurred in the pre-crisis period and that focused press attention on Grenada was the June 1983 visit by Prime Minister Bishop to the United States (Pastor 1990, pp. 203–204). Bishop's expressed purpose was to meet with President Reagan in an attempt to improve relations between the two countries. This visit was reported by *The Times* in three bylined news reports by its Washington correspondent Ali and in one unattributed final report. (Ali 1983a; 1983b; 1983c; and *The Times* 1983).

The tone of all these pieces was generally one of conflict resolution rather than of conflict intensification. While the Cold War framework was central to the analysis contained in all items, the dominant theme that emerged was Bishop's desire to improve relations with the United States, even though it was evident that the Americans were not willing to meet Bishop even half way. Bishop was portrayed as a non-belligerent leader seeking a reconciliation. In one item there was a direct reference to a shift away from anti-American rhetoric in Bishop's speeches. There was, however, no speculation that this softening in his attitude toward the United States might lead to domestic repercussions within Bishop's ruling PRG (Nylen 1988, p. 22). The final piece in *The Times* prior to the October crisis appeared on September 10 and dealt with Sir Eric Gairy's deportation to the United States by the Barbados government. It was mentioned that Gairy was wanted in Grenada on a charge of murder.

All things considered, press coverage of Grenada in *The Times* during the pre-crisis period was not at all helpful in preparing readers for the events that occurred in Grenada beginning on October 15. While the conflict between Grenada and the United States was certainly not downplayed, the more radical charges made by Bishop and others in the PRG that the United States was either planning or supporting a military invasion of the island were not mentioned. Nor was there any hint of a domestic power struggle within the PRG. In fact, Bernard Coard, Bishop's chief political rival was never mentioned in *The Times* reporting in the six months preceding Bishop's arrest. The dominant impression of Grenada gleaned from reporting in *The Times* was one of a leftist revolutionary government, of which Bishop was the uncontested leader, moving domestically to improve the quality and quantity of education and internationally to seek an understanding and better relations with its major adversary, the United States.

With one notable exception, the coverage of Grenada in *The New York Times* was only slightly more helpful in preparing readers for an American military intervention into Grenadian affairs. Coverage of Grenada during the period began in April, with a wire service report that Unison Whiteman, Grenada's Foreign Minister, had charged that the United States was supporting a "counterrevolutionary force of mercenaries and exiles" who were planning to invade the island (*New York Times* 1983d). The military invasion theme dominated the article and there was no hint of discord among the rulers of Grenada.

As was the case with *The Times*, four of the items on Grenada in *The New York Times* dealt with Bishop's June trip to the United States. The first of these was unattributed (1983a); the second came from the Associated Press (1983c), while Nossiter (1983b; 1983a) wrote the final two. While the dominant theme (that of Bishop seeking a reconciliation with a recalcitrant Reagan administration) was the same as that found in *The Times* reporting, two themes missing in the British press were discussed. The first was a restatement of the charge of a planned United States invasion, this time by Bishop himself. This was done, however, in the context of the invasion being "pushed back," although the threat of such an invasion was certainly "not entirely removed" (Nossiter 1983a). The second, and more important theme dealt with conditions in Grenada, where, in a press conference, Bishop was grilled on such questions as political prisoners, lack of a free press, and the absence of elections. Bishop seemed to have difficulty in justifying Grenada's policy on these issues and his responses were weak and unconvincing. Further, an indication of discord on the island was first mentioned, albeit the discord referred to was with Bishop's opponents outside the PRG. In the course of the press conference, Bishop did indicate that plans to hold an election were underway and promised a vote "as soon as reasonably practical" (Nossiter 1983b). There was no speculation regarding the impact that Bishop's attempted rapprochement with the United States and his promise to hold elections might have on his domestic power position. However, with the benefit of hindsight, we can point to the significance of these items in Bishop's eventual downfall. What was missing in this reporting was any discussion of political-ideological differences within the PRG (Nylen 1989, pp. 18–21).

It is precisely this variable that was mentioned (although not stressed) in what was overall the most perceptive piece of reporting on Grenada during the pre-crisis period in either newspaper — a front page article written by Crossette and datelined St. George's. This article, based on interviews with a wide range of Grenadians, posed the basic question, "Has Bishop lost control of the revolution?" (Crossette 1983). Crossette claimed that as Soviet-Cuban influence was increasing, public support for Bishop's government was "diminishing rapidly." In addition, Crossette cited the large number of political detainees, the absence of a free press and general intolerance of political dissent as areas where Bishop's government was being found wanting by the Grenadian population. Further to these observations, Crossette discussed the relationship between Bishop and Bernard Coard and his wife Phyllis. The Coards were described as "among the most radical members of the Government." Crossette also mentioned "a rift between the Coards and Mr. Bishop," but this was not elaborated upon. On the same day, excerpts from Crossette's interview with Bishop were printed, but these dealt mainly with Bishop's basic political philosophy rather than with current political problems (*New York Times* 1983e). The final *New York Times* piece on Grenada appeared on August 27 and dealt with unsuccessful United States opposition "on economic grounds" to a $14.1 million International Monetary Fund (IMF) loan to Grenada (1983b). Thus, while the reporting on Grenada in *The New York Times* was somewhat fuller than that found in *The Times*, especially with regard to the dispute with the PRG between Bishop and Coard, it lacked any real sense of an impending crisis; and certainly didn't hint at a crisis of the magnitude that would entail the deployment of American military forces in combat operations.

Conclusion

While the press may be an excellent indicator of what is actually happening in the world, it is far less reliable as a predictor of what tomorrow's crises might be. In the case of Grenada, we have to conclude that neither with respect to the volume of coverage nor the content of that coverage, did the press point with any degree of accuracy to an impending military operation there during the six months prior to its actual occurrence.

It certainly could be argued that this conclusion follows from an investigation of a highly atypical case. Nevertheless, significant military operations on the part of the United States actually did occur in this case in the Caribbean in the early 1980s. While this conclusion may be taken as laying the blame on the press for inadequate reporting, what apparently happened was a scenario of events so bizarre that even the governments of Britain and the United States seemed truly surprised and were unprepared for the final events (Nylen 1988, p. 25).

Because the United States moved swiftly and relatively decisively against the small island nation, some of the rough edges of the military operation are easy to overlook. While it is clear that the United States government opposed the Bishop government in Grenada and the press speculated about a military solution involving the United States along the lines of the 1954 exile invasion of Guatemala (see chapter 1), the idea that such an invasion would be triggered by Bishop's execution, stemming from a power struggle within his own government, seemed outrageous.

Bishop truly personified the Grenadian revolution, and it is doubtful whether his murderers could have succeeded in governing Grenada even without the benefit of the American intervention. Nevertheless, the small size of Grenada and its limited population masked the fact that the United States was really unprepared for military operations on the island. In spite of the Ocean Venture 81 military exercise, with the target state of "Amber and Amberdines" — widely assumed to be a dress rehearsal for an invasion of Grenada (Simmons 1985, p. 365) — it is apparent that the United States either did not have well-developed plans for an invasion or, if it did, didn't use them. In fact, the operation suffered from command, communication and intelligence problems, and given less-favorable circumstances, might have led to a major embarrassment.[2]

What seems to have characterized this military crisis is that it involved a highly improbable set of events. If surprise is one of the elements that constitute a crisis, should we reasonably expect the press to be less "surprised" than the major governments involved, which after all, do have considerable intelligence networks at their disposal? The answer to this question is an obvious No, yet this provides little comfort to those of us who depend to a great extent on the elite press for our understanding of unfolding international events.

Notes

1. This chapter is an edited version of "The Press as a Predictor of Military Conflict in the Caribbean: The Case of Grenada," which appeared in S. H. Surlin and W. C. Soderlund, eds., *Mass Media and the Caribbean* (New York: Gordon and Breach, 1990). It is published here with permission.
2. For example, Nylen reports that one of the two campuses of the U.S. Medical School in Grenada was "lost" and thus not secured until "forty-eight hours after the invasion had begun" (1988, p. 39).

Chapter 7

The Price of Censorship: Television Network News Coverage of the 1983 U.S. Invasion of Grenada

WALTER C. SODERLUND AND E. DONALD BRIGGS

In the early hours of October 25, 1983, elements representing virtually every branch of the American military began an armed invasion of Grenada, a geographically small island located in the southeastern Caribbean, with a population of approximately 100,000 people. Given the Cold War context of the Grenada invasion and in light of research demonstrating the congruence between the nation's mass media and its foreign policy (Paletz and Entman 1981; Herman 1985; Parenti 1986; Herman and Chomsky 1988; Bennett 1990), it should not have been an especially difficult task for the Reagan Administration to justify this extraordinary use of military force. Consequently, one would have expected American media coverage to be largely sympathetic to the objectives of the invasion, which the administration portrayed in the classic Cold War frame as "an encounter between U.S. virtue and Communist evil" (Parenti 1986, p. 185).

However, as Cuthbert's comparative study of newspaper coverage of the invasion in the United States, Canada, Europe and the Caribbean has shown, positive and negative directions of headlines in U.S. newspapers were virtually identical: 22.7% positive and 22.6% negative. Only among Caribbean newspapers was the invasion enthusiastically endorsed (1990). Similarly, another newspaper-based study failed to detect anything approaching a pro-administration "propaganda role" played by America's press in the invasion (see chapter 8).

This chapter investigates a further dimension of American media coverage of the Grenadian invasion—that of network TV news. As Bennett has observed, "The first important political observation about the American mass media is that to an important extent they regulate the content of public information and communication in the U.S. political system. Mass mediated images of reality set the limits of who in the world we think we are as a people, and what in the world we think we are doing" (1988, p. 14). Moreover, research has pointed out consistently that in the hierarchy of competing media, it is to television that Americans turn for their news and thereby obtain the "truth" regarding events in the world (Larson 1982; Larson 1984; Iyengar 1991). How then did this most important of all mass media report the invasion of Grenada to the American public in its major evening newscasts? Did television news take the balanced and critical role as evidenced in the nation's newspapers, or did it, as was clearly the case in the 1989 Panama invasion (see chapter 13), act as cheerleader for the invading American military forces in an important Cold War engagement?

Following generally poor relations with the United States based on Grenada's international alignment with the "Communist side" in the Western Hemisphere (Payne 1990), in the early summer of 1983 Bishop attempted a fence-mending trip to the United States (Nylen 1988, pp. 23–26). Not only did the visit fail to improve relations with the region's superpower, it also most likely increased tensions within the People's Revolutionary Government (PRG) between Bishop—increasingly seen as moderate—and the hard-line faction headed by Bernard Coard (Crossette 1983).

It was this split within the PRG that resulted in a power-sharing agreement between Bishop and Coard. Bishop's refusal to honor the deal occasioned his arrest, his release by supporters and his eventual murder at the hands of government troops. His death on October 19 left the government in the hands of hard-liners headed by General Hudson Austin, and served as the proximate cause for the U.S. military invasion of the island that began early on October 25 (Nylen 1988, pp. 27–30; Adkin 1989, pp. 28–81).

Methods

Data for this chapter were obtained from the Television News Archive at Vanderbilt University in the form of videotapes of news stories on the invasion appearing in the major evening newscasts on the ABC, CBS and NBC networks for a twelve-day period beginning on October 25 and ending on November 3, 1983. By the end of this period, all military operations had ceased and the focus of the invasion had shifted to restoring civilian rule to the island. The total number of news stories analyzed was fifty-nine: twenty on ABC, nineteen on CBS and twenty on NBC.

All coding was performed by the authors. On format variables (anchor/anchor-reporter, etc.), sources used, item placement and length, intercoder reliability was established at 96%. With respect to coverage of major issues, intercoder reliability was 90%, while on the evaluative dimensions, sources supportive or critical of U.S. policy, as well as text and visual support or opposition, intercoder reliability was 83% (Holsti 1969, p. 140).[1]

Actual descriptive language used with respect to President Reagan, Prime Minister Bishop and General Hudson Austin in the newscasts was recorded, compiled, collated and sent to a panel of six political scientists and communications scholars with instructions to judge whether each descriptive word or phrase used in reference to the three leaders involved in the crisis would be seen by the American people as positive, neutral/ambiguous or negative. (See the full list of descriptors and how they were coded at the end of this chapter.)[2] In order for a descriptor to be counted as either positive or negative, and thus appear in Table 7.5, five of the six panel members had to agree that such a judgment was appropriate. Intercoder reliability for this measure is, therefore, at least 83%.

Findings

Of the fifty-nine news stories dealing with the invasion, 68% were run in the first three placements, with 46% in the lead position. An additional 17% were featured as the last story in the newscast. The fact that only 15% of stories were scattered throughout the newscast gives an indication of the importance of the invasion as a news event. Further, only 24% of stories were of less than two minutes' duration, with fully 47% running over four minutes in length. With respect to format, 86% of stories featured anchors and reporters, 3% employed an "expert" commentator with an anchor, while 8.5% consisted of media commentary of the editorial variety. Only one story was in the anchor-read format. Ninety percent of stories included film. Clearly, the invasion has to be seen as an event attracting major attention from the nation's electronic media.

As is evident from data in Table 7.1, military dimensions of the invasion, not surprisingly, dominated the list of most important issues covered, accounting for seven of the top fourteen issues. Especially important in the view of the media were U.S. casualties, military operations underway and the role of Cubans in the fighting, which, in that order, were the top three issues overall in invasion coverage. A range of political considerations, including discussions of the U.S. political process, U.S. public opinion, press censorship, hemispheric security and implications of the invasion, filled out the agenda of major

Table 7.1
_____

Major Issues Covered in the Invasion of Grenada*

		Percentage of Stories Cited			
	ABC	CBS	NBC	Total	X^2
	N=20	N=19	N=20	N=59	Sig
1. U.S. Casualties	60%	47%	50%	53%	NS
2. Military Operations	45	53	45	48	NS
3. Role of Cuban Troops	55	47	40	48	NS
4. U.S. Political Process	40	47	40	42	NS
5. Link to Beirut Bombing	40	42	40	41	NS
6. Cuban Political Process	50	32	35	39	NS
7. Seizures of Weapons	30	32	45	36	NS
8. Return of Troops to U.S.	25	37	40	34	NS
9. Press Censorship	25	37	40	34	NS
10. Safety of Americans	35	42	20	32	NS
11. Implications of the Invasion	20	37	40	32	NS
12. Hemispheric Security	30	21	35	29	NS
13. Cuban Casualties	20	32	35	29	NS
14. U.S. Public Opinion	30	21	35	29	NS

*Since most stories dealt with many issues and all of these were coded, columns do not add to 100%.
_____

issues. That these issues would appear as important is not surprising and, indeed, statistical analysis reveals an underlying homogeneity on the part of the three networks regarding their judgments of what was newsworthy in invasion coverage.

There were, however, stylistic variations in network treatment of the invasion that merit commentary. In the early days of the invasion, ABC in particular relied heavily on the Pentagon for news, while CBS featured a wider range of independent sources. This resulted in the fullest background to the crisis being presented in CBS coverage. NBC was the network that attempted to put the invasion in a global context (i.e., a crusade against communism), while CBS focused its attention on more tactical aspects of the operation. Somewhat surprisingly, given Cuba's role as military opponent in the crisis, both ABC and NBC had reasoned and balanced coverage of Cuban involvement. CBS, through the tone of its commentary, appeared to be the most skeptical of the operation and the United States' role in it.[3]

Data in Table 7.2 deal with the first three newsmakers or sources in a story appearing either on-camera or quoted. It is evident from this table that to an extraordinary extent American sources (Sir Paul Scoon being the sole exception) dominated the list of those whose views were transmitted to the American public as major sources of news. Moreover, even within the context of American sources, we see "official" sources (the President, the Pentagon, U.S. forces in the field, and the State Department) given pride of place. The Pentagon, U.S. forces in the field, media commentators and President Reagan accounted for between 70% and 80% of lead sources on all three networks. What is interesting, however, is the extent to which television journalists themselves appeared as sources, mainly in an editorial capacity. This was particularly evident on NBC.

Given that the networks were forced to rely largely on what official American sources chose to feed them and had (at least until the invasion was a fait accompli) no investigatory capacity in the field of their own, it is not surprising that we see an overall balance of source commentary that was favorable to the American invasion. What is interesting, however, is that the balance toward favorable commentary is not *more* skewed. Among lead sources, while 63% presented information judged favorable to the invasion, 22% took the opposite position. Indeed, among second sources, positive positions dropped to 46%, while negative positions reached 39%. Leaving out of the

Table 7.2

Primary Sources Used in Grenada Stories

	ABC	CBS	NBC	Total
First Source	**(N=20)**	**(N=19)**	**(N=20)**	**(N=59)**
Pentagon	30%	37%	15%	27%
U.S. Forces in Field	25	11	20	19
Media Commentators	10	11	25	15
Ronald Reagan	10	21	10	14
	75%	80%	70%	75%
Second Source	**(N=19)**	**(N=18)**	**(N=15)**	**(N=52)**
U.S. Forces in Field	26%	28%	20%	25%
Media Commentators	21	6	/	10
Sir Paul Scoon	5	6	13	8
American Medical Students/ Administrators	5	6	13	8
Americans on Street	11	6	7	8
	68%	52%	53%	59%
Third Source	**(N=16)**	**(N=16)**	**(N=15)**	**(N=47)**
Pentagon	19%	13%	7%	13%
U.S. Forces in Field	13	/	27	13
State Department	13	6	13	11
	45%	19%	47%	37%

analysis those sources coded as neutral or ambiguous, among the remaining total of positive and negative sources used in all stories (N=279), 54% were favorable toward the invasion while 46% presented negative views (data not shown in tabular form).

When we examine data in Table 7.4 dealing with textual and visual components of news stories on the invasion, the situation becomes even more confused. Indeed, on the textual dimension, we find overall slightly more stories coded negative toward the American position (29%) than coded positive (27%). Moreover, this was the case with two of the three networks; only CBS had more stories with a positive rather

Table 7.3

Source Evaluation of American Invasion of Grenada

	ABC	CBS	NBC	Total
First Source	(N=20)	(N=19)	(N=20)	(N=59)
Favorable	65%	68%	55%	63%
Neutral/Ambiguous	20	6	20	15
Unfavorable	15	26	25	22
X^2=2.2860, DF=4, NS				
Second Source	(N=19)	(N=18)	(N=15)	(N=52)
Favorable	32%	56%	53%	46%
Neutral/Ambiguous	15	16	14	15
Unfavorable	53	28	33	39
X^2=3.0776, DF=4, NS				
Third Source	(N=16)	(N=16)	(N=15)	(N=47)
Favorable	56%	44%	47%	49%
Neutral/Ambiguous	13	18	33	21
Unfavorable	31	38	20	30
X^2=2.7441, DF=4, NS				

than a negative text. This tendency toward negativism, however, was not replicated with respect to visuals, where a favorable balance overall was recorded: 19% positive and 8% negative.

Data in Table 7.5 show the percentages of positive and negative descriptive words and phrases used with respect to Ronald Reagan, Hudson Austin and Maurice Bishop. They indicate an ambivalent treatment of the invasion on the part of American television news, especially with respect to President Reagan. First, Reagan was the individual actor receiving the majority of press commentary, and second, this commentary was very narrowly divided between positive and negative evaluations (52% positive and 48% negative). This is hardly the performance one would have expected of the American media in the circumstances of an American president ordering a military invasion in order to remove a communist government from

$Table$ 7.4

Text and Visual Evaluation of Invasion of Grenada

	ABC	CBS	NBC	Total
Text Evaluation	N=20	N=19	N=20	N=59
Pro-Invasion	25%	26%	30%	27%
Neutral/Ambiguous	45	53	35	44
Anti-Invasion	30	21	35	29

$X^2=1.4647$, DF=4, NS

	ABC	CBS	NBC	Total
Visual Evaluation	N=20	N=18	N=15	N=53
Pro-Invasion	15%	17%	27%	19%
Neutral/Ambiguous	80	72	66	73
Anti-Invasion	5	11	7	8

$X^2=1.3925$, DF=4, NS

$Table$ 7.5

Percentage of Descriptors Reflecting Positively or Negatively on Major Actors During the Invasion of Grenada

	Positive	Negative
Ronald Reagan (based on 42 positive and negative descriptors)	52%	48%
Hudson Austin (based on 22 positive and negative descriptors)	–	100
Maurice Bishop (based on 7 positive and negative descriptors)	43	57

power at a crucial period in the Cold War. General Austin was the recipient of no positive descriptors, while the very few descriptors applied to the late prime minister, Maurice Bishop, were, as was the case with Reagan, rather evenly balanced.

Conclusion

Given a classic Cold War confrontation, with American troops committed to combat against hostile forces; a set of news sources that by their composition should have supported the administration; and virtually no anti-invasion sources given prominence; how can we explain a media portrayal of American policy that was clearly lukewarm, if not openly critical?

Two factors appear to account for this situation. One can be seen as a legitimate concern on the part of media with an overextension and/or misuse of American military power. Literally days prior to the Grenadian invasion, American peacekeeping efforts in Lebanon ended in grief with the bombing of the marine barracks in Beirut causing horrendous casualties. Indeed, some of the troops used in the Grenada invasion had been diverted from assignment to Lebanon, where they were to have replaced those who were attacked. Bodies of soldiers arriving in the United States from two diverse parts of the world at the same time linked the two operations and gave legitimate cause for journalistic reflection regarding the commitment of American troops to hostile environments.

The second factor that might explain the media portrayal is one closer to home. Although the unique circumstances mentioned above were responsible for some of the negative commentary, in the final analysis the American decision to bar journalists from covering the fighting in Grenada, probably more than anything else, created the climate of confrontation between the press and the government that resulted in the less than enthusiastic way in which the media framed the coverage of the invasion.

This decision to bar journalists appears rooted in the dubious perception on the part of military officers who had served in the Vietnam War that "newsmen, especially television newsmen, were, at bottom, adversaries, neither trustworthy nor competent in military affairs, eager to dramatize American failings, possessing enormous power to undercut civilian backing for the men in battle" (Braestrup 1985, p. 20). As a consequence, no journalists were allowed to accompany the forces invading the island, resulting in voluminous coverage from disgruntled journalists in the field (many of whom had congregated in Barbados), focusing on attempts (all of them frustrated) to get to the scene of the fighting on their own. While the details of fighting were relayed to journalists in Washington by official government sources, these were interspersed with coverage from journalists "in the field" who were forced to comment largely on their own unfortunate circumstances and to speculate about what was being covered up and why.

Added to this mix was the role of the TV editorial, a feature of network news that has to a significant extent been abandoned in recent years. In 1983, however, anchors and respected network correspondents did offer editorial pieces, and in the case of the Grenadian invasion, these painted an unflattering picture of the Reagan Administration. Commentators ridiculed the security-secrecy-safety arguments offered by the administration for the banning of the press and cited in counterargument the long-standing tradition of U.S. journalists covering military operations (the D-Day Normandy invasion being a favorite example). The editorials made it clear that the American people were being short-changed by an administration that was apparently afraid of them finding out the truth, thus making the press ban a matter of democratic principle.

After the initial fighting was over, American journalists were allowed limited and controlled access to the island, and indeed, in spite of a set of less than inspiring military operations, they by and large presented to the American people a favorable interpretation of events that were unfolding. This was noticeably the case with respect to the mistaken bombing of a mental hospital, where the primary Grenadian interviewed, in effect, absolved the Americans of blame. As well, there was literally no investigation of the military blunders that plagued the campaign from the outset, including the obvious fact that the numbers of Cubans on the island corresponded exactly to those reported by Fidel Castro rather than the wildly exaggerated figures offered by the Pentagon.

There is another dimension that needs to be considered. All three networks appeared taken by surprise by the events in Grenada that resulted in American troops engaged in a combat situation in the Caribbean. This is not entirely unreasonable, given that Grenada truly was not of major strategic significance in the Cold War. However, it was apparent in the early reporting that network researchers, news writers and producers had little background information on Grenada or the Eastern Caribbean more broadly. For example, the name of the island was frequently mispronounced (as in the city in Spain) and at least on one broadcast, it was obvious that the anchor had no idea what the Organization of Eastern Caribbean States was or what it was doing. Also, the continuing lack of coverage of Bernard Coard in favor of General Hudson Austin is indicative of a shallow understanding of power relations on the island.[4]

In terms of explaining negative framing of the invasion, the implications of this outcome are somewhat unclear. It is, however, our judgment that lack of independent knowledge of Grenada on the part of the networks should have strengthened the Administration's hand vis-à-vis journalists. For us, it serves as further evidence of the alienating effects produced by barring journalists from covering the invasion.

While the military did eventually get an easy ride on television news, the damage had been done. A "rally around the flag" frame of coverage would have been predictable in light of research on how American media cover armed hostilities involving American forces. But by its own initiative of denying journalists access to the invasion, the administration brought upon itself some serious and unwanted problems. As it turned out, Grenada was not destined to be a long-term military problem for the United States, and once the fighting was over, American military forces were gradually removed in favor of police forces from Caribbean countries. However, had Grenada proved to be an ongoing military problem, the consequences of the attempted censorship of the press might have been significant. The American people had been told clearly and often that their government had lied, that it had not consulted Congress and refused to acknowledge that the War Powers Act applied, and had engaged in an unprecedented campaign of press censorship. Given this negative framing, it would have been an extremely difficult task for the administration to rehabilitate the image of the invasion had hostilities and casualties continued for any length of time.

Notes

1. By the end of the coding process, each story had been viewed at least three times by both authors. Intercoder reliability was determined by comparing individual coding decisions on a sample of twelve stories. Prior to the final coding, all disagreements were resolved to the satisfaction of both authors.
2. It is significant that Bernard Coard, Bishop's chief political rival within the PRG, was mentioned in the network's coverage of the invasion in only two stories. Early in the invasion, ABC referred to him as "deputy

prime minister" and "a committed ideological Marxist." Late in the
invasion NBC referred to him as "the leader of the coup that started the
fighting."
3. Some of the above observations are not evident in the statistical
    analysis. They are based upon viewing in sequence and at one time, all
    stories on the invasion, network by network. The observations are
    thus qualitative rather than quantitative in nature.
4. Media do not stand alone. Arguing that "To all intents and purposes,
    before March 1979 U.S. policy toward Grenada did not exist," Nylen
    cites numerous intelligence failures on the part of the U.S. government
    with respect to the domestic political situation that led to Bishop's
    arrest and execution (1988, pp. 4, 25).

Chapter 7 Descriptors

Ronald Reagan
Words/Phrases Judged to Be Positive
Feisty/unusually combative/eager to take on critics
A decisive image projected
Decided on a show of force
Willing to study new Soviet proposals
His toughest week as president and his finest hour
Openly critical of the Marxist regime in Grenada
Not trigger-happy
Pursuing a prudent policy to combat communist influence that threatens
    U.S. interests worldwide
Pleased with the way things went in Grenada
Justified in going in
Sent his first string to Congress
Persuasive
No change in his demeanor in his toughest week in office
Taking this in stride
Cheerful
More confident now
Probably justified in going in
Hard at work
Had little choice [but to invade]
Celebrated the good news

Words/Phrases Judged to Be Negative
His crisis support will fade
Eventually will be remembered as trigger-happy/trigger-happy
Reckless
His foreign policy is stupid
Particularly caustic

Lying about the number of foreign troops on Grenada
Produced a bureaucrat's dream—nobody's watching
His White House lied to its own press office
He didn't consult with Congress
Ducked the War Powers Act/ did not properly report under the War Powers
  Act/never acknowledged that the War Powers Act applied
Put out the most sweeping and dictatorial censorship directive in the history
  of American government
Received surprisingly little support from American allies
If he did not supply arms to the Contras, there would be peace in Nicaragua
Blocked news sources/is imposing censorship/[news coverage]/pattern to
  restrict information
Monster
Assassin/fascist assassin

Words/Phrases Judged to Be Neutral or Ambiguous
President/head of government
If the right signal goes out to Cuba, Nicaragua and the U.S.S.R., he will be
  one happy fellow
If American lives were in jeopardy, then the president acted wisely
Worried that the Revolutionary Council might take American hostages
A receptive audience for a request for an American invasion
Believed the world was moving toward Armageddon
Does not make crisis decisions himself
Not surprising that he would consider the use of force

Hudson Austin
Words/Phrases Judged to Be Positive
[None]

Words/Phrases Judged to Be Negative
Captured
Fugitive military leader of the Revolutionary Council
Reported cornered/trapped by American troops
Marxist extremist
Reported holding hostages
Radical
His attempt to seize power sparked the American invasion
Leader of hard-line Marxist coup
Cuban-trained military leader of Grenada/Cuban-trained general
Leftist
Untrustworthy
Shot and killed Bishop and several cabinet ministers
Held on the *USS Guam* for this own protection from the citizens of Grenada
Grenadian who overthrew Maurice Bishop in a bloody coup

Words/Phrases Judged to Be Neutral or Ambiguous
General
Leader of coup that overthrew and later killed Bishop
Held on U.S. warship *Guam*
Seized power a week ago
Leader of Military Council/leader of Grenada's Revolutionary Council/
running Grenada's ruling Council
Demanding safe passage to Guyana
Army commander
Head of government

Maurice Bishop

Words/Phrases Judged to Be Positive
Popular prime minister
Alarmed the Soviet Union

Words/Phrases Judged to Be Negative
Prime minister of a Marxist regime
Turned his country into an important Soviet-Cuban outpost in the Caribbean
Leftist

Words/Phrases Judged to Be Neutral or Ambiguous
Prime minister
Killed in a military coup
Ex-leader of Grenada
Under house arrest
Killed
Often predicted an American invasion would come to the island, but didn't
live to see it
Showed signs of wavering toward democracy

Chapter 8

Press Portrayals of Maurice Bishop: A Balance Theory Hypothesis[1]

WALTER C. SODERLUND AND STUART H. SURLIN

In the context of the American invasion of Grenada in the fall of 1983, an intriguing question is whether there was a conscious effort on the part of the U.S. military in the field and/or the government in Washington to "rehabilitate" the image of the assassinated prime minister, Maurice Bishop. While alive, in the view of the Reagan Administration, Bishop was clearly grouped with Nicaragua's Sandinista leader Daniel Ortega as an ally of Fidel Castro, and hence an enemy of the United States (Pastor 1990, pp. 198–201). However, following his execution by more radical elements in his government, American policy was now aimed at overthrowing his murderers. In these circumstances, was there a propaganda advantage to be gained by adopting a posture of avenging the death of the admittedly popular revolutionary leader?

Precisely such speculation was raised in two pieces included in the authors' edited volume *Media in Latin America and the Caribbean* (Soderlund and Surlin 1985). In his analysis of Grenada, Hoogendoorn levels the following charge:

> When Bishop was killed, the U.S. could no longer go after him and vilify him with the usual media labels "revolutionary," "Marxist," and so on. So within the Cuban framework, the so-called hardliners become the new Cuban-Grenadian, and in the most detestable label reversal of all, Maurice Bishop becomes the posthumous

hero and victim of evil forces. From the despised marxist leader the media now convert him into "the charismatic leader," and even "President Bishop." (1985, p. 267)

Writing about media coverage of the Grenada invasion in Jamaica, Habermann makes a very similar observation: "Jamaica's participation in the military operation in Grenada...was hailed by...*The Daily Gleaner* as a patriotic contribution to Caribbean autonomy. One small but perhaps important difference appeared: the once evil Maurice Bishop suddenly became a popular hero" (1985, p. 225).

A Balance Theory Hypothesis

In terms of pure pragmatism, because a military operation was underway, there were obvious propagandistic advantages to the United States and its Caribbean allies appearing to take the side of the slain and popular leader against his murderers. Since a "psychological operations" team from Fort Bragg, North Carolina, accompanied the invasion forces (O'Shaughnessy 1984, pp. 208–209), the potential for the type of image manipulation alluded to above is not entirely fanciful. There are, in addition, broader theoretical reasons why a shift in media portrayals of Bishop following his death might have been expected.

News reporters feel obligated to serve their readers' needs. This professional virtue is reflected in the deep-seated norm of the profession to objectively report the news of the day to one's constituent readers "untainted by any personal bias or outside influence that would make it appear anything but what it is" (Charnley 1966, p. 23). In spite of these norms offered to prospective journalists through textbooks, a body of literature has emerged that concluded that reporters do not report the news of the day in an unbiased manner. The reasons for this phenomenon appear twofold.

First, reporters are socialized into their professional role through various overt and covert messages in their work environments that communicate appropriate journalistic behavior (Sigal 1973; Tuchman 1978; Gans 1979). Also, since one's professional behavior occurs within an identifiable social, cultural and economic setting, pressures develop that naturally bend the perspective of the individual. This can be described as the "systemic-symbiotic" theory of news. A previously advanced "symbiotic" theory of news lead researchers to predict that news stories will reflect the interests of the government in power (Bennett et al. 1985). Other research has shown that news stories reflect the political perspectives of media owners and managers (Merrill 1965; Halberstam 1979). Especially with respect to culturally held stereotypes and beliefs concerning foreign (particularly third world) news, newspapers would be expected to present views that correspond to conventional wisdom (Scanlon et al. 1978; Riffe and Shaw 1982; Cuthbert and Surlin 1985).

Second, reporters strive to serve the psychological and informational needs of their audience. Therefore, the information conveyed will parallel what is perceived to be conventional wisdom for the audience, thus offering the audience a sense of well-being, or a "psychological balance." News is presented in a fashion that can be read efficiently and digested without psychological trauma, and this is facilitated if the news corresponds to the audiences' normative belief system.

The concept of "cognitive consistency" has developed from work undertaken by a number of prominent social psychologists including Abelson, Aronson, Festinger, Fishbein, McGuire, Osgood, Rosenberg and Singer (see Feldman 1966). While it is not our intention to review this literature in detail, it is helpful for readers to know that "Common to the concepts of balance, congruity, and dissonance is the notion that thoughts, beliefs, attitudes, and behavior tend to organize themselves in meaningful and sensible ways" (Zajonc 1960, p. 280). While balance theory is usually employed to explain individual belief systems, it is posited here that in this vein, reporters attempt to retain normative psychological balance among their readers and thus attempt to reduce the level of dissonance in the information they convey.

Since dissonance produces psychological discomfort, it may be harmful to newspaper-reader relations. It may even result in financial loss for one's employer through disgruntled reader reaction and canceled subscriptions. Research has documented how audience dissonance leads to media behavior aimed at reducing levels of psychological discomfort. This could occur through the selection of sources for exposure (Donohew and Palmgren 1971; Tan 1973) or changing audience attitudes concerning the credibility of dissonant sources (Tan 1975). On the other hand, research also indicates that if audiences receive what they desire psychologically from a newspaper, a favorable newspaper-reader relationship develops. This is most clearly seen in the content of special-focus newspapers, such as black-oriented and heritage-language newspapers (Stevens 1970; Surlin and Romanow 1985). The systemic-symbiotic theoretic formulation suggests, therefore, that through the combination of reporter enculturation/ socialization and the desire to achieve a psychological balance *with* one's readers and *for* the benefit of those readers, news reports will inevitably be biased.

One method of presenting biased information occurs through the use of evaluative, valenced descriptions. Words and phrases can greatly affect the perceived reality of a person (Merrill 1965), a group (Shoemaker 1983) or an event (Hvistendahl 1979). As Corcoran argues:

> The key concept here is the power of the media to define, not merely reproduce reality through their narrative devices which actively make things mean. Reality is no longer viewed as a given set of facts.... Instead, it is the result of a particular way of constructing, through preferred meanings, a "reality" which would have credibility, legitimacy and a taken-for-grantedness. (1984, p. 49–50)

Methods

In this chapter we seek to document the extent of a possible media rehabilitation of Maurice Bishop's image based on a balance theory hypothesis. In order to carry out this research, we have employed a comparative design utilizing content analysis of the leading newspapers in three western countries: in the United States, *The New York Times;* in Canada, *The Globe and Mail;* and in Great Britain, *The Times/Sunday Times.* These newspapers were examined throughout the entire year of 1983 for material dealing with Maurice Bishop, and all words and phrases used to describe the Grenadian leader were recorded for future coding and analysis.

In all, Bishop was mentioned in 168 items of newspaper content: ninety of these items appeared in *The New York Times,* forty-six in *The Globe and Mail,* and thirty-two in *The Times/Sunday Times.* In this reporting, a total of ninety-four separate words and phrases were used to describe Bishop. These were coded by the authors as reflecting either positively or negatively on Bishop, in terms of how they would likely be interpreted by an American audience. (See the full list of descriptors and how they were coded at the end of this chapter.) Identified words and phrases included both political and personal descriptors. Political references such as "moderate," "moved toward democracy" and "wanted a better understanding with the United States" were coded as positive image-builders, while words and phrases such as "dictatorial," "authoritarian" and "suppressed the press" were coded as negative. Personal references were rated according to commonly accepted usage. Thus, references such as "conscientious," "honest" and "modest" were coded as positive, while references such as "irresponsible," "paranoid," "womanizer" and "betrayer" were coded as negative.[2]

These words and phrases appeared in stories that carried, in the main, Caribbean datelines (54%), with the remainder originating primarily in the United States, Canada and Great Britain. Local staff writers and special correspondents provided 73% of the Bishop-related items, with 20% coming from the major wire services. Fifty-seven percent of the items in which Bishop was mentioned consisted of inside page news, 21% were front page news, 17% were feature columns, 3% appeared as editorials, while 1% were letters to the editor. Fully 84% of press items appeared after Bishop was killed as opposed to 16% appearing prior to his death. For purposes of analysis, the data set was divided into two periods: (1) all those words and phrases printed between January 1 and October 19, 1983; and (2) all those printed between October 20 (the date Bishop's death was reported) through to the end of the year. Organized in this way, the data should allow us to make rather sensitive comparisons regarding Mr. Bishop's treatment in the press. If he had been vilified prior to the October coup that resulted in his execution, was there an attempt on the part of the press to present a new Maurice Bishop "reality" after his death?

Theoretically, three distinct streams of "balancing pressure" can be seen as acting to push American news coverage toward a positive portrayal of Bishop following his execution. First, the U.S. government would want to cultivate a more favorable image of Bishop to serve as justification for their invasion. Second, there are symbiotic pressures within the field of journalism to support government policy, reflecting, at least in part, the desire to remain on good working relations with the Pentagon. Third, pressures can be seen acting on newspapers to achieve a cognitive balance with their readers concerning events in Grenada. Since the Grenadian invasion was widely supported by the American people (Kenworthy 1984), readers presumably would want to believe that their government was justified in its actions and that a positive outcome would result. And, although not measured in this study, one would also expect that Bishop's opponents would be discredited following his death. Thus, a double-barreled strategy involving the glorification of Bishop and the vilification of his murderers can be seen as consistent with reducing cognitive dissonance over U.S. actions in Grenada.

Since neither the British nor the Canadian governments supported the American military invasion, there would be less reason for the image of Bishop to be "psychologically rehabilitated" in the press of these countries, other than what might be seen as the normal respect paid to one who has been killed under tragic circumstances. However, since a high percentage of international news appearing in Canadian newspapers is American in origin (Scanlon 1974), we would expect to find Canadian newspapers midway between American and British newspapers in terms of a possible image rehabilitation.

Findings

Data in Table 8.1 indicate the percentage of positive and negative references to Maurice Bishop, both pre- and post-death, for each country. Neutral or ambiguous descriptors were dropped from the analysis.

While it is apparent in these data that some image rehabilitation did occur, there are also some serious differences between the hypothesized and actual distributions. In each country, Bishop's image improved after his death: Positive descriptors increased by 8% in Britain, 7% in the United States and 21% in Canada. However, in the United States, where pressures to produce an image rehabilitation should have been greatest, the actual percentage change was roughly equivalent to the change found in Britain, where these pressures were predicted to have the least effect. Canadian data also present a problem. While an intermediate position between the United States and Great Britain was hypothesized, the positive percentage increase found there is three times that recorded for Britain and the United States. In order to visualize the degree of congruence between actual and hypothesized results, data from Table 8.1 are portrayed schematically in Figure 8.1.

Table 8.1

Percentage of Positive and Negative References to Maurice Bishop

	Pre-Death	Post-Death	Total
Great Britain	N=13	N=43	N=56
Positive	46%	54%	52%
Negative	54	46	48
United States	N=29	N=108	N=137
Positive	35%	42%	40%
Negative	65	58	60
Canada	N=14	N=64	N=78
Positive	21%	42%	39%
Negative	79	58	61

Figure 8.1

Percentage of Positive Descriptors of Maurice Bishop

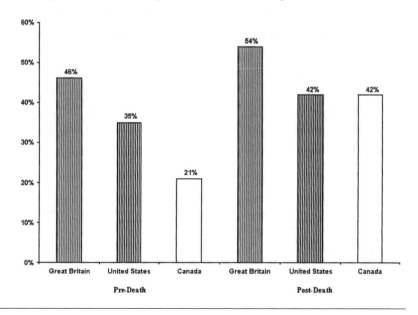

In order to gain a fuller understanding of these evaluative patterns, the words and phrases used most frequently to describe Bishop were further analyzed. The word "prime minister" was used most often. While this term can be seen as simply descriptive of the office he held, it must be remembered that Bishop assumed the "prime ministership" in 1979 as a result of a coup d'etat that deposed Sir Eric Gairy, and that his tenure in that office had never been legitimized by an election. Various derogatory terms are commonly used to describe leaders who have assumed power and ruled in this manner (see chapter 2). Given the circumstances, we believe that the common use of the term "prime minister" to describe Bishop could be construed as positive, as it served to legitimize his position. However, given the sheer volume of its use, to code it as positive would have greatly skewed the results. We therefore decided to code it as a neutral descriptor, and it is omitted from all analysis other than reporting the frequency of its use in Table 8.2.

The four positive descriptors occurring most frequently are "popular/likable/admired," "moderate/measured/non-extremist," "youthful/thirty-nine years old" and "lawyer/barrister/London-trained." Negative terms occurring most frequently are "Marxist/

Table 8.2

Major Words and Phrases Used to Describe Maurice Bishop

No. and Percentage of News Items in Which Word/Phrase Appeared

Word/Phrase (by frequency of mention)	N	Percentage
Prime Minister	133	79.2%
Popular/Likable/Admired	25	14.9
Marxist/Communist	24	14.3
Leftist/Left Wing	16	9.5
Moderate/Measured/Not Extremist	11	6.6
Ally of Fidel/Ally of Cuba/Pro-Cuban	11	6.6
Youthful/Thirty-Nine Years Old	10	6.0
Lawyer/Barrister/London-Trained	9	5.4
Abusive of Human Rights	7	4.2
Socialist	6	3.6

communist," "leftist/left wing," "ally of Fidel/ally of Cuba/pro-Cuban," "abusive of human rights" and "socialist."

When we examine the use of these descriptors, both before and after Bishop's death, by country, we find patterns that are not suggestive of any concerted propagandistic effort at image rehabilitation. For example, in Great Britain some positive descriptors see increased use following his death, but some negative ones do as well. Here the increase in positive references to Bishop after his death is clearly attributable to multiple positive descriptors, each used only one or two times. The same tends to be the case for the United States, with the exception that the descriptor "popular/likable/admired" was applied to Bishop only after his death. (Data not show in tabular form).

Because Bishop's image change undergoes the greatest transformation in Canada, the pattern of valenced descriptors in *The Globe and Mail* will be examined in greater detail.

Data in Table 8.3 show that while positive references to Bishop increased by 21% following his death, this took place in spite of a slight increase in the use of the negative terms "ally of Fidel/Cuba/pro-Cuban," "abusive of human rights" and "socialist." While the use of the negative descriptors "Marxist/communist" and "leftist/left

Table 8.3

Major Descriptors of Maurice Bishop in *The Globe and Mail*

Word/Phrase	Percentage of Newspaper Items in Which Descriptor Appeared		
	Pre-Death	Post-Death	Total
	N=5	N=41	N=46
Popular/Likable/Admired	0	22%	19.6%
Marxist/Communist	20%	14.6	15.2
Leftist/Left Wing	20	14.6	15.2
Ally of Fidel/Ally of Cuba/Pro-Cuban	0	7.3	6.5
Youthful/Thirty-Nine Years Old	40	2.4	6.5
Socialist	0	7.3	6.5
Moderate/Measured/Not Extremist	0	4.9	4.3
Lawyer/Barrister/London-Trained	0	4.9	4.3
Abusive of Human Rights	0	2.4	2.2

wing" did decline, the only positive descriptor to record a major increase in usage (as was the case in the United States) was "popular/ likable/admired." Thus, in the Canadian newspaper, as was true for the others, a large number of words and phrases, used only once or twice, accounted for the more favorable image of Bishop that emerged during the period after his death.

Conclusion

This study in the area of news coverage and balance theory is only mildly supportive of the hypothesis. As the theory predicted, the image of Maurice Bishop as projected to the reading publics in three major Western democracies did in fact improve after his death and coincident with the American invasion of Grenada. While neither the magnitude of the change, especially in the United States, nor the pattern of word usage suggest an orchestrated, government-directed propaganda campaign, it is evident that following his death reporters did find new and different words to present Bishop in a favorable light to their readers.

Moreover, this improvement in Bishop's image could theoretically have worked to reduce dissonance and increase balance for most readers in the United States. However, in Canada and Great Britain, where the pressures operating to improve Bishop's image were theoretically not as great or even non-existent, the degree of image improvement was either at a comparable level (Britain) or much greater (Canada). Clearly there were forces at work here that cannot be explained by balance theory. One factor that perhaps contributed to the small improvement in Bishop's image in the United States was the relatively sparse coverage of Grenada and Bishop before the critical events of October 1983 (see chapter 6). There is no doubt that Bishop was not a household word in the United States. Without a negative image of Bishop firmly fixed in American public opinion, there would be less pressure to radically reconstruct his image to fit a reconstructed reality. Had Bishop achieved the notoriety of a Saddam, a Qaddafi or a Fidel, we suggest that balance theory would have had greater predictive accuracy.

There are a number of interesting research questions that emerge from the study. Do different media in different cultures or countries hold differing beliefs regarding the need to offer cognitive/affective balance to their audiences? Does the pressure to maintain balance differ from one topic to another? How do reporters interpret the "public psyche" in order to determine the direction of the "bias" needed to achieve balance? Is there an ideal balance that can be achieved or should be achieved? What happens when news coverage does not attempt to achieve psychological balance for its audience?

We believe that balance theory is a formulation that with refinement can both predict and explain the biasing of news information. Essentially this biasing occurs for the purpose of achieving a cognitive/affective balance between medium and audience. Further research will either confirm, modify or refute the usefulness of the theory.

Notes

1. This chapter is an edited version of "Press Images of Maurice Bishop, Prime Minister of Grenada: A Pre- and Post-Death Comparison," originally published in *Canadian Journal of Communication*, Vol. 13, Nos. 3 & 4 (Fall 1988). It is published here with permission.
2. All coding was performed by the authors. Initial agreement was achieved on the coding of 87% of the "positive" and "negative" references. Agreement was not reached on the contextual meaning of six words, and these were then placed in the "neutral/ambiguous" category and omitted from the analysis. All other disagreements were resolved to the satisfaction of both authors.

Chapter 8 Descriptors

Maurice Bishop
Words/Phrases Judged to Be Positive
Popular/likable/admired
Moderate/measured/not extremist
Youthful/thirty-nine years old
Lawyer/barrister/London-trained
Tall/six feet tall
Relaxed
Resonant voiced
Charismatic/crowd-gripping
Articulate
Humanitarian
Entertaining
Brave
Hero
Pragmatic

Dedicated Grenadian
Good international image
Everybody loved him
Wanted better understanding with the U.S.
Created a state
Began move toward democracy
Has ability to inspire/instill confidence
Has ability to unite masses
Intelligent
Realistic
Noble/modest/unselfish
Tolerant and trustworthy
Non-authoritarian
Honest and moral leader
The nicest chap
Did much for Grenada
A God-Saint
Died to free country
Conscientious and honest
Developed agricultural resources
Deserved support of the Caribbean
Great leader
Good to work with
Handsome

Words/Phrases Judged to Be Negative
Leftist/left wing
Marxist/communist
Socialist
Comrade
Protégé of Fidel
Ally of Fidel/ally of Cuba/pro-Cuban
Radical/revolutionary firebrand
Abusive of human rights
Suppressed the press
Did not hold elections
Authoritarian
Betrayer
Womanizer
Autocrat
Tired and ill/depressed and quiet
Doomed
Detested
Dictatorial
Chilly toward the U.S.
Irresponsible/crazy
Corrupted by power

Non-admitted communist
Lacked leadership qualities
Hostile to criticism
Power and authority went to his head
Refused to negotiate and compromise
Sitting in underpants (under house arrest)
Seized power
Headed an illegal government
On American hate list/U.S. cool to him
Lacks brilliance in strategy and tactics
Paranoid

Words/Phrases Judged to Be Neutral or Ambiguous
Prime minister
Populist
Martyr
Nationalist
Bearded
Too charismatic
Too popular
Well intentioned, but price too high
In touch with Sir Eric Gairy
Disgraced the revolution and party
Defied the collective will
Not sufficiently Marxist
Too slow in enacting socialist policy
Petit bourgeois
Anti-colonialist/anti-imperialist
Onemanism
Exceptional/true revolutionary
Set on a pedestal
Came from a well-to-do family
Victim of a trap
Intended to use counterrevolutionaries

Chapter 9

Demonstration Elections? El Salvador, Nicaragua and Grenada 1984[1]

WALTER C. SODERLUND

A "demonstration election," as outlined by Herman and Brodhead (1984), is one where the main purpose is not the selection of a domestic government, but rather to provide an aura of international legitimacy for a particular ruling group. The research in this chapter focuses on North American press coverage of three elections held in the Caribbean Basin in 1984: El Salvador (March), Nicaragua (November) and Grenada (December).

The research employs content analysis to focus on differences in press coverage of these elections between leading newspapers in Canada and the United States. Herman has observed that in the American press "the media often treat similar events differently, depending on their political implications for U.S. interests" and suggests the appropriateness of a "propaganda framework" for analyzing American media coverage of international events (1985, pp. 136–137). The research design is based on the principle of "most similar systems," holding that, of all nations on earth, Canadian press coverage of international events should be closest to that of the United States. Key elements leading toward similarity in press coverage are shown in Figure 9.1.

In addition to likenesses in press coverage derived from general societal similarities (factor 1), we can see that there are other, more specific reasons to expect rather homogeneous press coverage of international events. Some research literature suggests that the American press is sensitive to pressures that create a "congruence"

Figure 9.1

Factors Leading to Similarity Between Canadian and U.S. Press Coverage of International Events

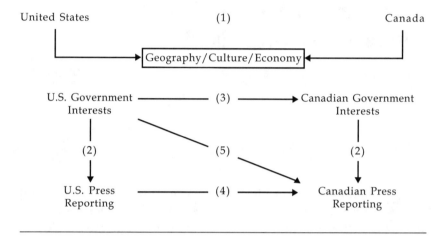

between press reporting and U.S. government policy (Kreisberg 1946; Herman 1985; Bennett et al. 1985; Parenti 1986; Herman and Chomsky 1988). These would include direct economic and political pressure and indirect effects of cultural biases and socialization to pro-government positions (factor 2). We expect these same general pressures to be operative in Canada.

While Canada is clearly an independent nation with a set of interests and a foreign policy distinct from those of the United States, the extent to which the Canadian export-based economy is dependent on American markets gives the U.S. considerable leverage to keep Canadian policy "on side" with respect to the Caribbean Basin, an area of the world not vital to Canadian national interests (Baranyi 1985; Morales 1985; Lemco 1986a; Haglund 1987; Rochlin 1988). Thus, we hypothesize a "government to government" channel of influence (factor 3), difficult to document but nevertheless working in subtle ways to keep official policy differences to a minimum. An additional channel of influence leading to a congruence in international press coverage may be seen in the "press to press" linkage (factor 4), since the major Canadian wire service, Canadian Press (CP), gets the bulk of its international news from foreign wire sources, primarily the American Associated Press (AP) (Scanlon 1967; Scanlon 1974; Canada 1970; Cumming et al. 1981). In fact, we would argue that the only channel of influence that is not operative (factor 5) is the one linking the American government directly to Canadian press organizations.

If, however, Herman is correct in his assessment that the American press functions as a propaganda conduit for the American government, it is precisely this government-to-press channel that would be critical in getting a "planned" government message across in the press in the case of specific events occurring over a relatively short time span (e.g., elections). Because Canadian newspapers are far less susceptible to direct pressures emanating from an American administration to take a position that is in agreement with American policy (factor 5), we maintain that Canadian newspaper content should be less propagandistic than American, in spite of the shared values and perceptions that characterize the two countries generally and the other more specific channels of influence that we have examined.

Since elections are a major component of the American concept of democracy, and because governments in disfavor with the United States — such as Cuba — are routinely castigated for not holding them (Frederick 1985), it is our assumption that each of these three elections presented the Reagan Administration with distinct foreign policy challenges. With respect to El Salvador and Grenada, which were clearly client states of the United States at the time of the elections, we have quintessential cases of demonstration elections. On the other hand, Nicaragua was perceived by the Reagan Administration as an enemy — a "communist state" — having fallen under the influence of Cuba and the Soviet Union.

There is, then, a legitimate question of whether the Nicaraguan election is a true demonstration election in the sense intended by Herman and Brodhead. Most clearly, Nicaragua was not a client state of the United States. Nevertheless, there were significant international pressures, coming chiefly from European and Latin American governments sympathetic to the Sandinistas as well as from the Socialist International, for Nicaragua to hold an election (Brumberg 1985). The reported views of various Sandinista leaders regarding the non-efficacy of elections (Brumberg 1985), combined with the realization, as expressed by Comandante Tomas Borge, that "the battle for Nicaragua will be won or lost in the United States" (quoted in

Zwerling and Martin 1985, p. ix), makes it reasonable to treat the Nicaragua election as being of the same species as the other two, albeit one with a radically different anticipated set of U.S. policy concerns and media portrayals.

In Latin America and the Caribbean, democratic elections of a conventional North American variety are only one of a number of methods used to achieve political power (Stokes 1952). And given the level of political instability and/or violence present in all three of these countries in 1984, it can hardly be argued persuasively that elections in any one of them were necessary, strictly in terms of domestic situations.[2] Thus, a strong case can be made that the "demonstration election" designation, positing that the elections occurred essentially to provide a veneer of international legitimacy on the governments winning the elections, is indeed appropriate (Herman and Brodhead 1984, p. vii).

In the scenario of a demonstration election, the American media play a key role. Their importance lies in the fact that for the vast majority of people living outside of the country in which a particular election is taking place, press reporting is the major channel through which information and perceptions regarding those elections are conveyed (Smith 1980). Herman and Brodhead have identified a number of characteristics common to coverage of a demonstration election:

- "Massive publicity" — a demonstration election is "a *media event* above all else";
- Construction of an appropriate agenda of election issues "carefully focused on the right issues, and avoiding the wrong ones" — the criteria here being whether a particular issue legitimizes or discredits the election;
- "Reliance on the proper sources of information" — i.e., U.S. government or local government officials supported by the U.S.;
- Portrayals of the election "as a dramatic confrontation between the forces of good and evil";
- Legitimizing the election in the minds of the U.S. public by getting "credible sources" (including foreign observers) to praise the election.

All of these factors are combined in a media public relations campaign to make "a pseudo-event look real" (Herman and Brodhead 1984, pp. 153–173).

Indeed, for Herman and Brodhead, the role of the American media in a demonstration election borders on serving as the handmaiden for U.S. foreign policy objectives:

> The subservience of the media to government political and propaganda aims is illustrated throughout the book, as the staged elections which we have examined have all been public relations triumphs and only by virtue of a level of media cooperation that amounts to propaganda service. (p. x)

From the research reported in this chapter we will not only be able to ascertain differences in American press coverage of three basically *similar* events, but also determine what differences, if any, occurred between American and Canadian press reporting of the *same* events. If Herman's propaganda framework is substantially correct, we should see key differences between American and Canadian reporting on each election, as well as among strictly American reporting on the three different elections.

Two assumptions underlie the research. The first is that each election studied presented the Reagan Administration with unique foreign policy opportunities and challenges. The Salvadoran and Grenadian elections required a strategy of "legitimization" — in the former to reduce Congressional intransigence in providing continued foreign aid to a government widely perceived to be abusive of human rights and ineffective, and in the latter to provide the proper psychological perception of stability so that private sector economic investment would begin to flow into the island. The Nicaraguan election, in contrast, required a strategy of "delegitimization" — that is, to portray it as a "sham" and a "farce." The second assumption is that the press would be the major vehicle through which the American government would attempt to communicate its positions to its citizens. If these assumptions are correct, we hypothesize that American newspapers would present their readers with substantially more favorable portrayals of the Salvadoran and Grenadian elections, while Canadian papers would present their readers with a substantially more favorable portrayal of the Nicaraguan election.

Methods

In order to test these hypotheses, we studied the three elections in a matched sample of Canadian and American newspapers: (1) national newspapers — *The Globe and Mail* (Toronto) and *The New York Times*; (2) capital newspapers — *The Citizen* (Ottawa) and *The Washington Post*; (3) elite-oriented newspapers — *Le Devoir* (Montreal) and *The Christian Science Monitor* (Boston); (4) eastern regional newspapers — *The Chronicle-Herald* (Halifax) and *The Atlanta Constitution*; (5) mid-continent regional newspapers — *The Winnipeg Free Press* and *The Chicago Tribune*; and (6) western regional newspapers — *The Vancouver Sun* and *The Los Angeles Times*.

Every item of content on each of the elections generated by newspaper sources for a forty-one-day period beginning thirty days prior to the election and continuing ten days past the election was included in the study.[3] The total data set consists of 637 news items. Through the application of content analysis methods, a number of dimensions of press coverage theoretically relevant to demonstration elections were examined: (1) total volume of coverage, (2) dateline of news items, (3) the relative salience of various specific issues treated in the context of each campaign (i.e., the "media agenda" for each election), (4) the evaluation of political parties and their leaders, and (5) whether headlines or textual language either "legitimized" or "delegitimized" the election reported.[4] The actual coding for the study was done primarily by the author along with two student research assistants.[5] Intercoder reliability was established at 84.6% (Holsti 1969, p. 140).

Findings

General Characteristics of Press Coverage

During the forty-one-day periods of study surrounding each election, there were 374 items of newspaper content dealing with the Salvadoran election (58.7%); 203 items dealing with the Nicaraguan (31.9%); and 60 items dealing with the Grenadian, accounting for a mere 9.4% of the total of 637 cases. Clearly, of the three elections, the Salvadoran generated the lion's share of press coverage, with the Grenadian trailing significantly in last place.

Moreover, when we examine the relative percentages of material appearing in the American as opposed to the Canadian newspapers, we find evidence of variation in patterns of electoral coverage in the two countries. For the Salvadoran election, roughly one-third of the items (N=122) appeared in the Canadian newspapers, while two-thirds (N=252) appeared in the American sample. For the Nicaraguan election, 40% (N=81) appeared in the Canadian sample, while 60% (N=122) appeared in the American papers. The coverage of the Grenadian election, however, does not follow this pattern. Not only was Grenadian coverage the most fragmentary, there was actually a slightly higher percentage of items (52%) in Canadian newspapers compared with the American papers (48%).

In reference to the concept of the demonstration election, in examining these data, two points are worthy of comment and both concern the Grenadian election. First, that election was by far the least reported of the three, evidence that casts doubt on its status as a demonstration election. Second, there is the rather curious phenomenon of the election generating roughly equal amounts of press coverage in Canada and the United States. This finding is at variance with the pattern found in both the Salvadoran and Nicaraguan elections, and it is not easily explained, as there were no particular Canadian ties to Grenada, as would be the case with Haiti, for example. For whatever reason, our conclusion is that the Grenadian election appears to have been underreported in the American press, a situation quite out of keeping with Herman and Brodhead's expectations regarding American press behavior in a demonstration election.

With respect to item datelines, for both the Salvadoran and Nicaraguan elections approximately two-thirds of the items originated from the actual country where the election was taking place. For the Grenadian election, fully 80% of items originated from the island. Washington, D.C., was the only other location from which a significant number of stories were filed for any of the elections. For the Salvadoran election, 25% of American press items carried a Washington dateline (by far the highest among the three elections), while 11% of Canadian reporting originated in Washington. For the Nicaraguan election, only 8% of American and 5% of Canadian items carried a Washington dateline, while the analogous figures for the Grenadian election were 17% and 7% respectively. In terms of direct U.S. government input into election coverage, both the Salvadoran and Grenadian elections yield figures on datelines that are at least congruent with such a role.

The Issue Agendas

Salvadoran Issues

Table 9.1 presents the major issues discussed in press treatment of the Salvadoran election. These issues, taken as a whole, constitute what Herman and Brodhead refer to as the "press agenda" for the election. This agenda, they maintain, is manipulated in order to highlight certain issues favorable to the U.S. interpretation of the election and to downplay those issues that run counter to the U.S. preferred view.

If we examine this agenda item by item, five issues are found where the differences in Canadian and American coverage are statistically significant: (1) U.S. aid to El Salvador, (2) a possible run-off election, (3) background discussions of history and political parties, (4) implications of the election and (5) the question of foreign observers to the election. The first and last can be explained by the fact that each

Table 9.1

Major Issues in the Salvadoran Election
(due to multi-coding, columns do not add to 100%)

	Percentage of Items in Which Issues Are Mentioned				
	Can	US	Total	Phi	Sig
Issue (by frequency of mention)	N=122	N=252	N=374		
Comment/Activity of U.S.	49%	60%	57%	.10	NS
U.S. Aid	31	44	40	.12	.05
FMLN Activity	34	43	40	.09	NS
Run-Off Election	44	29	34	.15	.01
Background/History and Political Parties	48	21	30	.28	.001
Background/Leaders	32	24	28	.08	NS
Human Rights Abuses	23	27	25	.04	NS
Implications of the Election	32	19	23	.14	.01
Foreign Observers	39	13	22	.30	.001
Campaign Strategy	25	16	19	.10	NS

constituted a particular political issue for the country where they received premier coverage. The patterns of coverage of the issues of a run-off election (made necessary if no candidate received 50% of the vote), the background discussion of history and political parties, and the implications of the election seem consistent with the demonstration election scenario. Herman and Brodhead specifically mention "the background and context of the election" and "ignoring the sequel" as "off-the-agenda items" (1984, pp. 163–167), and indeed the American newspapers were comparatively less interested in reporting these issues than were their Canadian counterparts. One could argue, however, that since these issues appear among the ten leading issues covered in the election, it would be inaccurate to say that they were "omitted" from American coverage of the election.

Such a case can be made, however, for coverage of the non-participation of the forces of the left in the election. While, as we shall see, the boycott of rightist opposition parties in the Nicaraguan election received premier coverage (appearing in fully 60% of newspaper items), the analogous non-participation of the left in El Salvador merited comment in only 8% of items dealing with that election, with this percentage being virtually identical in both Canada and the United States. While the relatively prominent coverage given to attempts by the Faribundo Marti National Liberation Front (FMLN) to disrupt the election is congruent with what Herman and Brodhead would expect to be "on the agenda," the coverage given to government human rights abuses in El Salvador is not.

Nicaraguan Issues
Table 9.2 addresses the substantive treatment of the Nicaraguan election. When this issue agenda is examined item by item, it is found that on only the final three items are differences in coverage statistically significant: The American papers covered the "Contra factor" to a greater extent than did the Canadian papers, while on the issues of foreign observers and reporting of election results, it was the Canadian papers that led the American in reporting.

In terms of the composition of the agenda, there is strong evidence that the Reagan Administration's scenario to delegitimize the election was in fact reflected in press coverage of the election, since a total of 60% of total news items mentioned the boycott of the election by parties to the right of the Sandinista National Liberation Front (FSLN). Further,

Table 9.2

Major Issues in the Nicaraguan Election
(due to multi-coding, columns do not add to 100%)

Issue (by frequency of mention)	Percentage of Items in Which Issues Are Mentioned			Phi	Sig
	Can	US	Total		
	N=81	N=122	N=203		
Boycott by Opposition	65%	57%	60%	.09	NS
Comment/Activity by U.S.	57	58	58	.01	NS
Political Freedom	31	34	33	.04	NS
Background/History and Political Parties	27	27	27	.00	NS
Date of the Election	20	30	26	.11	NS
Campaign Strategy	21	28	25	.08	NS
Possible U.S. Invasion	22	27	25	.05	NS
Contra Activity	15	30	24	.17	.05
Foreign Observers	36	11	21	.30	.001
Reporting of Election Results	28	14	20	.18	.05

33% discussed the status of political freedom in Nicaragua, while 26% focused on the date of the election, both major reasons given for the boycott by the opponents of the Sandinistas. While much of this discussion occurred within the same stories, virtually all of this type of coverage tended to delegitimize the election. In fact, one could make the argument that in the eyes of the press, the boycott of the election was nearly as important as the holding of the election itself. Differences between Canadian and American coverage are statistically significant on three of these issues. However, on two of the issues, Canadian coverage surpassed American coverage.

There are also three issues appearing on the election agenda that tended to legitimize the election, although their role in this respect is not as clear as was the case with the three delegitimizing issues: a threatened U.S. military invasion of Nicaragua, the activities of the American-backed Contras, and the role of foreign observers in the election. While these issues do make the top ten, they are not as prominently placed on the agenda as the delegitimizing issues. Also, the discussion of threats of a possible invasion and activities of the Contras received premier coverage in the American papers, while the question of foreign observers was covered to a greater extent in the Canadian press. However, the issue of whether to send official election observers to Nicaragua, just as it was with the Salvadoran election, was a hot political question in Canada. Thus, a good deal of Canadian coverage focused on this dimension rather than on the actual reports of the election observers, which tended to be quite positive.

On balance, what is evident in the issue agenda presented on the Nicaraguan election in the press of both Canada and the United States is a selection and ordering of material that would work to delegitimize the election in the eyes of readers. While legitimizing dimensions of the election were not ignored, they were not given prominence equal to the delegitimizing factors. In this pattern of coverage, there are, however, few significant differences between Canadian and American reporting. Thus, there is no compelling evidence that the American press especially followed the lead of the American government in its ordering and reporting of the major issues in the election.

Grenadian Issues
Table 9.3 shows the most frequently mentioned substantive issues surrounding the Grenadian election. Looking at amounts of coverage given specific issues, on only two are there statistically significant differences: background discussions of history and political parties, where Canadian newspapers lead in coverage, and economic development and foreign investment, which is the virtual preserve of the American press.[6] While not statistically significant, measures of association of .25 and .22 on the new airport and the reporting of election results indicate a greater attention to these issues among Canadian newspapers. An interesting finding in this data is that the percentage of newspaper items focused on commentary/activity on the part of the United States is very nearly as high in the Canadian as in the American papers, making that issue overall (as was the case with El Salvador) the most salient in the coverage of the election.

In terms of Herman and Brodhead's "right" and "wrong" agenda issues, the comparison of the Canadian and American press agendas

Table 9.3
___

**Major Issues in the Grenadian Election
(due to multi-coding, columns do not add to 100%)**

	Percentage of Items in Which Issues Are Mentioned				
	Can	US	Total	Phi	Sig
Issue (by frequency of mention)	N=31	N=29	N=60		
Comment/Activity of U.S.	68%	72%	70%	.05	NS
Background/History and Political Parties	84	48	67	.38	.001
Background/Leaders	65	45	55	.20	NS
Presence of Foreign Troops	58	52	55	.06	NS
Reporting of Election Results	45	24	35	.22	NS
Implications of the Election	29	38	33	.09	NS
Economic Development and Foreign Investment	7	48	27	.47	.001
New Airport	36	14	25	.25	NS
Campaign Strategy	29	17	23	.14	NS
Voting Irregularities	29	17	23	.14	NS
Election Day Voting Process	26	14	20	.15	NS
Source of Campaign Funds	19	21	20	.02	NS

on this election is inconclusive. Clearly, comment and activity on the part of the United States is central to coverage in both Canada and the U.S. Herman and Brodhead posit an active American role as indicative of press treatment of a demonstration election. On the other hand, election day turnout, another item that Herman and Brodhead see as an "on the agenda" item, while included in the major issues under "results" and "voting processes," is stressed considerably more in the Canadian as opposed to the American press (1984, pp. 163–167).

Also, when the "off the agenda" items are examined, there is not a clear pattern indicating that the American press played the role assigned to it by Herman and Brodhead in their demonstration election scenario. One issue that Herman and Brodhead argue should not be reported — background and context of the election — while more heavily covered in Canada, is nevertheless the third most frequently discussed topic in American election reporting. Of the twelve major issues appearing in Table 9.3, three — presence of foreign troops, alleged voting irregularities and sources of election funding — tended to discredit the election. On two of these issues Canadian reporting is higher than American, but in no case is the difference statistically significant.

With respect to issue coverage, there is one theme that is noticeably absent: any sustained evaluation of economic effects of the forced removal of the New Jewel Movement and the People's Revolutionary Government from power. Two items in *The New York Times* referred to "a continuing recovery" as well as problems hindering recovery such as high unemployment, heavy taxes and administrative red tape (Treaster 1984b; 1984a), but only in *The Christian Science Monitor* do we find the observation that "Grenada's economy, long based on spice and tourism, is worse off today than it was before the U.S. intervention" (Goodsell 1984). Besides these references, there was simply no analysis of what had happened on the island, socially and economically, in the year following the American invasion. Considering that the vast majority of reporting in both Canadian and American newspapers originated from Grenada, and since there seemed to be little in the way of "horse race" type campaign news to cover, one might have expected that socioeconomic stock taking a year following the invasion would have been a natural topic of interest and find its omission curious. While we can only speculate, it appears that this may have been an off-the-agenda item for this election.

The Image-Supplying Role of the Press

There is a growing controversy in North American journalistic practice regarding whether any reporting is in fact "objective" (Martin and Chaudhary 1983). If bias does enter into reporting, one way of measuring it is to analyze the descriptive words and phrases used in press reporting. As Corcoran argues, narrative devices employed by journalists in their reporting are capable of shaping the meaning attached to an event or person. Words are for the print journalist the basic materials upon which an interpretation of an event or person is built, and are therefore chosen carefully for the desired effect. For

Corcoran, the result is "a particular way of constructing, through preferred meanings, a 'reality' which would have credibility, legitimacy and a taken-for-grantedness" (1984, pp. 49–50).

For each election, we will examine this image-supplying role of the press with respect to four dimensions: (1) major political parties, (2) major political leaders, (3) language used in story texts that can be considered as either "legitimizing" or "delegitimizing," and (4) whether headlines shared the legitimizing or delegitimizing attributes of their stories.

Political Party Evaluation
Data in Table 9.4 deal with the evaluation of political parties and indicate that with respect to El Salvador, the press did tend to favor one major party, the Christian Democrats (PDC), over the other, the Partido Alianza Republicana Nacionalista (ARENA). Overall, 8% of items reflected favorably on the PDC (5% of Canadian and 10% of American), while 20% of items reflected unfavorably on ARENA, with but marginal differences between Canadian and American portrayals. While negative commentary on the PDC was at about the same level as positive in the Canadian press (4%), the American newspapers had little in the way of unfavorable commentary on that party.

In the case of the Nicaraguan election, data indicate that evaluative commentary of political parties was confined almost entirely to the ruling Sandinistas (FSLN), with again but minor differences between Canadian and American patterns of evaluation. Overall, the Sandinistas were criticized in 25% and praised in only 3% of total newspaper items.

For Grenadian political parties there is clear evidence in support of the "forces of light/forces of darkness" syndrome advanced by Herman and Brodhead as characteristic of a demonstration election. The New National Party (NNP), supported if not created by the United States, appeared in a favorable light in 58% of news items overall: 69% of American and 48% of Canadian items. Also, the party was mentioned in an unfavorable context in only 3% of items in each country. On the other hand, the Grenadian United Labor Party (GULP) was mentioned in a favorable context in only 2% of content overall, and was presented unfavorably in 38% of total items: 45% of American and 32% of Canadian. While the pattern of evaluation of these two parties is roughly similar in the two countries, the American press was both

Table 9.4

Percentage of Newspaper Items Reflecting Favorably and Unfavorably on Major Political Parties

	Can	US	Total
El Salvador	N=122	N=252	N=374
Pro-Christian Democrat	5%	10%	8%
Anti-Christian Democrat	4	1	2
Pro-ARENA	0	.5	.5
Anti-ARENA	19	22	20
Pro-National Conciliation	0	2	1
Anti-National Conciliation	2	2	2
Nicaragua	N=81	N=122	N=203
Pro-FSLN	5%	3%	3%
Anti-FSLN	28	24	25
Pro-Democratic Coordinator	1	0	.5
Anti-Democratic Coordinator	0	1	.5
Grenada	N=31	N=29	N=60
Pro-New National Party	48%	69%	58%
Anti-New National Party	3	3	3
Pro-GULP	0	3	2
Anti-GULP	32	45	38
Pro-Maurice Bishop Patriotic Movement	0	0	0
Anti-Maurice Bishop Patriotic Movement	6	0	3

more pro-NNP and anti-GULP, stances consistent with what would be expected from press performance in a demonstration election.

Leader Evaluations
Data in Table 9.5 focus on press evaluation of the major political leaders in the three elections and are derived from coding as "positive" or "negative" key words and phrases used to describe these leaders. An

American perspective was employed in making this evaluation, with those descriptors that were seen a either neutral or ambiguous omitted from the analysis. (See the full list of descriptors and how they were coded at the end of this chapter.)

Party leader data for El Salvador indicate that, far and away, Roberto D'Aubuisson, leader of ARENA, was the chief focus of press attention, and furthermore that the profile of D'Aubuission that emerged was highly negative in newspapers in both countries. The other two candidates, José Napoléon Duarte (PDC) and Francisco Guerrero of the National Conciliation Party, received nearly identical patterns of evaluation overall, with the balance highly skewed toward positive descriptors. Duarte received a higher percentage of positive commentary in the American press, while Guerrero (although not the object of very much attention in Canadian newspapers) emerged with a highly favorable portrayal in the coverage he did receive.

With respect to leader evaluation in the Nicaraguan election there is strong evidence for a congruence between American reporting and stated goals of American foreign policy. While there were far more descriptors applied to FSLN candidate Daniel Ortega than to his most visible opponent, Arturo Cruz (standard-bearer of the Democratic Coordinator), the pattern of these evaluations is different in Canadian and American newspapers. In Canadian reporting, Ortega received a relatively balanced evaluation (47% positive and 53% negative), while in the American press, approximately two-thirds of his descriptors were negative. While the total number of Cruz descriptors came nowhere near matching Ortega's total, the differences between the evaluation in the two countries is much greater. On the Canadian side 73% of the Cruz descriptors were negative, while in the American press, 100% of descriptors were positive in orientation.[7]

In Grenadian election reporting as well, political leader evaluation provides evidence that the American press did play a legitimizing role with respect to the treatment of the two major party leaders. Canadian newspapers were far more likely to use descriptors in references to GULP's Sir Eric Gairy,[8] while the American press used more descriptors in discussing NNP candidate Herbert Blaize. Consistent with party evaluations, while Blaize had a favorable image in both Canadian and American newspapers (78%), he was referred to more positively in the American press. Differences in the treatment of Gairy were even more pronounced: in Canada 48% favorable and 52% negative, while

Table 9.5

Percentage of Descriptors Reflecting Positively and Negatively on Major Political Leaders

	Can	US	Total
El Salvador			
Duarte	N=32	N=98	N=130
Positive	63%	72%	70%
Negative	37	28	30
D'Aubuisson	N=50	N=152	N=202
Positive	16%	18%	17%
Negative	84	82	83
Guerrero	N=11	N=40	N=51
Positive	82%	65%	69%
Negative	18	35	31
Nicaragua			
Ortega	N=15	N=22	N=37
Positive	47%	36%	41%
Negative	53	64	59
Cruz	N=11	N=9	N=20
Positive	27%	100%	60%
Negative	73	0	40
Grenada			
Blaize	N=38	N=50	N=88
Positive	74%	82%	78%
Negative	26	18	22
Gairy	N=46	N=37	N=83
Positive	48%	27%	39%
Negative	52	73	61

in the American press nearly three-quarters of Gairy descriptors were negative.

Of all leaders involved in the three elections, Roberto D'Aubuisson received the highest percentage of negative descriptors (83%),

142

Media Definitions of Cold War Reality

surpassing by a large measure the negative 61% recorded by Sir Eric Gairy and the negative 59% recorded by Daniel Ortega. Turning to positive evaluations, Herbert Blaize led the list with 78%, followed by José Napoléon Duarte with 70%, Francisco Guerrero with 69% and Arturo Cruz with 60%. In terms of leader evaluation, evidence tends to confirm the "good guy" vs. "bad guy" framing suggested by Herman and Brodhead. Also of significance is the comparative lack of attention paid to Sandinista leader Daniel Ortega. As is evident from the data, the relatively unknown third-party candidate in El Salvador received more press commentary than did the Sandinista leader. The same is the case with both Herbert Blaize and Sir Eric Gairy, although the gap was not as great.

Legitimizing and Delegitimizing Textual Language
Data in Table 9.6 portray the use of language within newspaper items that would tend to either "legitimize" or "delegitimize" the three elections. With respect to El Salvador, while differences on these two dimensions are not statistically significant, delegitimizing language predominates in both Canadian and American papers, with less legitimizing and more delegitimizing language appearing in the Canadian papers. On this important dimension, for the Nicaraguan election the dominant finding is that in both Canada and the United States, delegitimizing language appeared in the same percentage, 43% of total news items. Contrary to the demonstration election expectations, however, American papers actually used 3% more legitimizing language than did their Canadian counterparts, although it must be pointed out that this difference in not statistically significant.

For the Grenadian election the data are consistent with the American press playing a more legitimizing role, since twice as many items (35% of American as opposed to 16% of Canadian) employed legitimizing language. Conversely, there was almost no language that would tend to delegitimize the election in American newspapers, while in Canada such language was almost as prevalent as legitimizing language (13% as opposed to 16%), and dealt chiefly with fairness of the election occurring under what was in effect a military occupation.

Legitimizing and Delegitimizing Headlines
Data in Table 9.7 show the percentage of headlines coded as "legitimizing," "neutral" or "delegitimizing" for each election. In the

Table 9.6

Percentage of Items Using Legitimizing or Delegitimizing Language

	Can	US	Total	Phi	Sig
El Salvador	N=122	N=252	N=374		
Legitimizing Language	6%	10%	9%	.07	NS
Delegitimizing Language	21	13	16	.10	NS
Nicaragua	N=81	N=122	N=203		
Legitimizing Language	14%	17%	16%	.05	NS
Delegitimizing Language	43	43	43	.00	NS
Grenada	N=31	N=29	N=60		
Legitimizing Language	16%	35%	25%	.21	NS
Delegitimizing Language	13	3	8	.17	NS

Table 9.7

Percentage of Headlines Coded Legitimizing or Delegitimizing

	Can	US	Total
El Salvador	N=122	N=252	N=374
Legitimizing Headlines	3%	2%	2%
Neutral Headlines	82	90	87
Delegitimizing Headlines	15	8	10

X^2=4.951, DF=2, NS, Cramer's V=.12

	Can	US	Total
Nicaragua	N=81	N=122	N=203
Legitimizing Headlines	6%	4%	5%
Neutral Headlines	82	83	82
Delegitimizing Headlines	12	13	13

X^2=0.457, DF=2, NS, Cramer's V=.05

	Can	US	Total
Grenada	N=31	N=29	N=60
Legitimizing Headlines	16%	10%	13%
Neutral Headlines	81	83	82
Delegitimizing Headlines	3	7	5

X^2=0.787, DF=2, NS, Cramer's V=.01

case of El Salvador, while differences are not statistically significant and over 85% of the headlines were neutral, consistent with findings on textual language, there were in fact more delegitimizing headlines in both Canadian and American newspapers, with the percentage of such delegitimizing headlines greater in the Canadian papers. For Nicaragua, again, while over 80% of headlines were neutral, of those remaining, slightly over twice as many were delegitimizing than were legitimizing. While this could be seen as evidence supporting a demonstration election interpretation, there were no discernable differences between Canadian and American reporting. With respect to Grenada, while it must also be stressed that over 80% of headlines were neutral, there were actually more legitimizing headlines in Canadian papers and delegitimizing ones in American papers. This is a situation where headlines do not reflect the stories they caption, and thus weakens the case supporting a conscious legitimizing role played by the American press in the Grenadian election.

Conclusion

In assessing conclusions emerging from this research, two dimensions need to be explored. First are differences between Canadian and American coverage on each of the three elections. Such differences have been the primary focus of the research reported, and here we will highlight the major findings that have been discussed. Second, we will attempt to address the more difficult question related to differences in coverage among the three elections.[9] As a final point, we will attempt to incorporate both dimensions into an overall evaluation of the demonstration election hypothesis.

Comparing Canadian and American Coverage, by Election

El Salvador

With respect to the volume of coverage, the Salvadoran election generated by far the greatest amount of press coverage among the three elections included in the study. Comparatively, the level of press interest is quite compatible with the demonstration election scenario, especially given the high level of attention in the American press. However, when we examine other dimensions of press coverage, the evidence ranges from mixed to contradictory. The issue agenda presents us with mixed conclusions. In certain respects, items predicted by Herman and Brodhead's concept of the demonstration election appear on the agenda: the focus on the U.S. role in the election and the disruption from the forces of the left. Also, the electoral non-participation of political parties opposed to the government (the major issue in coverage of the Nicaraguan election) receives only scant attention. Finally, although they do appear prominently on the American press agenda, a number of items embarrassing to the United States do receive greater attention in the Canadian press. On the other hand, human rights abuses on the part of the Salvadoran government, actually receive more coverage in the American newspapers.

The evaluation of political parties and their leaders also leans in the direction of confirming the demonstration election hypothesis. The PDC received more favorable mentions in the American press, while ARENA was scathed in both American and Canadian papers. The pattern is even clearer when we examine coverage of the presidential candidates. Roberto D'Aubuisson was the virtual incarnation of "evil," while both his opponents received highly positive portrayals. While these trends are evident in Canadian as well as American reporting, they are stronger in the American press.

Evidence that runs counter to the demonstration election hypothesis is found in the use of legitimizing and delegitimizing language in both text and headlines. On both of these dimensions there is actually more delegitimizing than legitimizing content on the election. Although these trends are stronger for Canadian reporting, one cannot make the case that there was a concentrated effort to legitimize the election through the use of language in the American press.

Nicaragua

With respect to the volume of coverage, the Nicaraguan election occupies a mid-position between the Salvadoran and the Grenadian elections. Given that the Nicaraguan election had to compete directly with the American presidential election in the fall of 1984, the actual volume of coverage probably cannot be taken as evidence of suppressed American press coverage of the event. This appears confirmed by the ratio of American to Canadian coverage.

There are of course very clear indicators that American press coverage of the Nicaraguan election did serve to delegitimize it.

However, on most of these dimensions, Canadian press coverage was equally delegitimizing. Thus, it becomes difficult to sustain the thesis that the American press slanted its reporting to curry favor with the Reagan Administration.

The pattern of delegitimizing coverage in both countries is clearly seen with respect to the issue agenda, which gives very high prominence to the boycott strategies of the three center/right opposition parties. Given the volume of coverage on this issue, virtually any reader who was aware that an election was taking place would also be aware of the boycott. Further, it was mainly the opposition boycott that made the election suspect. Because the three opposition parties decided on the boycott option at different points during the campaign, the issue remained in press focus literally from the first reporting of the election to the termination of post-election commentary.

On the various evaluative dimensions of press reporting, the Nicaraguan data are not consistent. True, the FSLN was evaluated negatively, but there are no differences between Canadian and American perceptions in this regard. The same conclusion holds true for the use of delegitimizing and legitimizing language both within stories and in headlines. The only area where the American press evaluation departs from the Canadian pattern in the direction of greater congruence with administration policy is in the language used to describe Daniel Ortega and Arturo Cruz.

Grenada

First on the list of evidence that tends to cast doubt on the legitimizing role of the American press in the Grenadian election is the scant volume of coverage it generated. Over forty-one days, an average of fewer than five items of content per newspaper appeared on the election in the American sample of newspapers, actually two fewer items than appeared in the Canadian sample. While something of a case can be made for heightened Canadian press interest based on the Commonwealth connection, contrary to expectations, the election proved to be a rather low salience event for the American press. In truth, given the comparative figures for El Salvador and Nicaragua, it would be difficult to consider the level of coverage in either country as constituting "media hype."

However, when American and Canadian press coverage of the election is compared on other dimensions, some of the data reveal differences that point to a limited legitimizing role in the election on the part of American newspapers. Contrary to the American pattern, in the Canadian press the percentage of delegitimizing language was nearly as high as the percentage of legitimizing language. Also telling is what did not appear on the American press agenda: an analysis of Grenadian society a year after the termination of the revolution by an American military invasion. In this case, however, neither did this type of analysis appear in Canadian newspapers, which to some extent weakens the argument. Combined with this topic of non-coverage, we of course find that a key American agenda item (not found in Canada) was the role that the election would play in bringing the political stability needed to spur foreign investment (mainly American) to promote the economic development of the island.

When political parties and their leaders are discussed in the news, we see the clearest evidence of the American press playing a legitimizing role in the election. The election is acted out as a morality play with the key actors being in the center and on the right. The NNP and Herbert Blaize are portrayed as the "good guys," while GULP and Sir Eric Gairy are seen as the "bad guys." While the same trends are also evident in Canadian reporting, they are not visible to the same extent.

The use of legitimizing language in stories and headlines presents mixed evidence. Legitimizing headlines are actually more numerous among the Canadian papers and delegitimizing ones more numerous in the American press. Within the stories, however, it is the American press that used legitimizing language and refrained from using language that would tend to delegitimize the election in the eyes of readers by casting doubts on either its validity or its efficacy in solving the island's problems.

Comparing Press Coverage Across Elections

In attempting to assess differences in coverage among the elections perhaps the most obvious comparison deals with relative salience. The three elections clearly were not regarded as equally newsworthy events. The Salvadoran election captured the attention of both Canadian and American reporters to a degree unmatched by the Nicaraguan and especially the Grenadian election. The dearth of reporting on the Grenadian election in the American press appears to be a case of systematic underreporting, although reasons for this are unclear.

In addition to these marked differences in overall salience of the elections, it is our assessment that each election was "played" differently in press reporting. Moreover, with the exception of the Grenadian election, which revealed real differences between Canadian and American reporting, the elections seemed to evoke a similar pattern of interpretations in Canadian and American reporting.

El Salvador

The Salvadoran election was covered in both Canadian and American reporting as a genuine electoral contest in which three parties and their leaders would play a role in its outcome. Thus, in a macro sense, press reporting of the election can broadly be seen as "legitimizing." Further, in the evaluation of parties and candidates, press reporting in both countries tended to favor the Christian Democrats and the National Conciliation Party while attacking the credibility of ARENA and especially its leader, Roberto D'Aubuisson. However, in the use of language in text and headlines, the press in neither Canada nor the United States played a legitimizing role. The Salvadoran election certainly had its share of warts, and these received coverage prominent enough that it would be difficult to sustain the demonstration election hypothesis.

Nicaragua

The Nicaraguan election presents the clearest case of a unified and consistent portrayal of an election in newspapers of both Canada and the United States. Morever, this is the case in spite of rather wide and significant foreign policy differences between the two countries with respect to Nicaragua under Sandinista rule. What the data tell us is that in both Canadian and American reporting, the election was not portrayed as a legitimate electoral contest. The uniqueness of a supposed communist government holding elections in which parties of both the left and the right were allowed to contest for power, was not the frame in which the Nicaraguan election was placed. Rather, press attention focused on the boycott strategy (which some say was orchestrated in Washington), and the interpretation of the election that emerged was that the boycott fundamentally flawed the election. Thus, press reporting of the Nicaraguan election did indeed serve to delegitimize it, but curiously, for the logic of the demonstration hypothesis, this pattern of negative evaluation characterized Canadian reporting nearly to the same extent as it did American. Certainly the possibility must be entertained that the election truly was flawed, that both Canadian and American reporters saw it in that light, and that consequently their reporting was accurate.

Grenada

Of the three elections, the Grenadian generates the highest number of unanswered questions. If Grenada were no more than the tiny Caribbean island with a population that would fit into Michigan Stadium, there would be little reason to expect more than perfunctory international press coverage of an election occurring there. Of course, Grenada's importance lies not in this reality but rather as a symbol of a great American foreign policy "success" in the worldwide struggle against communism. The invasion occurring when it did — following the bitter Vietnam experience, the humiliation of the Iranian hostage crisis and the agony of peacekeeping efforts in Lebanon — made Grenada far more important to the U.S. than an island of 100,000 people would seem to warrant. With the victory against a perceived pro-communist and pro-Cuban government in Grenada in 1983, America's ideological stock market value rose, and the election of December 1984 marked the consolidation of that gain. Thus, the Grenadian election was a prime candidate for Herman and Brodhead's "demonstration election." In this scenario, the election was conceived to demonstrate to Americans and to the world that democracy, not dictatorship, followed in the wake of American military intervention.

Differences between Canadian and American reporting were found to be greatest on the Grenadian election. However, these differences cut in opposite ways with respect to confirming the demonstration hypothesis: In the area of content and style, the evidence is positive, in the area of volume it is negative. In American newspapers the election was portrayed in a propaganda framework. The virtues of Herbert Blaize were exaggerated as were the deficiencies of Sir Eric Gairy. The left was ignored and the election was portrayed to set the stage for large-scale American investment. Canadian reporting was similar to both countries' reporting of the Salvadoran election, with coverage balanced and focused on positive and negative features of the election alike. If, in fact, the volume of election coverage in the American press had been greater, one would have concluded that the Grenadian election did constitute confirmation of the demonstration election hypothesis. However, in the absence of such amplification, the election appears primarily as a puzzling case, where at best only half of the legitimizing role of the press was performed.

Assessment of the Demonstration Election Hypothesis

On the basis of the three case studies examined in this chapter, it is difficult to confirm the type of active, propagandistic role of the American press consistent with demonstration elections. Indeed, in the case of every election there are some features of press reporting that, if taken in isolation, would appear to be convincing evidence in favor of the hypothesis. The totality of election coverage, however, leads to the conclusion that the American press is far more pluralistic in its interpretation of these kinds of electoral events.

On the whole, there are subtle yet measurable differences that point out that the American press is more likely to present a given election in ways that appear compatible with American foreign policy goals. However, these differences are certainly not of the magnitude that would be consistent with an overt propagandistic role of the press; rather, they are more consistent with a symbiotic theory of news reporting (see chapter 8 in this volume and Bennett et al. 1985). Finally, in one case — that of Grenada — where the style of American reporting is consistent with the demonstration election hypothesis, we find evidence of significant underreporting of the election, negating to a large degree the stylistic evidence. It is possible to see how Herman and Brodhead could, by focusing on specific and limited aspects of press coverage, legitimately perceive the propagandistic role of the American press, which would constitute a demonstration election. However, a systematic investigation of these three cases leaves little doubt that such a role is an oversimplification of a reality that is far more complex.

Notes

1. This chapter is an edited version of "Canadian and U.S. Coverage of Latin American Elections," which appeared in *Newspaper Research Journal*, Vol. 13 No. 3 (Summer 1992). It is published with permission.
2. Grenada's election certainly was the most peaceful. However, even there, arguments were raised against calling an election. According to Lloyd Noel, a former attorney general who had been dismissed and imprisoned by Bishop, "We need a long time to organize ourselves politically after what has happened. If we rush into elections in a year we will end up with people in power who have not been properly assessed by the population, and these people will be peddling half-baked ideas." The case for early elections was put by George Louison, former minister of agriculture in the Bishop government. "I am in favour

of quick elections. The quicker we have a government the people recognize as their own the better. The people want the programs of the revolution to continue and I think a party espousing the ideas of the New Jewel Movement would be popular" (Fishlock 1983).

3. Letters to the editor were not numerous and were not coded.

4. "Legitimizing" is defined as any statement made by either the newspaper or another source and reported by the newspaper that enhances the image of the election as democratic or as a step likely to help solve the country's problems. Conversely, "delegitimizing" is defined as any statement reported by the newspaper that detracts from the election as being democratic or questions its efficacy in helping to solve the country's problems.

5. The author wishes to thank Jana Truka and Mark Restoulle for their assistance in coding and Robert Burge for assistance in computer-related aspects of the study. Thanks go also to the Canadian Studies Center at Duke University and the School of Journalism and the Institute for Research in Social Science at the University of North Carolina for assistance provided during the author's sabbatical leave working on this project during the 1985–1986 academic year.

6. Under this issue were coded references to investors, mainly American, who were waiting for a sign of political stability prior to initiating various economic development projects on the island.

7. The major difference in the language used is that Canadian papers referred to Cruz as a "former Sandinista ally" and a "former member of the Sandinista Government," while no such references to his former association with the Sandinistas was made in the American press.

8. Although the leader of GULP, Sir Eric Gairy, was not himself a candidate in the election, it was widely speculated that if his party won a majority of seats, one of the victorious candidates would resign and Gairy would run in the by-election.

9. This question is the more difficult of the two because we cannot assume that the three events, although all "elections," were necessarily equal events. In the preceding analysis focusing on differences in coverage of each election, this assumption is possible, as we compared and contrasted Canadian and American reporting of the same event.

Chapter 9 Descriptors

José Naploéon Duarte
Words/Phrases Judged to Be Positive
Political moderate/moderate/moderate left
Reformer
Tough
Centrist
Father figure
Comfortable

Confident
Fervent supporter of capitalism
Dynamic
Decent
Trusted
Architect of land reform
Best-known politician
Front runner
Liberal
Preferred by U.S./popular with Congress
Combative
Stellar politician
Democrat
Official winner

Words/Phrases Judged to Be Negative
Accused of vote fraud in 1982
Communist/communist in disguise/pro-communist/soft on communism
Allied with military
Provoked exodus of progressives from party
Crazy/crazy man
Presides over unstable government
Liar
Leftist
Traitor/traitor to the people
Persona non grata
Reputation badly damaged
In autumn of his political career
Enemy of the people
Fool
Self-centered

Words/Phrases Judged to Be Neutral or Ambiguous
Former president
Civil engineer
Veteran politician
Melodramatic
Plump
Flawed champion
Former junta president
Least right wing
Distrusted by army and oligarchy
Party founder
Lesser of two evils
Populist/burly populist
Former two-term mayor of San Salvador

Roberto D'Aubuisson
Words/Phrases Judged to Be Positive
Anti-communist
Effective
Smiles easily
Boyish looking/Eddie Fisher look-alike
Tough
Handsome
Aglow
Young/youthful
Sex appeal of a rock star
Hero
Forthright fighter
Es un hombre
Muscular
Has crowd appeal
Charismatic
Relaxed humorous style
Good stump politician
Front-runner
Restrained
Low-keyed
Conciliatory

Words/Phrases Judged to Be Negative
Pathological killer
Champion of the far right
Right wing/rightist
Linked to death squads
Slick
An assassin
Nazi/fascist
Upstart young military man
Godfather
Arch conservative
Notorious
Immoral
Opposed by Washington/opposed by U.S.
Cashiered army major
Dashing cashiered major in elevator shoes
Defender of privileges of oligarchy
Nervous
Militant strongman
Anarchic psychopath
Lacks moral qualities
Demagogue

Cynical
An anathema
Supports Nazi-fascist terrorism
A murderous thug
Ruthless
Political liability
Hold democratic institutions and human rights in contempt
Enemy of the people
Pariah
Linked to murder of American nuns
Unsavory international image

Words/Phrases Judged to Be Neutral or Ambiguous
Former army intelligence officer
Head of National Guard Intelligence/intelligence officer
Forty years old/ Forty-five years old
Fiery/firebrand
President of Constituent Assembly
Spellbinder
Nationalist
Controversial

Francisco José Guerrero
Words/Phrases Judged to Be Positive
Moderate
Effective negotiator
Man of concord and renewal
Politically adept
Centrist/center-right
Has ready laugh
Warm
Affable/amiable/backslapping/glad handing
Consummate politician
Smiling
Relatively clean image
Backed by U.S.

Words/Phrases Judged to Be Negative
Heads party of corruption and graft
Colorless
Rightist
Likely to finish third
Corrupt
Shopworn remnant
Not a reformer
Lacks popularity

Words/Phrases Judged to Be Neutral or Ambiguous
Dark horse
Likely king-maker
Conservative
Fifty-eight years old/ Fifty-nine years old
Lawyer
Politically between Duarte and D'Aubuisson
Veteran politician
Rotund/chubby
Short/stocky/heavy-set
Malleable
Lacks political ideology
Least polarizing
Uninspiring
Ex-cabinet minister
Old Pol
Classic L.A. version of a smooth-talking, hard-nosed U.S. ward healer

Daniel Ortega
Words/Phrases Judged to Be Positive
Famous
Bible school teacher
Energized
Pragmatist
Moderate
Modest
President-elect

Words/Phrases Judged to Be Negative
Marxist
Not charismatic
Not a good speaker
Ill-suited for a political role
Awkward
Super-sensitive
Ill-informed
Has negative attitude toward democracy
Leftist
Revolutionary/revolutionary leader
Introverted
Shy
Doesn't smile
A high-security-risk head of state
Strident Marxist rhetoric
Hardened guerrilla fighter
Crying wolf
Has less than infectious personality

Words/Phrases Judged to Be Neutral or Ambiguous
First among equals
Former guerrilla commander
Formal
Leading member of the Sandinista government
Nicaraguan leader
Current junta coordinator/leader/chief
Junta boss
Chief of state
Thirty-eight years old
Poet
Indian face
Laborer's son
Reserved
Austere

Arturo Cruz
Words/Phrases Judged to Be Positive
Well liked
Well respected
Has integrity
Main opposition leader

Words/Phrases Judged to Be Negative
Former Sandinista ally
Former Sandinista junta member

Words/Phrases Judged to Be Neutral or Ambiguous
Former ambassador to U.S./Nicaraguan envoy in Washington
Former ambassador to the U.N.
Former banker and diplomat
Former official of the World Bank

Herbert Blaize
Words/Phrases Judged to Be Positive
Middle of the road/moderate
Soft spoken
Honest/reputation for honesty
Favored by U.S./favored by Reagan
Front-runner
Mentally sharp
Grandfatherly
Reassuring
Has integrity
Quiet
Self-effacing
Steady/solid

Levelheaded
Respectable
Radiant
Strong of voice
Likely winner
Highly respected
Grenada's favorite son
Intellectually impressive
Morally impressive

Words/Phrases Judged to Be Negative
Colorless
Dominated by Gairy
A retread
Unremarkable
Unimpassioned
Weary
An invalid
Frail
Has no popular appeal

Words/Phrases Judged to Be Neutral or Ambiguous
Sixty-six years old
Former P.M.
Elected leader
Arthritic
Former chief minister
Lawyer/solicitor/attorney
Partly paralyzed
Not so newly born
Former civil servant
Walks with a cane
Flinty
Fiscal conservative
Legislator
Slightly built
Devout Anglican

Sir Eric Gairy
Words/Phrases Judged to Be Positive
Generous
Popular with women
Peasants' hero
Dominant political figure
Charismatic speaker
Well known
No bloody fool

Words/Phrases Judged to Be Negative
Guilty of financial irregularities/corrupt
Vengeful
Eccentric
Autocratic
Mysterious
Bogeyman
Inexplicable
Despotic
Repressive
Bizarre
A ghost
Likened to a UFO
Right wing
Almost invisible
Ready to do the deeds of U.S. imperialism
Exploitive
Authoritarian
Abusive of human rights
Associated with black magic
An embarrassment
Venial
Brutal
Has a somewhat negative rating
Erratic
Harsh
Dictatorial

Words/Phrases Judged to Be Neutral or Ambiguous
Labor organizer
Mystic
Former/ex-P.M.
Black man
Inexplicable
Wealthy
Sixty-two years old
Populist

Chapter 10

Constructing the Agenda: Ronald Reagan and Aid to the Contras 1986[1]

WALTER C. SODERLUND, RICHARD G. PRICE, RONALD H. WAGENBERG AND ROBERT M. KRAUSE

W hile the American political system is based on the principle of checks and balances, most scholars acknowledge that since the time of Franklin Delano Roosevelt, the president has emerged as the dominant figure in the making of the nation's foreign policy. In addition to constitutional powers granted the president related to foreign relations, which through use and judicial interpretation have been enhanced at the expense of Congress, an important informal power has developed: the power of political communication. According to Kumar and Grossman,

> It was during the Nixon years that the various segments of a president's political communication were brought together. In the sense that Franklin Roosevelt "established" the modern presidency, Richard Nixon "created" the modern White House. He understood that political communications is at the core of presidential power, and that strong and effectively managed White House operations makes possible the use of that power. (1986, p. 94)

In the research reported in this chapter we intend to examine President Ronald Reagan's ability to use the mass media to convey to the American people his point of view on the issue of renewed military aid for the Nicaraguan "Contras" — a key element in his strategy to overthrow the Sandinista government, which had come to power in July 1979 following the successful revolutionary struggle against the Somoza dictatorship (see chapter 4). In January 1986, Reagan asked Congress to resume aid to the Contras in the amount of $100 million, $60 million of which would be in the category of military aid. Military aid had been cut off by a congressional vote in the summer of 1984, while $27 million in "humanitarian" aid was set to expire at the end of March 1986 (North 1991, p. 237).

From the revelations of the Iran-Contra scandal, we now know the extent to which the Reagan Administration had circumvented congressional will through illegal arms for cash deals with Iran. Nevertheless, the effort to reestablish the legitimacy of U.S. military aid to the Contras was a major foreign policy goal of the administration (North 1991). That the press would play a major role in this strategy, conditioning both congressional (Cohen 1963) and mass public (Shaw and McCombs 1977; Erbring et al. 1980; Weaver 1984) attitudes on the question, appears beyond dispute.

Reagan Administration officials believed that communication policies had a high cash value. By keeping focus on the president and the positions he wanted to emphasize, they thought they could develop and maintain momentum and thus gain political support for the president. There is no doubt that Reagan officials tended to regard communications as a key ingredient of leadership (Kumar and Grossman 1986, p. 95).

Methods

In order to investigate presidential influence in agenda setting, we examined all press coverage on the question of renewed aid to the Nicaraguan Contras in two leading American newspapers, *The New York Times* and *The Christian Science Monitor*. This was done for a period of four months, beginning on January 1 and concluding on April 30, 1986. This period encompasses the initiation of the request for renewed aid and the first House and Senate votes on the question. *The New York Times* was chosen for study due to its preeminent status as the "newspaper of record" in the United States (Cohen 1963) and *The Christian Science Monitor* for its particular interest and reputation in the area of international affairs (Barney and Nelson 1983). Thus, our choice of newspapers was based on an attempt in the study to see how well the president was able to "structure the news" to his advantage in organs with premier reputations in international reporting.[2]

Every item of newspaper coverage dealing with aid to the Contras (including editorial cartoons and letters to the editor) appearing in these two newspapers over the period of the study was coded. Variables examined included dateline, length, type and source of content. In addition, items were coded for "primary newsmaker"; that is, the first source cited in an item, and up to three additional newsmakers. As well, each item was coded for substantive thematic coverage, an overall assessment as to whether the item was "pro-aid", "neutral" or "anti-aid," and whether the language used to describe key players in the item — the Sandinista government and the Contras — was, from an American perspective, positive or negative. Coding for the study was done primarily by a graduate student research assistant,[3] with intercoder reliability established at 86% with that done by the authors (Holsti 1969, p. 140).

Findings

The total data set for the study consists of 362 cases, approximately two-thirds of which appeared in *The New York Times* and one-third in *The Christian Science Monitor*. Press coverage of the aid to the Contras issue began slowly in January (5% of the total), increased marginally in February (9%), peaked in March (58%) and began to fall off in April (28%). Not surprisingly, Washington, D.C., was the dateline for 43% of total news items, with 11% originating from Nicaragua and 6% from Honduras. Twenty-five percent of items carried no dateline. Not only did *The New York Times* focus more attention on the issue of aid to the Contras in terms of volume of coverage, but it also tended to run longer items, with 45% running sixteen paragraphs or longer. *The Christian Science Monitor* ran approximately equal percentages of short, medium and long items, while *The New York Times* ran far fewer short items (15%).[4]

Data in Table 10.1 show the type of content on the question of aid to the Contras featured in the two newspapers. Again, major differences are apparent. For *The New York Times*, front page and inside page news accounted for 77% of total items, while for *The Christian Science Monitor* these categories contributed only 56% of content. *The Monitor* also ran far more letters to the editor and editorial cartoons (23%), categories

Table 10.1

Type of Content About Aid to the Contras

	NYT N=242	CSM N=120	Total N=362
Front Page News	13%	18%	14%
Inside Page News	64	38	56
Editorials	4	6	5
Features	17	15	16
Letters to the Editor	2	17	7
Cartoons	0	6	2

X²=54.52, DF=5, Cramer's V=.39, Sig<.001

Table 10.2

Source of Content About Aid to the Contras

	NYT N=242	CSM N=120	Total N=362
Local Staff/Special Correspondent	74%	54%	67%
American Wire Services	13	0	9
Other American Sources	4	17	8
Non-American Sources	6	11	8
Unknown	3	18	8

X²=62.48, DF=4, Cramer's V=.42, Sig<.001

which were hardly represented in *The New York Times*. There is virtually no difference between the two papers in percentages of editorials and features.

Data in Table 10.2 show that with respect to source of material on the aid to the Contras issue, the two newspapers seemingly used different sets of sources. *The New York Times* relied extensively on its own local staff and special correspondents for material (74%) and secondarily on American wire services (13%). *The Christian Science Monitor* used local staff and special correspondents for slightly over half of its total items. Also, as letter writers (more numerous in the coverage of *The Monitor*) were coded in the category of "other American sources," it is not surprising that this category occupies a position of greater prominence in that newspaper's coverage (17%) than in that of *The New York Times* (4%). As well, "non-American sources" accounted for a larger percentage of *Monitor* items (11%) than was the case for *The New York Times* (6%). The 18% of "unknown" items in the coverage of *The Christian Science Monitor* consist chiefly of very short items, which although unidentified as to source, most likely came from wire services. If this is indeed the case, the actual differences in source of material are probably not as great as the data would suggest.

Data in Table 10.3 show the "primary newsmaker," that is, the person or office first cited as a source of information in a news item. In this case we are looking at two primary newsmakers: President Reagan and a variety of American government officials. In all, the president (11%), his administration — named and unnamed — (12%) and the State Department (5%) were the primary newsmakers in just over a quarter of items, with *The New York Times* more likely to cite these sources (33%) than was *The Christian Science Monitor* (16%). The latter newspaper was far more likely to feature non-Nicaraguan Latin American sources as primary newsmakers (14%). For most primary newsmakers, differences between use in the two newspapers are not statistically significant.

If we extend the examination to newsmakers cited as first to fourth sources of information not much changes, as we see an overall similarity to the data dealing with just the primary newsmaker. With respect to differences between the two newspapers, "other American" (non-governmental sources), the president himself, "unattributed" administration sources, Democratic congressmen and Nicaraguan government spokespersons were relied on more extensively by *The New York Times*, while, as was the case with the primary newsmaker, non-Nicaraguan Latin American sources were used more often by *The Christian Science Monitor* (data not shown in tabular form).

Turning to data in Table 10.4, we examine the substantive coverage of the Contra aid issue. In spite of differences in volume of coverage, length of item, type and source of content, as well as primary newsmakers relied upon, there were no great differences in the

Table 10.3

"Newsmakers" as First Source of Information About Aid to the Contras, by Newspaper

	NYT N=242	CSM N=120	Total N=362	Phi	Sig
President Reagan	12%	8%	11%	.05	NS
Non-Government American Sources	12	8	11%	.05	NS
Latin American Non-Nicaraguan Sources	7	14	9	.12	.05
Unattributed U.S. Administration Sources	9	3	7	.12	.05
Democratic Congressmen	5	6	6	.00	NS
Republican Senators	5	6	6	.00	NS
Nicaraguan Government (Sandinistas)	7	3	6	.07	NS
Reagan Administration (Named Sources)	6	3	5	.08	NS
State Department	6	2	5	.10	NS
Non–American/Non–Latin American Sources	3	3	3	.02	NS

dimensions of the Contra aid story upon which the two newspapers focused attention. In fact, each paper gave primary attention to the same three issues: Reagan's political strategy, the vote in the House and the vote in the Senate. And on only two of twelve major substantive issues coded, are differences in coverage statistically significant. *The Christian Science Monitor* devoted substantially more coverage to the Contadora peace process, while *The New York Times* focused more attention on the repressive policies of the Sandinista government aimed specifically at the Catholic church. Further, although differences in coverage are not statistically significant, it is apparent that *The Monitor* focused more attention on the Contras (atrocities, military capabilities and leadership) than did *The New York Times*.

In terms of evaluation of the newspapers' positions on the Contra aid issue, data in Table 10.5 indicate the extent to which items overall

Table 10.4

Major Issues Regarding Aid to the Contras
(due to multi-coding, issues do not add to 100%)

	NYT	CSM	Total	Phi	Sig
	N=242	N=120	N=362		
Reagan Political Strategy	64%	60%	62%	.04	NS
House Vote	53	49	52	.04	NS
Senate Vote	40	45	41	.05	NS
Sandinista Subversion in Hemisphere	22	14	19	.09	NS
Sandinista Domestic Repression	15	17	16	.02	NS
Role of Cuba	15	17	16	.02	NS
Contadora Peace Process	10	21	13	.16	.01
Sandinista Military Incursion into Honduras	12	11	12	.02	NS
Contra Military Capabilities	9	14	11	.08	NS
Contra Atrocities	8	13	10	.09	NS
Contra Leadership Capabilities	7	13	9	.11	NS
Sandinista Repression of Catholic Church	11	2	8	.16	NS

were judged to take a pro-aid, anti-aid, or balanced or neutral position. The results are interesting. While the majority of items either took a balanced or no stance on the question (74%), with respect to those expressing an evaluative opinion, only 6% favored renewed aid, while 20% opposed it. Differences between the two newspapers on this dimension are negligible.

Table 10.6 presents data on our final evaluative dimension—the actual language used to describe the Sandinista government of Nicaragua and its Contra antagonists. To arrive at the percentages shown in Table 10.6, first of all the actual descriptive words and phrases used with respect to the Sandinistas and the Contras were recorded. These were then evaluated by the authors as to whether, from an American perspective, they reflected positively or negatively on the two actors. Those upon which the authors could not agree

Table 10.5

Percentage of Items Deemed Pro-Aid, Neutral or Anti-Aid to the Contras

	NYT	CSM	Total
	N=241	N=119	N=360
Pro-Aid	6%	8%	6%
Neutral/No Position	75	70	74
Anti-Aid	19	22	20

X^2=1.05, DF=2, Cramer's V=.05, NS

Table 10.6

Percentage of Descriptors Reflecting Positively and Negatively on the Sandinistas and the Contras

	Positive Descriptors	Negative Descriptors	Total
Sandinistas	N=6	N=176	N=182
	3%	97%	100%
Contras	N=93	N=45	N=138
	67%	33%	100%

unanimously were omitted from the analysis. (See the full list of descriptors and how they were coded at the end of this chapter.)

The data thus produced are quite revealing. For the Sandinistas, scarcely a positive descriptor can be found. This is the case in spite of the fact that both newspapers ran far more material opposed to aid to the Contras than supported it. Moreover, although from data in Table 10.5 one could hardly describe the Contras as the solution to Nicaragua's problems, when actual language used to describe them is examined, they were in fact portrayed in positive language twice as often as they were in negative language. In the war of words, the raw materials from which meaning is shaped (Corcoran 1984), we see a clear victory for the supporters of Contra aid.[5]

Conclusion

With respect to aid for the Contras, this study demonstrates both the power of the president to shape foreign policy and the limitations in his ability to structure the environment totally to his way of thinking. The chief power of the president is in getting an item on the press agenda. The president is by definition news, and if he decides to publicize an issue, it is virtually impossible for the press to ignore it. Ronald Reagan certainly subscribed to this view, as the following quotation makes clear:

> The biggest advantage a modern president has is the six o'clock news. Presidents can be on the news every night if they want to – and usually they do. They can easily make themselves the focus of every news report, because the president of the United States is the most powerful individual in the world. (quoted in Kegley and Wittkopf 1987, p. 286)

The reality that emerges from this particular case study, however, is that while the press cannot ignore the president, it does make an attempt to give expression to opposition viewpoints. The president may well be the dominant newsmaker, but he does have to compete with opponents whose views are given greater visibility as an issue increases in salience. Also, it is clear that the press cannot be counted upon to act as an advocate of the foreign policy positions advanced by the president. Thus, although the president was clearly able to establish the *issue* of renewed aid to the Contras as an important one on the foreign policy agenda, in terms of a balance between pro-aid and anti-aid stories, neither *The New York Times* nor *The Christian Science Monitor* supported the president's position on the issue.

In spite of this lack of support, the study reveals that the pro–Contra aid position put forward by the president dominated the vocabulary battle. Although over twice the number of press items opposed Contra aid than supported it, virtually no complimentary descriptors were applied to the Sandinista government of Nicaragua. Thus, opponents of renewed aid to the Contras conceded the point that the Sandinistas were enemies of the United States. What is perhaps more surprising is that, in spite of an anti-aid plurality with respect to newspaper items, in descriptive language, the Contras were actually referred to in positive terms twice as often as in negative ones.

To investigate this finding further, we selected from the total data set, only those stories in which the president, the administration (attributed and unattributed) or the State Department were used as newsmakers (N=138). In analyzing this sub-set, we are able to see the power of the government to shape reality, as fully 82% of the language used to describe the Contras was positive. To be a newsmaker is clearly an important prerequisite to get your point of view across.

The Sandinistas had been established as the "bad guys" long before the campaign for renewed aid to the Contras began in January of 1986, going back to press coverage of the revolution itself (see chapter 4) and of the 1984 election (see chapter 9). In these circumstances, opponents of aid to the Contras were working under a severe disadvantage, since images, once established, are difficult to change (Duetsch and Merritt 1965). If everyone agreed that the Sandinistas meant no good to the United States, the focus then was on assessing the character of the Contras. We find in the study that the image of the Contras found in press reporting can be best described as fluid. Although neither newspaper supported renewed aid to them, it would appear that their portrayal in 1986, given their lineage, military tactics and accomplishments, was more charitable than would seem to have been deserved.

Notes

1. This chapter is an edited version of "La presidencia y los medios," originally published in CHASQUI: Revista Latinoamericana de comunicacion No 29–30 (Enero–Junio 1989). It is published here with permission.
2. If a similar study were done today, *The Christian Science Monitor* would not be chosen.
3. The authors wish to express their thanks to Anne Mander who not only did the bulk of newspaper coding, but keyed the data into the computer as well.
4. Short items ran between one and five paragraphs, medium items between six and fifteen paragraphs and long items over fifteen paragraphs in length. Due to high correlations between measure based on number of items and space, column inches of material were not coded (Stevenson and Shaw 1984, p. 35; Merrill 1962).
5. Oliver North disagrees, claiming, "With few exceptions, the Sandinistas received unusually gentle treatment in the American press." He also believes that "the public relations effort on behalf of the resistance could have been far more successful if the Contras had produced a charismatic leader...who could have effectively symbolized their struggle as an anti-Communist Ho Chi Minh, or Fidel, or Che" (1991, p. 233).

Chapter 10 Descriptors

Sandinistas

Words/Phrases Judged to Be Positive
Duly recognized government
Pragmatic
Flexible
Not totalitarian

Words/Phrases Judged to Be Negative
Very bad guys/ not nice guys
Subversives
Marxists/Marxist regime/evil Marxists/Marxist leaning/Marxist led/Marxist junta/Marxist dominated/Marxist rulers
Despised/unpopular
Communist/communist regime/dedicated communists/communist dictatorship/hard core communist regime
Repressive/increasingly repressive
Small band of Marxist-Leninists
Totalitarian/totalitarian regime
Support terrorism
Behavior gets worse and worse/have gone from bad to worse
Undemocratic/anti-democratic
A cancer in Central America that has to be removed/a cancer
Authoritarian/authoritarian and truculent/strongly authoritarian
Fundamentally evil
Soviet backed/Moscow backed/Soviet proxies/Moscow's puppet regime/ Soviet client regime/Soviet lackey
Dictatorial/dictators/dictatorship of the left
Leftist
The Soviet Union's Western Hemispheric distributors of aggression
Communists at war with God and Man
Corrupt
Reds
Stalinists
Outlaws/outlaw regime
Tyrants
Oppressive/run a bad repressive government
Want total power in their hands
Anti-Semitic
Rascals
Taking Nicaragua to Marxism-Leninism
No friends of the United States
A threat to stability in Central America
Myth of well-meaning revolutionaries

Generally appalling leadership
Deeply involved in drug trafficking

Words/Phrases Judged to Be Neutral or Ambiguous
A new order of Franciscan monks
Inept democrats
Nationalists
Revolutionary

Contras
Words/Phrases Judged to Be Positive
Democratic opposition
Democratic resistance forces
Freedom fighters/good freedom fighters
The good guys
Jeffersonian democrats
The moral equivalent of the Founding Fathers
Anti-Soviet/anti-communist
United States supported/United States backed
Brave
Not led by Somocistas
Forces of freedom
Guerrillas for democracy
Flexible

Words/Phrases Judged to Be Negative
Not a unified and credible alternative to the Sandinistas
A dirty word/repugnant
Small, fragmented and squabble-ridden/deeply divided
A handful of tyrants
Mercenaries/mercenary forces/isolated mercenaries
Thugs
Losers
Non-democratic
A machine that was badly damaged and is now falling apart
A small-bore gang of pistoleros/a gang that can't shoot straight
Illiterate farmers and cutthroats
An exile army with no impressive following
Terrorists/terrorist killers of unarmed civilians/mistreating civilians
Corrupt
A stateless army organized by the CIA/proxy gang of fighters
Do not have the capability to defeat the Sandinistas
Bandits
Unwelcomed guests
Lazy
Armed, frustrated group
Inadequate

Words/Phrases Judged to Be Neutral or Ambiguous
Guerrillas
Rebels
Exiles
Anti-government
Counterrevolutionary
Moral equivalent of Filipino revolutionaries
Organized by the CIA/only an arm of the U.S./controlled by the U.S
Armed rebels against the Nicaraguan government
Anti-Sandinista
Adventurers

Part III

The End of the Cold War, and Democratic Transitions: Haiti, El Salvador, Nicaragua, Panama and Cuba

Chapter 11

Transition to Democracy?
Elections in Haiti, 1987–1990[1]

RALPH C. NELSON AND WALTER C. SODERLUND

The Duvalier dynasty ruled in Haiti from 1957 to 1986. It created the infamous Tonton Macoutes, murdered and tortured Haitian citizens, pillaged the country and, at the time it ended, when Jean-Claude Duvalier — Baby Doc — went into luxurious exile, the army held political power (Fauriol 1988). Between 1986 and the end of September 1991, Haiti experienced five successful coups d'etat (plus the unsuccessful attempt in January 1991 by Roger Lafontant) as well as three presidential elections: one annulled, one fixed and one fair. Following the restoration of President Aristide in the fall of 1994, and a subsequent election in 1996, the situation in the country is still not stable. The government and police force are barely able to function and the international community is increasingly losing patience in its attempt to deal with a seemingly unsolvable set of problems. In short, the restoration of a legitimate government through free and fair elections, while perhaps a necessary condition to solve Haiti's problems, has certainly proven to be less than a sufficient one.

The history of Haiti since its liberation from France in 1804 has been characterized by autocratic rule and the political role of the army. The armed forces, disbanded by Aristide following his return to power in 1994, owed its structure to the American occupation (1915–1934), for the United States Marine Corps reorganized the Haitian army before it departed. Indeed, as Bellegarde-Smith noted, the Haitian army continued "to play a major role as 'arbiter' save for a brief period under François Duvalier" when it was "macoutized" (1990, p. 137). The notion that the National Council of Government (CNG in French) that took power after Duvalier's departure would support the popular aim of *déchoukage* (uprooting, eliminating the Tonton Macoutes from positions of power and influence) was dashed by the complicity of the army in the savage rampage of the Macoutes on "Bloody Sunday," November 29, 1987: the slaughter that led to the annulment of that election by General Henri Namphy and his associates (Abbott 1988, pp. 1–7).

Dealing with Haiti in the context of the literature on democratic transitions is not an easy task (O'Donnell et al. 1986; Diamond et al. 1989; Karl and Schmitter 1991). As Crassweller, writing in *Foreign Affairs* has pointed out,

> The culture of Haiti is in all possible respects so unlike that of the Western World from which assistance in the processes of change must come that the transmission of that change will inevitably be hindered by a thousand obstacles as yet hardly even suspected. Haitian society is not the transitional variety with which American and European assistance technicians are familiar, but truly a traditional society. (1971, p. 326)

Writing in the same journal over fifteen years later, Rotberg offered a similar pessimistic assessment regarding the possibility of democratic change:

> Unhappily, given Haiti's tragic history and the legacy of three decades of Duvalierism, it is very difficult to persuade jejune observers that Haiti can be transformed from within. It lacks a viable political culture, basic literacy, natural resources and a germ of prosperity. It also has little faith in itself. (1988, p. 96)

Haiti's economic underdevelopment, a key component in hindering the growth of democracy, has been analyzed extensively (Lundahl 1991), and combining factors cited by Lundahl with those offered by Garcia-Zamor yields the following list:

1. The interaction between the growth of population and soil erosion;

2. The lack of technological progress in agriculture (which is where the vast majority of the population earn their living);
3. The predatory nature of the governments that have ruled the country for more than one and a half centuries; (Lundahl 1989, p. 2)
4. Language dualism;
5. The rigidity of administrative structures. (Garcia-Zamor 1989, p. 410)

Maingot (1986–87) has linked Haiti's sociocultural and political history specifically to the problems of a democratic transition in the post-Duvalier period. In his analysis, he identified six problems:

1. Tendencies in Haitian political culture that were not uprooted "by the fall of Duvalier and which place definite obstacles in the path of liberal democracy";
2. Too many would-be leaders participating in the political system without coordination;
3. The problem of "outguessing regress"; i.e., "Haiti's propensity for making decisions without firm grounds on which to base them is exceptional";
4. "The presence of a large number of risk-free participants...key actors who are exogenous to the system," e.g., the United States and long-time political exiles;
5. The "problem of asymmetry of motivation," chiefly between totalitarians and moderates;
6. The "problem of the manipulated agenda," in terms of establishing the rules of the game for the democratic transition. (Maingot 1986–87, pp. 88–94)

Much has transpired in Haiti since Maingot's formulation (see Maguire 1997). Rather than attempt to update his analysis, we should like to base our assessment of Haiti's democratic transition on the more general observations of the noted student of democracy, Robert Dahl. The political neutrality of the armed forces is one of the conditions that Dahl cited for the establishment of political democracy, and another is the establishment of stable democratic institutions. He discussed those conditions most favorable to the development and maintenance of democracy; conditions that are necessary though not always sufficient to achieve this purpose. An examination of these conditions throws some light on the great difficulties encountered in the democratization of the Haitian polity. Dahl emphasized three such conditions, while not excluding others discussed in his more systematic writings on democracy or polyarchy (1971):

1. An adequate level of social and economic development;
2. Traditions supportive of democratic values;
3. A military that is politically neutral. (Dahl 1984, pp. 17–19)

It would not take a researcher long to conclude that these three conditions were all absent in Haiti in the post-Duvalier period.

Background

Social and Economic Development

With respect to the socioeconomic situation, the long years of the Duvalier regime left the economy in a catastrophic situation. The monumental greed practiced by the regime and its allies, the transfer of great amounts of wealth out of the country (Maingot 1986–87, pp. 84–88) and the squandering of foreign assistance, all form a part of a familiar and deeply depressing story resulting in terrible poverty, misery and illness in the population (Hector 1988, pp. 6–7).

It is possible to study Haiti by using class analysis, race analysis or elite theory (Nicholls 1996). The long-standing foundation for the great distance between the rich and the poor, in a country with a very small middle class, is usually tied to the opposition between the wealthy mulattoes and the poor blacks. Abbott (1988) in particular pointed out the great significance of racial differences in explaining class differences in Haiti. Papa Doc Duvalier had been an adherent of the *noiriste* cause (similar to Leopold Senghor's concept of *négritude* in Senegal), which if not racist was race-based. In one place in her book someone is said not be to a Haitian because that person is a mulatto. There are terrible accounts of the slaughter of whole families of light-skinned Haitians in Jérémie by the forces of Papa Doc. The racial difference and social difference are accentuated by the fact that the mulattoes were educated and the blacks for the most part were not. While it is necessary to be tentative on this point, the two groups are divided on religious grounds as well, one Roman Catholic, the other basically voodooesque (practitioners of vodun or voodoo). This is a complicated issue in Haiti, where people often seem to combine the two beliefs, practicing voodoo yet going through a baptism or marriage ceremony at the Catholic church (Aristide 1991, p. 109). And if all of these cleavages were not enough, there is the difference between the elite, who speak French, and the masses, who speak Creole. Garcia-Zamor reports that French and Creole "are not mutually interchangeable or comprehensible...[and] only 5% of the population speaks both Creole and French fluently, 10 to 15% are bilingual, and 80% understand only Creole" (1989, p. 417). One writer describes these differences as

> the wound that from the beginning had cut through Haitian culture, dividing their highly sophisticated, predominantly mulatto elite that spoke French, attended Mass and followed Parisian fashion, from the illiterate peasants who knew only Creole, practiced voodoo and lived their daily lives as their ancestors had done in West Africa four centuries before. (Danner 1991, p. 18)

Hence, Haiti is a country deeply divided on racial, class, religious and linguistic lines, with accordingly a great gap between the social elite and the masses. A social elite means those who control power, possessions and knowledge (*le pouvoir, l'avoir, et le savoir*). As to the political elite, it would be important to investigate the relative standing of civilians, including educators, lawyers, businesspeople, church leaders and labor leaders. Another issue is whether the army remained an enclave in which the traditional mulatto elites continue to dominate the officer class. This has been suggested in the case of General Raoul Cédras, the leader of the 1991 coup against Aristide.

Democratic Values

The history of Haiti since its liberation from France reveals no tradition, no cultural foundation for democracy, except for the rather recent appearance of liberation theology (Wilentz 1989; Aristide 1991, pp. 110–113). And yet there is a great popular desire for democratic elections among Haitians, for the right to choose those who will lead them. But popular support, particularly of an elected president, does not mean an endorsement of the kind of democratic politics implied in the Constitution of 1987,[2] in which an elected president is to work in conjunction with an elected bicameral parliament.

One must assume that the great mass of the Haitian population that voted for Aristide in 1990 assumed that they were voting for a strong leader, even an elected autocrat, since how many of them were likely to have paid much attention to the Constitution of 1987? However, that Constitution clearly envisaged an executive that would be administratively strong but politically weak. While the president would control the administration and would have some input into the legislative process, he would have neither veto over legislative acts, as in the American case, nor the power to issue decrees, as in the French case. Nor could the president stand for immediate reelection. The Constitution unequivocally stipulates that the president may only appoint the prime minister without consultation if the Chamber of Deputies is controlled by the president's party (Haiti 1987, p. 13). Since this was not the case with Aristide, he was required to choose the prime minister in consultation with the parliamentary leadership. Following the coup, the negotiations that led to the nomination of René Théodore as prime minister were in conformity with the Constitution, even though the actual regime that resulted was illegitimate.

The events preceding the coup d'etat of September 1991 indicate how great was the opposition between presidential rule and parliamentary prerogative, especially when the president's party did not control the parliament. As the French would say, it led to a very uneasy *cohabitation*.[3] The real danger for the fledgling Haitian democracy was perceived by the drafters of the 1987 Constitution as caesaro-populism: the elected leader relying on the masses to overwhelm, and perhaps crush, opponents in the parliament. After the long (thirty-year) reign of the Duvaliers *(père et fils)*, the masses had been socialized to unitary leadership and not to the division and separation of powers. Ironically, a constitution designed to thwart dictatorship, a constitution that includes an unusual provision prohibiting the cult of personality,[4] may replace the danger of dictatorship by the spectacle of political deadlock.

Political Role of the Army

Finally, one turns to the role of the army in Haitian political life. During the long Duvalier dynasty, a parallel armed force was created and the power of the army, now overwhelmingly inferior numerically to the new group (the dreaded Tonton Macoutes), was effectively pushed aside and its ranks frequently purged by Papa Doc (Crassweller 1971, pp. 317–319). The overthrow of the Duvalier dynasty in 1986 made the army again the real arbiter of power in Haiti. General Namphy first blocked democratic elections, then rigged the election that brought Leslie Manigat to power. He was then replaced by General Prosper Avril who, in turn, succumbed to another General, Hérard Abraham (characterized as "upright" and "respected") (Abbott 1988, p. 372), who supported an interim government led by Ertha Pascal Trouillot, which organized the elections of December 1990 in which Jean-Bertrand Aristide became president. In September 1991 the new president was ousted by the army under the leadership of General Raoul Cédras. There were suggestions at the time of the coup that not only did Aristide want to diminish the influence of the army, but also that he, like his predecessors, was considering a kind of praetorian or palace guard to protect him from the army's interference. Thus, one might say, the sorry logic continued; the same conditions existed, the same temptations arose, the same methods were considered and used.

Given these circumstances, this chapter seeks to analyze the way in which the mainstream press in Canada and the United States reported on Haiti's quest for democracy between the overthrow of the Duvalier dictatorship in 1986 and the election of Aristide in December of 1990. It will do so specifically by focusing on press coverage of three critical points in the transition process (Weiner and Ozbudan 1987; Booth and Seligson 1989): the presidential elections of November 1987, January 1988 and December 1990. Underlying the research is the assumption that for its information about and evaluations of international events, mass publics in Canada and the United States rely to a significant degree on press reporting. We have opted to focus on the elections, as they attracted concentrated press coverage and, of necessity, forced reporters to interpret Haitian politics for North American readers, thus allowing us to determine what issues and which leaders were covered, with what evaluative judgments.

Research Methods

For each of the three elections, all items in a matched sample of Canadian and American newspapers dealing with Haiti that appeared thirty days prior to and ten days following polling day were studied.[5]

The sample of newspapers was as follows: (1) newspapers of record —
The Globe and Mail (Toronto) and *The New York Times*; (2) capital
newspapers — *The Citizen* (Ottawa) and *The Washington Post*; (3) elite
opinion-leading newspapers — *Le Devoir* (Montreal) and *The Christian
Science Monitor* (Boston); (4) eastern regional newspapers — *Le Soleil*
(Quebec City) and *The Atlanta Constitution*; (5) mid-continent
newspapers — *The Winnipeg Free Press* and *The Chicago Tribune*; and (6)
western regional newspapers — *The Vancouver Sun* and *The Los Angeles
Times.*[6]

First, variables such as dateline, source of content, and length and
placement of items in the newspapers were coded. Following this, items
were read and coded for references to major campaign issues and
political leaders. On this later dimension, descriptive words and
phrases used with respect to major political figures in all three elections
were recorded and subsequently recoded into "positive," "negative"
and "neutral/ambiguous" categories.[7] (See the full list of descriptors
and how they were coded at the end of this chapter.) Headlines were
also read for language that would project to readers either positive or
negative images of Haiti and its leaders as well as the efficacy of the
elections in helping to solve the set of vexing problems besetting the
country.

Findings

With respect to the volume of press coverage, the three elections present
interesting contrasts. The 1987 election generated 369 items of press
commentary (49% Canadian and 51% American); the 1988 election
429 items (57% Canadian and 43% American); while coverage of the
1990 elections fell off to only 116 items, again with 57% of these
appearing in Canadian newspapers as opposed to 43% in American
papers. Thus, press interest began at a fairly high level in 1987, peaked
in 1988 and declined dramatically in 1990.

For all three elections the majority of items carried Haitian
datelines: 70% in 1987, 65% in 1988 and 87% in 1990. Hard news
(event-driven news of the day) dominated coverage in all elections:
82% in 1987, 87% in 1988 and 72% in 1990, with 16%, 13% and 17% of
total items garnering first page placement in the three elections
respectively. Editorials comprised between 6% and 7% of total coverage
in each election, while feature articles accounted for 9% of coverage in

both 1987 and 1988, increasing to 18% in 1990. In summary, the press coverage of the three elections consisted by and large of Haitian-based reports of the elections as they developed on a day-to-day basis. Only in the 1990 election did in-depth, interpretive material exceed 20% of the total, but it must be pointed out that the base against which that percentage is calculated is reduced considerably from the earlier elections (data not shown in tabular form).

Tables 11.1, 11.2 and 11.3 present, in turn, the leading substantive issues of the three elections. Each table, taken as a whole, can be said to constitute the "press agenda" (i.e., the media were telling readers that those issues were important in the respective elections) (McCombs and Shaw 1972).

Table 11.1

Major Issues in the 1987 Election in Haiti
(due to multi-coding, columns do not add to 100%)

	Percentage of Items in Which Issues Are Mentioned				
	Can	US	Total	Phi	Sig
Issue	N=181	N=188	N=369		
Violence	87%	77%	81%	.12	.05
(Nov. 29 Massacre)	50	38	44	.12	.05
Role of CNG	57	62	60	.05	NS
Role of Army	38	42	40	.05	NS
Comment/Action by U.S.	23	56	40	34	.001
Role of Tonton Macoutes	26	33	30	.08	NS
Dissolution of CEP	28	27	28	.01	NS
History of Duvalier Dictatorship	15	25	20	.12	.05
Comment/Action by Canada	36	7	19	.30	.001
Role of Foreign Observers	21	17	19	.07	NS
U.S. Aid	13	25	19	.09	NS
Disqualification of Duvalierists	16	22	19	.09	NS
International Intervention	14	21	18	.10	NS

Table 11.2

Major Issues in the 1988 Election in Haiti
(due to multi-coding, columns do not add to 100%)

Issue	Percentage of Items in Which Issues Are Mentioned			Phi	Sig
	Can	US	Total		
	N=245	N=184	N=429		
Violence	43%	59%	50%	.15	.01
(Nov. 29th Massacre)	41	56	47	.15	.01
Role of CNG	51	46	49	.05	NS
Election Boycott	41	50	45	.09	NS
Comment/Action by U.S.	17	57	34	.42	.001
Comment/Action by Canada	47	14	33	.35	.001
Role of Army	21	32	26	.12	.01
Appointment of New Electoral Council	25	22	24	.03	NS
Dissolution of CEP	19	27	22	.09	NS
Election Fraud/Irregularities	20	24	22	.04	NS
Election Rules and Procedures	19	26	22	.08	NS
Disqualification of Duvalierists	16	25	20	.11	.05
International Intervention	15	26	20	.13	.01
Implication of Election	17	23	20	.08	NS

The legacy of the Duvalier dictatorship and electoral violence were the dominant frames of reference in which both the 1987 and 1988 elections were interpreted. In November 1987, presidential candidates associated to a significant degree with the Duvalier dictatorship were disqualified, as called for by the new constitution. The disqualification included the self-proclaimed leader of the Tonton Macoutes, Roger Lafontant. Following this disqualification, electoral violence, which included murder and arson, increased, culminating in the early morning election-day massacre (Bloody Sunday) on November 29. Moreover, not only was violence the prime focus of press reporting,

Table 11.3

Major Issues in the 1990 Election in Haiti
(due to multi-coding, columns do not add to 100%)

	Percentage of Items in Which Issues Are Mentioned				
	Can	US	Total	Phi	Sig
Issue	N=66	N=50	N=116		
History of Duvalier Dictatorship	46%	66%	54%	.20	.05
Background/Political Leaders	52	56	53	.04	NS
Role of Foreign Observers	49	46	47	.02	NS
Implication of Election	47	36	42	.11	NS
Role of Army	29	56	41	.27	.01
Violence	42	36	40	.06	NS
(Nov. 29 Massacre)	29	42	35	.14	NS
Economic Conditions	42	22	37	.21	.05
Comment/Action by U.S.	15	48	29	.36	.001
Role of Tonton Macoutes	30	26	28	.05	NS
Reporting of Election Results	38	16	28	.24	.01
Role of UN	17	36	25	.22	.05
Social Class Divisions	20	30	24	.12	NS

virtually all other major issues were treated in the context of electoral violence. Thus the disqualification of Duvalierist candidates, the role of the CNG, the Haitian Army and the Tonton Macoutes in the election were treated in terms of causes of violence, while the dissolution of the CEP [Provisional Electoral Council], reports of foreign observers, statements of both Canada and the United States, the termination of U.S. aid to Haiti and discussions of a possible international intervention were treated as consequences of the violence which terminated the election." (Soderlund and Nelson 1990, pp. 380–382)

It is also clear from an examination of Table 11.2 that violence continued to provide the framework through which the January 1988 election was interpreted, although paradoxically the election itself was relatively violence free. Thus, it was anticipated acts of violence, combined with the retelling the events of November 29, that provided the dominant frame through which the second election was reported. The leading presidential candidates in the November 1987 election (Marc Bazin, Gerard Gourge, Sylvio Claude and Louis Dejoie III) all boycotted the January 1988 election, serving to delegitimize the second vote, and the boycott received major play as a story. Also, the likelihood and necessity of some type of international intervention in Haiti should the anticipated violence indeed occur, attracted considerable press commentary.

As is evident from data in Table 11.3, the December 1990 election not only saw a marked reduction in press interest, but also a shift in the pattern of press coverage. While the specter of violence (largely associated with Roger Lafontant) remained a part of the press agenda, it was the candidacy of the charismatic and controversial Roman Catholic priest Jean-Bertrand Aristide that dominated coverage of the third in this series of Haitian elections. Aristide, who had earlier questioned the efficacy of elections in Haiti and was not a candidate in the previous ones, announced his candidacy in 1990 as the champion of Haiti's most impoverished classes. His candidacy caught fire, and opinion polls reflected that he held a considerable lead over his main opponent, Marc Bazin. Given Aristide's lead, press coverage focused on the possibility of violence forestalling his election or potential difficulties his presidency might face given his domestic radicalism and international anti-Americanism. The role of foreign observers in the election, particularly the activities of the UN in assuring free and fair elections, also received a good deal of press attention.

Political parties were not well developed in Haiti, and those movements that did exist tended to be extensions of particular candidates (Lundahl 1989, pp. 16–17). Thus, it was the political leaders themselves, rather than the parties they represented, that tended to be the chief focus of press reporting.

As data in Table 11.4 illustrate, in the first two elections it was General Henri Namphy — rather than any of the actual candidates — who received primary press attention. This attention was well deserved, as he effectively terminated the first election and arranged for Leslie Manigat to win the second (Sunshine 1988, pp. 55–56). Bazin,

Table 11.4

Percentage of Items Dealing with Major Political Figures in the Haitian Elections (due to multi-coding, columns do not add to 100%)

Political Figure	November 1987 Can N=181	US N=188	January 1988 Can N=245	US N=184	December 1990 Can N=66	US N=50
Marc Bazin	13%	19%	27%	29%	59%	46%
Louis Dejoie III	11	13	30	31	29	2
Sylvio Claude	19	19	23	25	21	2
Gerard Gourge	9	14	22	25	–	–
Leslie Manigat	2	3	22	27	–	–
Jean-Bertrand Aristide	–	–	–	–	88	78
Henri Namphy	43	49	41	42	–	–
Roger Lafontant	–	–	–	–	24	26

Dejoie, Claude and Gourge competed fairly equally for press coverage in the November 1987 election, and in all cases their press coverage increased in the January 1988 election, which they all boycotted. Leslie Manigat, a candidate in both the first and second elections, attracted significant press attention only in the second, in which he emerged the "winner."

The December 1990 election properly may be called the "Aristide election," for although Bazin was commented on in over 50% of total stories, this paled in comparison with Aristide, who was covered in fully 84%. Claude and Dejoie were still treated as factors in Canadian press coverage, but failed to attract the attention of the American press. Roger Lafontant, who was to lead an unsuccessful coup against Aristide in January 1991, was clearly perceived to be a player, appearing in about a quarter of the press items.

Data in Table 11.5 show the relative percentages of positive and negative descriptors used with respect to Marc Bazin over the three elections, Leslie Manigat in the first two elections and Jean-Bertrand Aristide in the December 1990 election. Of the three political leaders, it is Bazin who draws the most favorable coverage, albeit there were somewhat more unfavorable references to him in the third election

Table 11.5

Percentage of Descriptors Reflecting Positively and Negatively on Political Leaders in Haiti (neutral or ambiguous descriptors omitted from analysis)

	November 1987			January 1988			December 1990		
Leader	Can	US	Total	Can	US	Total	Can	US	Total
Bazin	N=12	N=35	N=47	N=15	N=23	N=38	N=43	N=35	N=78
Positive	91%	100%	98%	100%	95%	97%	79%	86%	82%
Negative	9	0	2	0	5	3	21	14	18
Manigat	N=0	N=7	N=7	N=52	N=56	N=108	–	–	–
Positive	–	71%	71%	56%	66%	61%	–	–	–
Negative	–	29	29	44	34	39	–	–	–
Aristide	–	–	–	–	–	–	N=104	N=108	N=212
Positive	–	–	–	–	–	–	63%	44%	53%
Negative	–	–	–	–	–	–	37	56	47

than in the previous two. Manigat and Aristide, although they both maintained an overall positive balance of descriptors, did not fare nearly so well. In 1988 Manigat received the highest percentage of negative descriptors in the Canadian newspapers, while in 1990, for Aristide, it was the American press that proved to be more critical.

Data in Table 11.6 are based on an analysis of headline language and indicate the percentage of headlines that were coded "reputation enhancing" or "reputation discrediting" with respect to Haiti, its political leaders and the election processes. On this dimension, we see a dramatic change in evaluation over the course of the three elections. While there was only a slight increase in the percentage of reputation-enhancing headlines between 1987 and 1990 (4% to 6% in Canada, and 3% to 10% in the U.S.), there was a dramatic decline in the percentage of headlines coded as reputation-discrediting over the same period (71% to 5% in Canada, and 56% to 6% in the U.S.). Since a sizeable majority of press items consisted of hard news, it is apparent that as the level of violent activity declined from election to election, so too did the number of headlines that reflected negatively on the Haitian political situation.

𝒯𝒶𝒷𝓁ℯ   11.6

Percentage of Reputation-Enhancing and Discrediting Headlines in the Haitian Elections

	November 1987			January 1988			December 1990		
	Can	US	Total	Can	US	Total	Can	US	Total
	N=181	N=188	N=369	N=245	N=184	N=429	N=66	N=50	N=116
Reputation Enhancing	4%	3%	3%	5%	5%	5%	6%	10%	8%
Neutral	25	41	34	38	43	40	89	84	87
Reputation Discrediting	71	56	63	57	52	55	5	6	5

Conclusion

In terms of the data analyzed in this chapter, there appear to be two important and related deficiencies in press reporting on Haiti's transition to democracy in the North American press. In both the 1987 and 1988 elections, preoccupation with tracking the level of violence, and speculation regarding possible acts of violence yet to come, seriously distorted the set of fundamental socioeconomic and political problems facing Haiti. Similarly in the 1990 election, Aristide's candidacy and the tendency of the press to focus on him, served the same function. This is not to say that these factors were not important; they certainly were. Likewise, much of the analysis of the political role played by the army and the Tonton Macoutes domestically, and the impact of American and Canadian foreign policy initiatives along with the supervisory functions performed by the UN in particular, was both germane and perceptive.

The problem, and this is especially apparent in coverage of the 1990 election, was the absence of analyses of the Haitian Constitution of 1987 and the all too obvious incongruity between a campaign in which Aristide's candidacy symbolized the expectation of a drastic shift in political power to the Haitian masses, and a set of constitutional rules that severely limited presidential power. These problems would be especially troublesome in circumstances where the president did not command a legislative majority, as was almost certain to be the case with an Aristide victory. In short, the political problems that led to the September 1991 coup that removed Aristide from power were far from unpredictable: high expectations for political change, combined with a constitution that virtually guaranteed immobility. Moreover, as we are all too aware from the history of numerous Latin American and Caribbean countries in the nineteenth and early twentieth centuries, when socioeconomic realities and constitutional provisions differ, it is usually the latter that fall by the wayside.

Notes

1. This chapter is an edited version of "Press Definitions of Reality During Elections in Haiti," which originally appeared in *Media Development*, Vol. 39, No. 3 (1992). It is published here with permission.
2. *Constitution de la République d'Hàiti, 1987.* We are indebted to the Haitian Embassy in Ottawa for a copy of this document.
3. *La cohabitation* refers to a situation under the Fifth Republic in which the president of the Republic and the prime minister belong to different parties. Such a situation occurred briefly when François Mitterand, the Socialist president, had to "cohabit" with Jacques Chirac, the leader of the right. This is the only instance of the situation in the Fifth Republic.
4. The clause is found in Title 1, Chapter 1, Article 7 of the Constitution of 1987 and states: "The cult of personality is strictly prohibited. The images and names of living persons cannot figure on money, stamps or labels. The same is the case for public buildings, streets and works of art."
5. For the second election, there are seven additional days added to the pre-election period; that is, coverage began on December 10 rather than on December 17. Fifteen press items appeared during this period, so even if we subtracted these from the total for that election, the January 17 election still received the heaviest press coverage of the three.
6. Efforts were made to ensure equivalency of newspapers, a problem central to all cross-national press studies (see Edelstein 1982, pp. 45–60). Intercoder reliability for 1987–1988 and 1990 leader and issue coverage was 88% (Holsti 1969, p. 140). Students helping with coding the 1987–88 data were Elizabeth Burton and Ann Boyd, while assisting in coding the 1990 data were Elizabeth Ng, Livianna Tossutti and Laura Hytenrauch. Robert Burge assisted with computer analysis of the 1987–88 data as did Laura Hytenrauch with the 1990 data. The authors wish to thank all of these talented students for their help.
7. For 1990 data, words and phrases used to describe the various political leaders were compiled and sent to a panel of six political science and communication studies professors with instructions to identify those that, from an American perspective, reflected either positively or

negatively on the candidate. In order to qualify as "positive" or "negative," five of the six-member panel had to agree, thus intercoder reliability is 83%. For 1987–1988 data, this coding was performed by the authors.

Chapter 11 Descriptors

Marc Bazin (1987 and 1988 Elections)
Words/Phrases Judged to Be Positive
Former World Bank employee/economist/official/senior official/ administrator/leading expert at World Bank
Paris trained lawyer and economist
Most popular candidate
Favorite of U.S. policy makers/candidate of the Americans/a leading presidential candidate/leading candidate/main candidate/top candidate/ prominent candidate/major candidate/ most important candidate/ principal candidate
Likely winner in run-off
A front-runner/top contender/top politician
Prominent opposition leader/opposition leader
Centrist
An honest man/only uncorrupted finance minister in Haitian history
Able administrator
Middle of the road
Mainstream
Finance expert
Moderate
Best-known candidate internationally
Mr. Clean
Chief of the Division of International Organizations at the World Bank
World Bank representative at the UN
Has best organized campaign/well organized
Has broad support
Image of competence
Most likely to win
Social democrat
Aims for efficiency and modern management

Words/Phrases Judged to Be Negative
Radical
In third place
Former/ex-Duvalier finance minister/minister of finance under Jean-Claude Duvalier
Won't get the popular vote

Words/Phrases Judged to Be Neutral or Ambiguous
Fifty-five years old
Center-right
Exile
Economist
Lawyer
Former IMF official
Unacceptable to high-ranking military officer
Liberal
Conservative
French educated
Leader/founder of movement to install democracy in Haiti
Candidate of the political class, intellectuals and businessmen
Supported by non-Duvalierist right
Runs media-style campaign

Marc Bazin (1990 Election)
Words/Phrases Judged to Be Positive
Mr. Clean
Former World Bank official
Political centrist
Moderate
Experienced
Favorite of the U.S./the American candidate/acceptable to U.S.
Strongest challenger/main rival
Leading candidate in 1987 election
Backed by the middle class
Sober
Honest
Pragmatic
Confident
Well intentioned
Moderate

Words/Phrases Judged to Be Negative
Too old
Identified too strongly with the U.S.
Courted the Duvalierist vote
Not a man of the people
Trailing

Words/Phrases Judged to Be Neutral or Ambiguous
Former cabinet minister
Economist
Conservative
U.S.-style candidate
Has penchant for smart blue suits

Lacks charisma
Campaign coffers bulging
Bureaucrat
Economic liberal
Most serious rival of Aristide

Leslie Manigat (1987 and 1988 Election)
Words/Phrases Judged to Be Positive
Skillful
Astute
Has quick intelligence/intelligent
Respected academic
Strong-willed
Ambitious
Man of reconciliation and unity
Energetic
Has most impressive credentials/has world-class credentials
Shrewd
Comes from family of educators and politicians
Educated at Sorbonne/French educated
A democrat/ has democratic credentials
Has anti-Duvalier credentials
Has long record of opposition to dictatorships
Distinguished
Centrist
At top of list of candidates/a leading candidate
Able
Most likely to be the winner/a good bet to win
Imprisoned and exiled by Duvalier
No friend of current junta
Leading Caribbean intellectual
Has political savvy/savvy politician
Brilliant at politics
Jovial
Exudes confidence
Urbane
Realistic
Prominent figure in Haitian exile politics
Pragmatist
Not a puppet

Words/Phrases Judged to Be Negative
Unpredictable
Machiavellian
The military's choice/the military's hand-picked candidate
Badly tainted
Used to be a democrat

All over the map
Political chameleon
Has no constituency
Marxist-socialist
Military sympathizer
Utter opportunist
Does not embarrass easily
Former ally of deposed Duvalier dictatorship
Mani-Doc
Attitude is Duvalierist
Demagogue
Considered a socialist; politically weak
Has no direct political or administrative experience
Authoritarian
Vindictive
Intolerant of dissent
Government puppet
Discredited

Words/Phrases Judged to Be Neutral or Ambiguous
Former political science professor/political scientist/professor of political
    science
Professor/ex-professor/university professor
Fifty-seven years old/fifty-eight years old
Conservative
New president/president-elect
Rotund
Gravel-voiced
Exile/former exile/twenty-three years in exile
Rightist
Paradox
Did not finish doctoral thesis
Linked to Socialist International
Right of center
Complex
Calculating
Without blood on his hands
Large
Garrulous
An inoffensive compromise
Historian
Has close ties to the junta and the U.S. government
Nationalist
Conciliatory to the media
Manigance

Jean-Bertrand Aristide (1990 Election)
Words/Phrases Judged to Be Positive
Front-runner/undisputed front-runner/leading candidate
Idol of the poor
Charismatic
Gifted linguist/speaks and writes six languages/eight languages
Has always been with the people
Activist
Champion/defender of the poor
Unassuming
Savior/God-sent savior
Soft spoken/quiet
Has toned down strident anti-foreign and revolutionary speeches
Wildly popular/popular/has strong support
Pure spiritual leader
Self-effacing
Messianic/messiah
Successful politician
Haiti's Mandela or Martin Luther King
Very lucid politician
Has powerful mystique
Prophet
Threat to Duvalierists
Has mystical powers/mystical
Symbol of change
Honest
Voice of the people
Hero of mythic proportions
Freely elected president
Only anti-Macoutes candidate
A social democrat
Little father of the people
Guide to the people
Youthful
Head of popular church
Foe of military

Words/Phrases Judged to Be Negative
Leftist/left wing/on the left
Expelled/ousted from the Salesian order/defrocked
Firebrand/fiery/fire-breathing
Inexperienced/has no government experience
Loner
Radical
Hostile/resentful/distrustful of Washington/anti-American
Destabilizing influence

Rabble-rouser
Revolutionary
Ultra-communist
A cross between the Ayatollah and Fidel Castro
Volatile
Uses violent language
Divisive influence
Fomented class warfare
Economic programs are incoherent
Has chip on his shoulder
Nervous
Nervy
Timid
Frail
Vaguely socialist
Demagogue

Words/Phrases Judged to Be Neutral or Ambiguous
Priest/Roman Catholic priest
Slightly built/small/diminutive/slim/5'4"/wispy/thin/slender/
   physically unimposing
Thirty-seven years old/born in 1953
Survived three assassination attempts
Studied psychology
Montreal educated/studied at the University of Montreal
Proponent of liberation theology
Titid
Serious threat
Populist
Has no ties to the country's elite
Priest-politician/priest turned politician
Reverend/Father
Nationalist
Preached drastic change for five years
President-elect
Anti-establishment
Retiring
"Coq kalite" (good rooster)
Can become either the father of Haitian democracy or just one more of its
   betrayers
An orphan
Ordained in 1982
Formerly impetuous
Bespectacled
Slum priest
Son of modest peasants

Chapter 12

The Cold War Retreats:
Elections in El Salvador 1989
and Nicaragua 1990[1]

WALTER C. SODERLUND

While the circumstances leading to civil strife in El Salvador and Nicaragua differed considerably, beginning in 1982 in El Salvador and 1984 in Nicaragua, elections were held both as a means of dampening the level of societal violence and embarking the respective countries on paths of democratic selection of their governments (see chapters 5 and 9). To evaluate the achievements of El Salvador and Nicaragua in accomplishing these goals, one must distinguish between cynicism on the one hand and euphoria on the other, and avoid the pitfalls inherent in adopting either stance. Following the end of the Cold War, the situation in both countries was clearly "better" than the pervasive violence that had existed during the decade of the 1980s. However, significant problems remained to impede progress toward the achievement of meaningful democratic systems.

During the 1980s, first the demise of a number of autocratic regimes around the world, and then the collapse of communism in Eastern Europe and in the 1990s the Soviet Union, established the study of "democratic transitions" as a topic of scholarly interest (O'Donnell 1973; O'Donnell et al. 1986; Diamond et al. 1989; Karl and Schmitter 1991). In the Latin American context, much of the democratic transition literature focused on the reestablishment of democracy in Argentina, Brazil and Chile, where Cold War imperatives combined with pressure stemming from working class political mobilization had led in the 1960s and 1970s to the overthrow of democratic governments and their replacement by "national security regimes" (Stohl and Lopez 1986; Moriera Alvez 1988; Weinstein 1988; Stepan 1988). While this literature is quite useful in gaining an overall appreciation of democratic transitions, it is not particularly helpful in understanding the specific problems associated with the establishment of democracy in El Salvador and Nicaragua. Not only are these countries poorer than their southern cone counterparts, they also have literally no experience in democratic governance; since the 1930s both have experienced virtually uninterrupted dictatorial rule, albeit more obvious in Nicaragua than in El Salvador (Anderson 1971; Millett 1977; Crowley 1979; Diederich 1981; Dunkerley 1982; Montgomery 1988).

More helpful in understanding the problems confronting the establishment of democracy in El Salvador and Nicaragua is the analysis of Dahl, made in the context of United States policy toward Central America during the 1980s. Dahl argued that three conditions were necessary (but not sufficient) to achieve democracy in the region: (1) an adequate level of social and economic development, (2) traditions supportive of democratic values, and (3) a politically neutral military. He concluded with respect to El Salvador and Nicaragua (as well as Guatemala and Honduras) that these conditions were either non-existent or, at best, only weakly present (1984, pp. 17–19). McSherry, in addition to emphasizing the economic and military problems identified by Dahl, specifies what would be required to fulfill the category of supportive democratic values: the establishment of the rule of law and the creation of an impartial judicial system, the promotion of respect for human rights, and increased political participation (1992, pp. 463–488).

It is not the intent here to review the performances of post-election Salvadoran and Nicaraguan governments in addressing this set of formidable problems (see Rivas-Gallont 1992; Serafino 1992; Montgomery 1993). Rather, the chapter focuses on the way in which the mainstream press in Canada and the United States evaluated the 1989 and 1990 elections as critical turning points in Salvadoran and Nicaraguan political development. Specifically, (1) how important were the elections seen to be, measured by volume of coverage, amount of material contributed by local staff and special correspondents, placement of material on the front page, as well as length of items? (2) How were issues common to both elections, as well as some unique to each, evaluated in terms of salience? (3) How were political parties and leaders evaluated? And finally, (4) in terms of both headlines and text, were the elections seen as promoting or subverting transitions to democracy in the respective countries?

Elections, while clearly not sufficient in themselves to bring about democratic governance, are unquestionably important milestones in that process (Weiner and Ozbudan 1987; Booth and Seligson 1989). Underlying this study is the assumption that mass publics in Canada and the United States rely to a significant degree on the press for their information on and interpretations of what is going on in the world beyond their immediate personal range of experience (McCombs and Shaw 1972; Gitlin 1980). Thus, we have chosen to focus on these elections as they attracted concentrated press coverage and, of necessity, forced journalists to interpret their implications for North American readers (Altheide 1982; Herman and Chomsky 1988; Dickson 1992).

Methods

For each election, all items in a matched sample of Canadian and American newspapers that appeared thirty days prior to and ten days following polling day were analyzed. The following newspapers were used: (1) newspaper of record — *The New York Times* and *The Globe and Mail* (Toronto); (2) capital newspapers — *The Washington Post* and *The Citizen* (Ottawa); (3) elite opinion-leading newspapers — *The Christian Science Monitor* (Boston) and *Le Devoir* (Montreal); (4) eastern regional newspapers — *The Atlanta Constitution* and *The Chronicle-Herald* (Halifax); (5) mid-continent newspapers — *The Chicago Tribune* and *The Winnipeg Free Press*; and (6) western regional newspapers — *The Los Angeles Times* and *The Vancouver Sun*. The question of equivalence is always a difficult one in comparative media research (Edelstein 1982, pp. 45–60), and while it is possible that other researchers might have selected a different paper in one or two categories, on the whole the selection of papers seems to be a reasonable one, given that the purpose of the research was to discover how the mainstream press in the two countries covered the elections.

Employing content analysis, a number of dimensions of press coverage were studied: (1) total volume of coverage, (2) source of content, (3) type of content, (4) length of items, (5) relative salience of issues, (6) whether language in headlines and text reflected positively or negatively on the election and the future of the country, and (7) relative salience and evaluation of political parties and their leaders.[2] On this latter dimension, descriptive words and phrases used with respect to major political figures involved in the two elections were recorded and subsequently recoded into positive and negative categories. (See the full list of descriptors and how they were coded at the end of this chapter.) Therefore, the data on leader images shown in Table 12.6 are based on total uses of positive and negative descriptors in newspaper reporting on the candidates.[3]

Findings

The Salvadoran election of March 1989 was covered in a total of 287 items of newspaper content, while the Nicaraguan election of February 1990 was covered in 521. Obviously the latter was seen as more important, especially in the United States, which accounted for 66% of total press content on that election, as opposed to only 53% for the Salvadoran election. The percentages of content appearing in the thirty-day pre-election period as opposed to the ten-day post-election period differed widely between the two elections: 65% pre- versus 35% post-election for El Salvador and 40% pre- versus 60% post-election for Nicaragua. Clearly the Nicaraguan election became a "hot" news item primarily after the defeat of the ruling Sandinistas.

Data in Table 12.1 show which sources supplied material to Canadian and American newspapers on the elections. The patterns are very similar for both elections, with local staff/special correspondents furnishing the vast majority of material to American newspapers and the major wire services, Associated Press (AP), Reuters and Agence France Presse (AFP) providing the largest amount of content to Canadian newspapers. Freelance journalists, politicians and academics were far more evident as sources for material on the Nicaraguan than on the Salvadoran election in both Canadian and American newspapers. That 77% of reporting in American newspapers for both elections was done by persons working for these newspapers indicates a considerably greater financial commitment to cover these events than was seen among their Canadian counterparts.

Data in Table 12.2 indicate where material on the respective elections appeared in the newspaper. "Hard news" (events of the day) appearing on the front and inside pages, not surprisingly, dominated coverage, over 70% in all cases except Canadian reporting on the

Table 12.1

Sources of Content on the Savadoran and Nicaraguan Elections (items of unknown origin omitted)

	El Salvador			Nicaragua		
	Can	US	Total	Can	US	Total
	N=119	N=146	N=265	N=172	N=332	N=504
Local Staff/Special Correspondents	27%	77%	55%	24%	77%	59%
Canadian Wire Services	3	0	1	5	0	2
American Wire Services	33	6	18	17	5	10
British Wire Services	12	0	5	9	3	5
French Wire Services	5	1	3	10	0	3
Combination	13	9	11	10	1	4
Other	7	7	7	25	14	17

Table 12.2

Type of Content on the Savadoran and Nicaraguan Elections

	El Salvador			Nicaragua		
	Can	US	Total	Can	US	Total
	N=135	N=152	N=287	N=179	N=342	N=521
Front Page News	8%	12%	10%	12%	19%	17%
Inside Page News	65	62	63	54	53	53
Editorials	6	8	7	5	4	5
Features	11	16	14	23	21	21
Other	10	2	6	6	3	4

El Salvador: $X^2=11.432$ DF=4, Sig<.05, Cramer's V=.20

Nicaragua: $X^2=6.395$ DF=4, NS, Cramer's V=.11

Nicaraguan election. Front page placement (an important indicator of how important an event is seen to be) was higher for American papers in both elections, while overall, the Nicaraguan election garnered more front page coverage in both countries. The percentage of editorials remained relatively constant, while the percentage of features increased fairly dramatically in both Canadian and American coverage of the Nicaraguan election.

Length of items, as measured by their number of paragraphs, also indicates that the Nicaraguan election was seen as the more important of the two and that American newspapers saw both elections as more important than did their Canadian counterparts. "Long" items (sixteen paragraphs or longer) comprised 41% of Salvadoran election items (26% of Canadian and 52% of American) and 51% of Nicaraguan election items (41% of Canadian and 55% of American).[4]

Thus, salience, as measured by four separate indicators, was higher for the Nicaraguan election, and both elections were seen as more "newsworthy" by American than by Canadian newspapers. Because the United States had been involved directly and significantly in the political processes of El Salvador and Nicaragua for over a decade, while Canadian involvement was far more circumscribed, this should not be seen as surprising (Haglund 1987; Rochlin 1988).

Table 12.3 shows comparatively the relative salience accorded international and domestic issues common to both elections in Canadian and American reporting, while Table 12.4 presents data on treatment of some key issues that were idiosyncratic to each election.

With respect to international issues, the greatest difference is seen in the extent to which a Cold War context was visible in reporting.[5] Cold War language was used in just over a quarter (27%) of items dealing with the Nicaraguan election as opposed to its use in just over half (52%) of items on the Salvadoran election, which was conducted approximately a year earlier. The role of Cuba was not seen as a significant factor in either election, while that of the United States obviously was of key importance for both. The issue of U.S. foreign aid was more significant in El Salvador, while the role of foreign observers received greater attention in Nicaragua.

Among the domestic issues common to both elections, similarities far outweighed differences. Those differences that did appear were greatest on the issue of violence, FMLN-instigated in El Salvador (52%) and Contras-instigated in Nicaragua (17%); human rights abuses by governments (35% in El Salvador versus 5% in Nicaragua) and implications of the elections (48% in Nicaragua and 27% in El Salvador). Major domestic issues of an idiosyncratic character that

Table 12.3

Common Issues Covered During the Savadoran and Nicaraguan Elections

	Percentage of Items in Which Issue Is Mentioned									
	El Salvador					Nicaragua				
	Can	US	Total	Phi	Sig	Can	US	Total	Phi	Sig
	N=135	N=152	N=278			N=179	N=342	N=521		
International Issues										
Cold War Language	50%	53%	52%	.02	NS	36%	23%	27%	.05	.01
Role of U.S.	33	63	49	.31	.001	47	49	48	.00	NS
Role of Cuba	2	1	1	.04	NS	3	4	4	.00	NS
Foreign Observers	7	10	9	.04	NS	30	34	32	.04	NS
U.S. Aid	21	32	27	.13	.05	13	13	13	.00	NS
Common Domestic Issues										
Background/ Leaders	22%	23%	23%	.00	NS	19%	15%	16%	.05	NS
Background/ Parties	20	26	23	.07	NS	24	20	22	.04	NS
"Horse Race"	16	13	14	.05	NS	21	15	17	.08	NS
Campaign Strategy	13	18	16	.07	NS	28	20	23	.09	.0
Implications	22	32	27	.11	NS	45	49	48	.04	NS
FMLN/Contras Violence	56	47	52	.09	NS	24	13	17	.14	.01
Human Rights Abuses	32	39	35	.06	NS	4	5	5	.02	NS

ranked high on the press agendas of each election indicate a somewhat greater American press interest in the unique political problems of El Salvador.

Data in Table 12.5 indicate the percentages of press items that reflected favorably or unfavorably on the major political parties that contested the two elections. In the case of El Salvador, none of the major parties were portrayed favorably, while it was the far-right ARENA party that garnered the most hostile coverage, 13% overall

Table 12.4

Unique Issues Covered During the Savadoran and Nicaraguan Elections

	Percentage of Items in Which Issue Is Mentioned				
	El Salvador				
	Can	US	Total	Phi	Sig
	N=135	N=152	N=278		
Election Postponement	25%	42%	34%	.17	.01
Party-FMLN Talks	16	31	24	.17	.01
FMLN Boycott	24	24	24	.00	NS
	Nicaragua				
	Can	US	Total	Phi	Sig
	N=179	N=342	N=521		
Economic Conditions	33%	35%	34%	.05	NS
Transfer of Power	29	35	32	.06	NS
Disarming of Contras	30	28	28	.02	NS
Role of Sandinista Army	27	24	25	.04	NS

(12% in Canadian as opposed to 15% in American newspapers). The Christian Democrats appear to have been written off by the Canadian newspapers, while American papers were more critical of this party (which during the 1980s had enjoyed the support of the American government) than supportive. Although the percentages are extremely low, the party of the left, the Democratic Convergence, was looked upon favorably in the Canadian and unfavorably in the American press.

Political parties contesting the Nicaraguan election were subjected to a good deal more evaluation than were their Salvadoran counterparts. The incumbent FSLN was given a relatively equal evaluation in Canadian newspapers (10% favorable as opposed to 12% unfavorable), while in the American papers only 4% of items were favorable while 11% were unfavorable. It is interesting that the victorious UNO coalition did not receive a favorable balance of coverage in the newspapers of either country, with Canadian newspapers giving the party exactly

Table 12.5

Percentage of Items Reflecting Favorably and
Unfavorably on Political Parties in El Salvador and Nicaragua

| | El Salvador | | | | Nicaragua | | |
	Can	US	Total		Can	US	Total
	N=135	N=152	N=287		N=179	N=342	N=521
Pro-PDC	0	2%	1%	Pro-FSLN	10%	4%	6%
Anti-PDC	0	6	3	Anti-FSLN	12	11	11
Pro-ARENA	0	3	1	Pro-UNO	5	3	4
Anti-ARENA	12%	15	13	Anti-UNO	12	5	8
Pro–Democratic Convergence	2	0	1				
Anti–Democratic Convergence	0	3	2				

the same unfavorable assessment as they had rendered with respect to the FSLN (12%).

Table 12.6 offers data reflecting the positive/negative balance in descriptive words and phrases used in reporting on major political figures involved in the two elections. Candidates on the left (Guillermo Ungo in El Salvador and Daniel Ortega in Nicaragua), while certainly not lionized in Canadian newspapers, fared particularly poorly in the American press. American and Canadian press evaluation of the two ARENA leaders (Roberto D'Aubuisson and Alfredo Cristiani), as well as the two Christian Democratic leaders (Jóse Napoléon Duarte and Fidel Chavez Meña) present interesting contrasts. In American newspapers nearly two-thirds of Cristiani descriptors are positive, while in Canadian there is a fifty-fifty split. D'Aubuisson acted as a lightning rod for journalistic venom in news reporting in both countries, with 83% negative descriptors in the United States and 93% negative in Canada. Thus, for the ARENA party, we see American reporting seeking to distance the new presidential candidate Cristiani from the "death squad" image of its past candidate D'Aubuisson. The pattern for Duarte and Chavez Meña is quite different. Retiring President

Table 12.6

Percentage of Descriptors Reflecting Positively or Negatively on Major Political Leaders in El Salvador and Nicaragua

	El Salvador				Nicaragua		
Total	Can	US	Total			Can	US
Chaves	N=5	N=13	N=18	Ortega	N=38	N=61	N=99
Positive	40%	38%	39%	Positive	50%	41%	44%
Negative	60	62	61	Negative	50	59	56
Cristiani	N=32	N=64	N=96	Chamorro	N=71	N=151	N=222
Positive	50%	64%	59%	Positive	55%	68%	64%
Negative	50	36	41	Negative	45	32	36
Ungo	N=6	N=10	N=16				
Positive	33%	20%	25%				
Negative	67	80	75				
Duarte	N=14	N=32	N=46				
Positive	50%	66%	61%				
Negative	50	34	39				
D'Aubuisson	N=44	N=53	N=97				
Positive	7%	17%	12%				
Negative	93	83	88				

Duarte received the same fifty-fifty split as did Cristiani in Canadian newspapers, while garnering a two-thirds favorable balance in the American press. The new Christian Democratic candidate, Chavez Meña, impressed neither Canadian nor American reporting, as over 60% of his descriptors were negative in both countries. Thus, American papers distinguished between the "bad" D'Aubuisson and the "good" Cristiani, as well as between the "good" Duarte and the "bad" Chavez Meña. Violeta Barrios de Chamorro also received a more favorable balance of descriptors in American newspapers than in Canadian (68% positive to 55% positive). The two eventual winners, Cristiani and Chamorro, were both presented more positively to the American mass public than they were to Canadian newspaper readers.

Two tables present data showing the pattern of positive and negative evaluations of the elections and the future of the countries in headlines (Table 12.7) and text (Table 12.8). These tables are organized to show differences between pre- and post-election assessments.

First, with respect to El Salvador, overall evaluations contained in both headlines and text are strongly skewed in the negative direction, with at least twice as many negative as positive appraisals. Canadian headlines reflect a more negative stance following the election, while in the area of text, it is the American papers that are more pessimistic after the ARENA victory.

For the Nicaraguan election, headlines overall show a much more positive orientation than seen for El Salvador, with little pre/post

Table 12.7

Percentage of Headlines Reflecting Positively or Negatively on the Election or Future of El Salvador and Nicaragua

	El Salvador					Nicaragua				
	Can		US		Total	Can		US		Total
	Pre	Post	Pre	Post		Pre	Post	Pre	Post	
Positive	3%	2%	0	4%	2%	21%	21%	20%	20%	20%
Negative	11	1	9%	10	10	10	10	13	8	10

Table 12.8

Percentage of Text Reflecting Positively or Negatively on the Election or Future of El Salvador and Nicaragua

	El Salvador					Nicaragua				
	Can		US		Total	Can		US		Total
	N=135		N=152		N=287	N=179		N=342		N=521
	Pre	Post	Pre	Post		Pre	Post	Pre	Post	
Positive	3%	9%	2%	17%	6%	36%	23%	13%	23%	23%
Negative	9	20	11	28	17	16	23	10	7	12

variation except that negative assessments dropped in American papers following the Chamorro victory. In the area of text, the Nicaraguan election is more complicated, as Canadian newspapers were both more positive and more negative than their American counterparts. When we look at the pattern of pre- and post-election evaluations, however, an interesting trend emerges. Positive assessments in Canadian newspapers decreased by 13% in post-election reporting, while negative assessments increased by 7%. Concomitantly, positive appraisals in American papers increased by 10% following the defeat of the FSLN, while negative appraisals decreased by 3%. Thus, while the Canadian baseline for both positive and negative evaluations is higher, data based on text language confirm that Chamorro's victory was interpreted as a positive development in the American press, while in the Canadian newspapers clearly it was not.

Conclusion

The 1989 and 1990 elections in El Salvador and Nicaragua respectively were not the first efforts at electoral democracy made in the two countries. El Salvador held elections in 1982 and 1984, while the Sandinistas held the first elections since the 1979 revolution in 1984. What made the 1989 and 1990 elections especially significant was that not only did the governments in power at the time of the election lose — the Christian Democrats in El Salvador and the Sandinistas in Nicaragua — but democratic transitions to governments of the opposition party actually took place.

It is clear in examining the press coverage of the two elections that the North American press was far more optimistic regarding the future prospects for Nicaragua than it was for El Salvador. In part this was due to a much clearer picture of the implications of the "collapse of communism," which occurred in the year between the two elections. Arguably, it was also based on an accurate reading of the complexity of the problems facing each country. In El Salvador, the replacement of the centrist Christian Democrats with the strongly anti-communist ARENA was not likely to lead to conflict resolution. Indeed the November 1989 FMLN offensive provided strong evidence that the election had, in the short run, actually hardened the respective positions of left and right. Indeed, the UN negotiated peace accords, which ended the civil war on December 15, 1992, were only agreed upon in January of that year. The effects of the election on the Nicaraguan situation were much more direct, as once the Sandinistas relinquished power to the U.S.-backed Chamorro government, the rationale for continued U.S. support for the Contras vanished. Thus, the election itself established the conditions for an end to that country's civil war.

Notes

1. Material on El Salvador in this chapter was published previously under the title of "Canadian and American Press Coverage of the 1989 Salvadoran Election" and appeared in J. Zylberberg and F. Demers, Eds., *America and the Americas*. St. Foy, Quebec: Les Presses de l'Université Laval, 1992. It is published here with permission.
2. Intercoder reliability on technical characteristics of content exceeded 90% for both elections; issue, party and leader coverage exceeded 86%, while the image data is reliable at 80% for the Salvadoran election and at 83% for the Nicaraguan election (Holsti 1969, p. 140). The author's thanks go to Elizabeth Burton, Elizabeth Ng, Laura Hyttenrauch and Liviana Tossutti for their diligent efforts at coding and to Jean Pignal and Jon Innes for data processing assistance.
3. Image data found in Table 12.6 are based on an evaluation of words and phrases used to describe various leaders in press reporting. Words and phrases were recorded, compiled, and sent to panels of judges who were asked to categorize each as to whether it would be seen as "positive," "neutral or ambiguous" or "negative" toward a particular leader by the American reading public. Salvadoran descriptors were judged by a ten-person panel, eight of which had to agree on a positive or negative evaluation, while the Nicaraguan descriptors were judged by a six-person panel, five of which had to agree on a positive or negative evaluation. Intercoder reliability on this dimension therefore was 80% for Salvadoran leaders and 83% for Nicaraguan leaders.
4. Column inches of material were not recorded due to the high correlations between measures based on number of items and space (see Stevenson and Shaw 1984, p. 35).
5. "Cold War" language was operationalized as words and phrases likely to cause the reader to interpret the events surrounding the election in the context of East-West conflict; for example, communist, communist-backed, leftist, left wing, right wing, Marxist, Marxist-Leninist, Cuban-backed.

Chapter 12 Descriptors

Fidel Chavez Meña

Words/Phrases Judged to Be Positive
Man of honor
Integrity never questioned
Moderate
Important candidate

Words/Phrases Judged to Be Negative
Technocrat/party technocrat
Appears stiff in public
Fallen in public opinion surveys
Straitlaced
Uninspiring speech maker/speeches are like listening to a record playing at
    too slow a speed
Failed to get his message across
Ran a lackluster campaign
Lagging badly
Biggest loser

Words/Phrases Judged to Be Neutral or Ambiguous
Political fixture
Senior minister/former government minister/foreign minister
Lawyer
Principal opponent
Life-long government official
Running second
Conservative

Alfredo Cristiani

Words/Phrases Judged to Be Positive
Enjoys a commanding lead/ahead in the polls/front-runner
Moderate/moderate talking/moderating force/projects a moderate image
Peaceful
Staunchly anti-communist
Lucid
Even-tempered
Mild-mannered
Conciliatory
Intelligent
Practical
Has a social conscience
Top candidate
Honest
Energetic

Free of human rights taints
Opposed to death squads
Progressive
Conservative democrat
Savvy
Poised
From a well-respected family
Shrewd
Has guts/stands up like a real leader
Smooth
Important candidate
Urbane
Would make a good diplomat
Stable
Charming
Articulate
Immaculate
Patient
Consensus builder
Very calm
Has an innate feel for the right position

Words/Phrases Judged to Be Negative
Frontman/figure head/facade
Ultra-conservative
Flat/wooden/dull as a door knob
Lacks purpose
"False face" for D'Aubuisson/mask for a monster
Shallow
Far right/extreme right
Mediocre
Inspires little confidence
Not so bright
Pretty boy
Immature
Inexperienced
To make his resume fill a page he had to list every sports team he's ever
    played on

Words/Phrases Judged to Be Neutral or Ambiguous
Pharmaceutical executive
Georgetown University graduate
Conservative
Former president of the Coffee Growers Association
Land owner/property owner
Affable
Free-market advocate

Balding
Industrialist
Political newcomer
Entrepreneur
Tall
Athlete/sportsman/sports star
Respectable face of party
Excellent in English
Abstemious
Not charismatic

Guillermo Ungo
Words/Phrases Judged to Be Positive
Braved death threats
Non-Marxist socialist candidate

Words/Phrases Judged to Be Negative
Butcher
Terrorist
Political ally of the FMLN/long-time rebel ally/ally of guerrillas
Running a weak fourth

Words/Phrases Judged to Be Neutral or Ambiguous
Lawyer
Leftist political leader/the left's candidate
Running third/expected to finish third
Returned from exile
Former university professor
Seven years in exile
Former leader of the rebel political wing
No ambition to win the election

José Napoléon Duarte
Words/Phrases Judged to Be Positive
Reinvigorated
Centrist/personification of the political center
Most respected PDC leader
Reformist
First popularly elected president in fifty years
Leader of U.S.-backed effort to curb a Marxist insurgency
Brave
Moderate
Washington's staunchest ally/supporter of U.S. policy
Courageous
Great patriot and champion of democracy

Words/Phrases Judged to Be Negative
Leader in name only
Failed to deliver
Cynical
Pawn of the U.S.
Ran one-man government
Corrupt/government mired in corruption/record of corruption/failed to stamp out corruption
Incapable of ending human rights violations
Incompetent

Words/Phrases Judged to Be Neutral or Ambiguous
Terminally ill/dying/suffering from cancer/ailing/in declining health
President
Sixty-two/sixty-three [actual age]
Unable to carry out duties
Couldn't end the war
Incumbent president

Roberto D'Aubuisson
Words/Phrases Judged to Be Positive
Most popular politician/popular
Colorful
Charismatic
Hypnotic speaker
Handsome
Rock star

Words/Phrases Judged to Be Negative
Extreme right wing
Rightist firebrand
Hitler/Hitler of El Salvador
Volatile
Cashiered army major
Notorious
Unsavory
Unacceptable face of the far right
Murderer
Major Blow Torch
Dark image
Rough edged
Gunslinging
Frenetic
Strongman
Linked to death squads
Pathological killer
Participated in paramilitary violence

Extremist image
Associated with the murder of Bishop Romero
Swaggering
Hard drinking
Wild man
Strident
Unacceptable to the U.S.

Words/Phrases Judged to Be Neutral or Ambiguous
Flamboyant
Fiery/fire-eating style
Top leader/maximum leader
Tough
Macho
Lost the presidency in 1984
Overshadows Cristiani
Natural leader of the upper class
Streetwise
Power behind the throne/most powerful/has real power
Founder of ARENA
Will not be in government
Former army major
Wild card in the election
Major Bob
Rightist
Majority leader in the National Assembly
Controversial
Former army/National Guard Intelligence officer
Honorary president of ARENA's Executive Committee
Has total power

Violeta Chamorro
Words/Phrases Judged to Be Positive
Widow of prominent democratic revolutionary mentor
Widow of crusading newspaper editor/wife of martyred newspaper editor
Ideal political compromise
Most visible and influential voice of opposition to the government
Casual, motherly style of conversation
Successful candidate
Newly elected democratic leader
Principled challenger
Personified promise of the revolution
Has motherly warmth/motherly charm/maternal aura
Has personal charm
Winner
Nicaragua's woman in white
Lady of unwavering will/will of steel

Complete lucidity of purpose
Talent for reconciliation
Handsome woman
Closer to the people
Symbol of the country
A good person/a good Nicaraguan
Symbol of unity
Nearly saintly public persona/imagery of a saint/saintly appeal
Courageous
Candidate of reconciliation
Family-oriented
Conciliator
Untainted by ambition for power
Image of purity
Has innate political acumen
Anti-communist
Decent woman
Strong
Elegant
Campaigned despite a broken leg
Friend of the U.S.
Mediator
Shrewd judge of character
Triumphant
May be more effective than Corazon Aquino
Has no debts
Favored candidate of the U.S./U.S. candidate/chosen candidate of the U.S./
    U.S.-backed
Victorious candidate/victor/victorious
Fiercest critic of the revolution
Tall and elegantly slim
Valiant
Polite
A contender
Not a cynical politician
Not a slick politician
Popular
Crusading
Asserting authority quickly
Respected
Seems to be no fool

Words/Phrases Judged to Be Negative
Stalking horse for Yankee imperialism/stalking horse for American
    militarists
Right-wing tool of the U.S./instrument of the imperialists/instrument of
    Washington

Has no political identity
Docile, if distinguished creature of her advisors
Has no political experience/inexperienced/lacks political experience
Puppet of the U.S.
Has little knowledge of economic matters
Relies heavily on her advisors
Elitist who intends to govern for the benefit of the few
Ability to fulfill promises in doubt
Stumbling
Neither politician nor orator
Right-wing tool
Airhead
Space cadet
Figurehead
Never conquered English
State Department's lackey
Stilted speaking style
Never graduated from high school
Has limited knowledge of world affairs
Has short attention span
Fragile
Political neophyte/political novice/no politician
Figurehead member of the FSLN government
Doesn't have any leadership abilities
Unschooled for the political task/knows nothing about politics
Image of a gringo puppet
Has weak grasp of details
Little more than a symbol/a weak political symbol
A vapid woman of no leadership ability
Not too bright/a person of few intellectual resources
Object manufactured for the campaign
Violeta the illiterate/illiterate
Ran an awkward campaign
Has no idea how to unify the country
Unimaginative
Lacks charisma

Words/Phrases Judged to Be Neutral or Ambiguous
Sixty years old
Widow/Nicaragua's most famous widow/Nicaragua's number one widow/
    widow of a Sandinista hero
Revered but not effective
Candidate/presidential candidate
Publisher
Client of the U.S.
Silver-haired/steel gray hair/gray-haired/white-haired
In a wheelchair/campaigning in a wheelchair

Mother of the Contras/seen as close to Contras/linked to Contras
A symbol of what might have been
Sheltered, upper-class girl
Candidate of President Bush/backed by Bush
Leader of UNO
Aristocratic bearing/regal bearing/patrician bearing
Doña Violeta
Owns one of three daily newspapers/newspaper proprietor/president and
    director general of *La Prensa*/publisher of *La Prensa*/owner/editor of *La
    Prensa*
Catapulted into politics
Had strong support from the Catholic church
Fragile and feminine
From land-owning family/from one of Nicaragua's wealthiest families/
    from one of the country's best-known families
Matriarch of a politically divided family
Lived for her husband and children
Depends heavily on family
Devout Catholic
Tall
Slim
Chiseled features
Matriarch
Suffers from chronic osteoporosis/suffers from chronic bone disease
Main rival/leading challenger/main opposition candidate/principal
    opponent/principal opposition candidate/challenger
Does not belong to any political party/unaligned with any political party
Mrs.
Snow White
Outsider
President-elect/elected president/new president
Charter member of the Sandinista five-person junta/one-time Sandinista
    government member
Conservative
Simple
Dressed in white
Maligned as a political lightweight
An early Sandinista supporter
Waves in expansive gestures
A Cory Aquino repeat
A metaphor for a warring nation
Rich/well-to-do
Member of the Social Democratic Party
Bourgeois woman
Benign matriarch
Underdog
An untested leader

Sidelined with a broken knee
Has no enemies
Owes her political legitimacy to status as widow of Pedro Joaguin Chamorro
Mystical
Representative of large Nicaraguan family that reigns on the left as well as
    on the right
Future president
Candidate of a united opposition
Head of opposition coalition
Crippled
Looks like a statue of the Virgin
Mother of four
Short-cropped hair
Housewife
Not a natural politician

Daniel Ortega
Words/Phrases Judged to Be Positive
Undisputed leader
Personally appealing
Evolved from an often strident revolutionary leader to an upbeat political
    performer who could easily be a teen idol/upbeat teenage idol
Behaving like a Western politician
Leads polls by 27%
Showed a remarkable demonstration of freedom and respect for human
    rights
Courageous
Graceful in defeat
Cultivating a youthful image/youthful
Making concessions
Converted the FSLN from a "party of zealots" bent on imposing a Marxist
    regime to an "electoral party"
Down-to-earth image
A man of his word
A real sport in transferring power
Boyish looking
Soft spoken
Snazzy electioneering
Man of conscience
Has dignity
Committed to democracy
Very conciliatory/language is conciliatory
Mature
Has the touch
Popular man
Excellent orator
Tough campaigner

Prepared to cooperate
Polished
Carefully groomed
Upbeat
Highly visible starring role
Has personal appeal
Modern hero
Celebrity
Confident

Words/Phrases Judged to Be Negative
No Lincoln
Hostile
Will not give up power
Leading revolutionary leader
Disheveled
Dour Marxist revolutionary
Loser
An uninvited animal at a garden party
Socially stiff
Leftist
Marxist/Marxist leader
Dictator
Leftist comandante
Rarely smiled
Tyrant
Self-acknowledged Marxist
Supporter of Central American leftist movements
Long-time Washington nemesis
Discredited
Very boring
Tedious
Soviet ally
Scraggly
Flirted with Marxism
Threatened to close Chamorro's newspaper and confiscate her house
Washington's other arch enemy
Skunk at a garden party
Little man in a military uniform/a little man
Cuba's favorite son

Words/Phrases Judged to Be Neutral or Ambiguous
Forty-four years old/in his forties
Jogs
Hugs babies/kissing babies
President
Seeking another six-year term/second term

Candidate for reelection
Mr.
Highly visible
Traditional
Civilian politician
Like a rock star/rock-star flavor/strutted like a rock star/rock-star
    presence/rowdy rock star/slightly hyper rock star on the comeback trail/
    rock-star image
Wardrobe strategically selected/chic wardrobe
Abandoned olive drab uniform
Contact lenses replaced designer glasses
Carter put him in office and Carter got him out
Lame-duck president
Diffident
Cheerleader enthusiasm
Packaged as a presidential candidate/making over his image—Madison
    Avenue style
Gamecock/rooster/el gallo/bantam rooster
Evangelical preacher
Key candidate
Sandinista leader/head of revolutionary Sandinista movement
Losing presidential candidate/defeated presidential candidate
Achieved national notoriety
Not known to harbor deep religious convictions
Incumbent president
Leader of losing party
Former guerrilla fighter/former guerrilla
Comandante
Symbol of Sandinista existence
Not humiliated
Spent time in jail under Somoza
Sexy
Campaigning as a single man
Introverted
Has severe myopia
Defiant
Emotional
Opponent of Somoza
Intellectual in fatigues
Old fashioned party boss
More traditional politician
Ascetic
Gone are the bad haircuts, bookworm glasses and olive drab uniforms
Lone ranger
Disco Dan
Survived a decade-long campaign against him
Has monastic personal tastes
Surprised at the results

Chapter 13

Cheerleader or Critic?
TV Network News Coverage
of the 1989 U.S. Invasion of Panama[1]

WALTER C. SODERLUND, RONALD H. WAGENBERG
AND IAN C. PEMBERTON

The role of mass media, especially television, in reporting United
States military operations is a subject on which there is
considerable interest as well as diversity of opinion. From at
least the time of the legendary assessment that when the U.S. "lost"
Walter Cronkite (following the Tet offensive of 1968), it lost the
Vietnamese War, the impact of media coverage on operational success
has been recognized by both supporters and opponents of American
use of military force. However, analysts disagree on whether the media
tend to be supportive or critical of such ventures.

According to the Report of the Twentieth Century Fund Task Force
on the Military and the Media,

> in the wake of the Indochinese War and the turbulent 1970s
> many of the nation's senior military officers, veterans of
> Vietnam, had developed a bitter consensus: newsmen,
> especially television newsmen, were, at bottom,
> adversaries, neither trustworthy nor competent in military
> affairs, eager to dramatize American failings, possessing
> enormous power to undercut civilian backing for the men
> in battle. (Braestrup 1985, p. 20)

This view of the role of the press is of course challenged by those
scholars who adopt the position that the media are subordinated to
state authority and are used effectively by the United States government

as channels of pro-government propaganda. For the Vietnam War, Herman and Chomsky's "propaganda model" brings a different perspective to media coverage:

> On its assumptions, we would expect media coverage and interpretation of the war to take for granted that the United States intervened in the service of generous ideals, with the goal of defending South Vietnam from aggression and terrorism and in the interest of democracy and self-determination. (Herman and Chomsky 1988, p. 169)

Obviously, two very different expectations regarding media behavior are contained in these opposing assessments. This chapter employs a detailed content analysis of actual TV news coverage to ascertain which of these roles characterizes press performance with respect to the United States invasion of Panama, which began on December 20, 1989.

The use of military power by the United States to achieve foreign policy goals in the Caribbean Basin has a long history. While the phenomenon of "yellow journalism" has been cited as a factor in getting the U.S. involved in the Spanish-American War (Wissan 1965), media coverage is increasingly seen as crucial to the success of initiated military operations. Once lives and resources are committed to battle, democratic governments are sensitive to the necessity of maintaining popular support for the operation through managed coverage. Since mass media, especially television, are able to bring the battlefield to the nation in living color on a nightly basis, the activities shown, and the "spin" placed on those activities, are seen to be a major factor in the perceived, if not real, success of any military operation (Sarkesian 1976; Gabriel 1962; Cohen 1984; Rockman 1987).

For the past forty-five years, anti-communism has provided the basic framework for United States foreign policy, no less so in the Caribbean Basin than elsewhere in the world. Beginning with political unrest in British Guiana resulting in the suspension of the constitution in 1953, and a revolution in Guatemala ended by a U.S.-sponsored exile invasion in 1954, continuing over the years with events in Cuba, the Dominican Republic, Jamaica, Grenada, El Salvador and Nicaragua, the Cold War injected itself in a major way into U.S.

decisions regarding whom to support and whom to oppose in the region. By the end of 1989 Soviet influence in Eastern Europe had collapsed; thus, Panama represents the first instance of post–World War II armed American intervention where anti-communism in the context of the global confrontation with the U.S.S.R. was not a primary motivating factor.

Rather, American domestic concerns — ranging from the war on drugs to presidential image making — predominated as motives for U.S. action. Indeed, General Manuel Noriega, who had risen to power as a CIA "asset" in the context of the Cold War, had become an expendable embarrassment, if not an intolerable irritant to President George Bush. The inability to deal more seriously with Noriega could spark the reemergence of the "wimp" image that Bush had to counter in the 1988 election campaign. Since the old ideological parameters within which the U.S. media had interpreted earlier interventions were no longer operative,[2] in what framework would the U.S. media present the Panama invasion to the U.S. population?

The Canadian perspective on U.S. involvement in the Caribbean Basin has always been more detached, and at times governments formed by both major parties have taken positions contrary to or not necessarily supportive of U.S. policy. Such differences are particularly evident with respect to Cuba, Grenada, El Salvador and Nicaragua (Dramin and North 1990; Baranyi 1985). Further to this, Canadian detachment had been symbolized by its long-time refusal to join the Organization of American States. That refusal had, at least in part, been predicated on the desire to avoid the consequences of appearing to be the junior Cold War partner of the United States in its hemispheric foreign policy. Nonetheless, after a period of observer status Canada did eventually join the OAS as a full member in January 1990, literally weeks after the invasion of Panama. This policy shift obviously gave the Canadian media, which has always been interested in the Caribbean Basin policy of the United States, additional reason to seek clarification of its own government's reactions to the strong U.S. military initiative. At any rate, the government control and media ownership factors, which Herman and Chomsky posit as crucial ingredients of the propaganda model, should operate to a far less significant extent in Canada than they do in the United States (see chapter 9).

Background

Panama has a unique relationship with the United States, created as it was in 1903 by American diplomacy, intervention and strategic need. The opening of the Panama Canal in 1914 tied the host nation's fortunes ever more closely to the United States. This created understandable frustration among Panamanian nationalists who saw their bisected nation as a victim of American power and ambition. In 1964, nationalist tension exploded into violence over the question of displaying Panama's flag in the American-controlled Canal Zone. In 1977, the Carter Administration appeared to have taken a major step toward reconciliation by negotiating treaties with the government of General Omar Torrijos, whereby Panama would control the Canal by the year 2000.

However, the decade of the 1980s would bring two issues to the fore that would ultimately have considerable impact on Panamanian-American relations. The first was the emergence of a Marxist-style Sandinista government in Nicaragua (and its apparent close ties to Cuba) following the revolution there in 1979, while the second was the domestic "war on drugs" in the United States (Griffith 1997a). General Manuel Antonio Noriega, by 1983, had assumed control of Panama after the death of Torrijos in 1981, and skillfully played a dual manipulative role in American policy on both these issues. An avowed anti-communist who, at least until 1986, cooperated in the covert American military effort against Nicaragua, Noriega also maintained friendly and cooperative relations with Cuba. However, it was in the international drug trade where he truly displayed his peculiar genius, working with the American Drug Enforcement Agency on the one hand, while being deeply involved in drug trafficking on the other (Dinges 1990; Scranton 1991). By 1987, the United States had decided that the multifaceted Panamanian general had become an acute liability and attempted to solve the problem by encouraging popular resistance to him, by the imposition of an economic embargo and by actually trying to negotiate his voluntary retirement into exile. Elections in May of 1989 (resulting in the election of the anti-Noriega candidate Guillermo Endara) were annulled by the dictator, further exacerbating the situation. The failure over two years of these efforts to remove Noriega brought about the massive invasion of Panama — Operation Just Cause — in the early hours of December 20, 1989.[3]

Methods

The research reported in this chapter is based on data gathered from content analysis of the news coverage of the United States invasion of Panama by the three major American television networks (ABC, CBS and NBC) and the two major English-language Canadian networks (CBC and CTV). The major nightly newscasts on these networks were compared for a twenty-three-day period from December 15, 1989 (five days prior to the invasion) to January 6, 1990 (three days following the surrender of General Noriega and his removal from Panama to the United States to stand trial on drug-related charges).[4] During this period, 197 news stories were gathered for analysis. Examined in the study are factors such as the volume of coverage (number and running time); format; placement of items in the newscast; substantive issues given prominence; news sources utilized, and whether these sources were favorable or unfavorable toward U.S. foreign policy positions; positive and negative "images" presented of the key actors involved (Manuel Noriega, Guillermo Endara and George Bush); and whether overall, in both text and visual impact, the story was likely to be interpreted as either pro- or anti-invasion by viewers. It is on the basis of these data that the cheerleader/critic roles of the press will be assessed.

Data for the U.S. networks were obtained from the Television News Archive at Vanderbilt University, while those for the Canadian networks came from the National Media Archive of the Fraser Institute.[5] American network content was received on videotape, which allowed us to judge the visual impact of news stories, while Canadian content was received in transcript format, which made this impossible. For all networks, some newscasts were missing: ABC, three days; CBS, five days; NBC, two days; CBC, five days; and CTV, three days. While this is unfortunate, we judged that the relatively few and non-systematically missing newscasts would not materially alter overall findings. Tests for intercoder reliability were conducted on a sample of taped and transcripted stories. On items of a format nature — for example, length,[6] placement, anchors, reporters, sources used and visuals — intercoder reliability was established at 94%. With respect to issues discussed in each story, intercoder reliability was 86%. On the dimensions of whether sources were supportive or critical of U.S. policy positions, and whether in text and visuals (for U.S. stories) material was pro- or anti-invasion, intercoder reliability was 83% (Holsti 1969, p. 140).[7]

Specific language used to describe General Noriega and Presidents Endara and Bush in each story was recorded, compiled and sent to a panel of ten political scientists, historians, communication scholars and professional researchers, with instructions to judge whether each leader descriptor would be seen by the American people as positive, neutral/ambiguous or negative. (See the full list of descriptors and how they were coded at the end of this chapter.) While the panel was not chosen on the basis of political alignment, it did include a reasonable political left-to-right mix. In order for a descriptor to be counted as either positive or negative, eight of the ten panel members had to agree on such a judgment. Thus, intercoder reliability for each descriptor is at least 80%. In most cases agreement on descriptors was at 90% or 100%.

Findings

At the risk of some oversimplification, the invasion of Panama can be likened to a morality play in four acts. Act I begins on December 15 when General Noriega proclaimed that Panama was in a state of war with the United States. Following this, a series of hostile encounters occurred between off-duty U.S. military personnel and their families and the Panamanian Defense Force (PDF). Precisely who was provoking whom was not entirely clear, but at least one U.S. officer was killed and one PDF member wounded. This period (December 15 to December 19) accounted for 10% of the total TV news coverage.

These threats to Americans established the crisis atmosphere leading to Act II (December 20): the actual invasion and subsequent manhunt for the elusive Noriega. A unique feature of the Panama invasion is that the initial military thrust was massive and multipronged. The PDF, wherever it was located, was overwhelmed in the first assault and was never able to regroup and confront the American invaders in other than nuisance operations. Noriega, however, managed to elude U.S. forces, and after a few days in hiding, presented himself on December 24 at the Vatican diplomatic compound where he was granted sanctuary. This period accounted for 30% of the total TV news coverage.

Act III deals with the possible fate of Noriega — whether he would be able somehow to "escape justice" — and the conflict between the United States and the Vatican over his continued diplomatic sanctuary, including the controversial blasting of the Vatican compound with rock music. Treated, as well, in this the longest of the Acts (December 24, 1989 to January 2, 1990) were the many problems facing the new Endara government, which had assumed power under U.S. protection. Criticism focused on military operations (from both tactical and intelligence perspectives) and assessments of the economic damage done to Panama as a consequence of the military action. This period accounted for 40% of the total TV news coverage.

Finally, Act IV begins on January 3, when Noriega surrendered and was flown immediately to Florida to stand trial on American drug charges. Issues given prominence in this period include background to the drug-running/money-laundering charges and how Noriega would be dealt with by the U.S. justice system, speculation on the impact of Noriega's trial on the reputation of George Bush, and the return of Panamanian exiles to their country. This period (January 3 to January 6) accounted for 20% of the total TV news coverage. At the end of "the play," the lesson is clear: Two weeks after the military operation against him began, the once-powerful Noriega resided in a Miami jail cell and his "mug shot" was displayed prominently on all TV network newscasts.

Indicators of Story Importance

In general, as one might expect given the direct involvement of U.S. troops in combat operations, the invasion of Panama was a "bigger" story in the United States than it was in Canada. The U.S. networks ran an average of 2.3 stories per day, while the Canadian networks averaged 1.7 stories per day. The U.S. networks also ran more "long" stories: 27% were over three minutes in length, as opposed to 17% of Canadian stories in that category. Conversely, Canadian networks featured more "short" stories: 23% were under one minute in length, while only 10% of American stories ran for less than one minute. Placement of stories in the newscast also indicates greater U.S. interest: 73% of U.S. stories were placed in the first three positions, with 31% running as the lead story; while 53% of Canadian stories occupied the first three positions, with 16% in the number-one slot. Format items as well point to a differential of interest between the two countries: stories employing just an anchor without reporters or experts comprised 24% of the Canadian and only 11% of the American total. U.S. networks used "experts" in 17% of their stories, while the Canadian percentage was 6. Finally, film accompanied 90% of U.S. and 74% of Canadian stories.

For Americans, the invasion was of course both a foreign-policy and a domestic story, while for Canadians it was strictly a foreign-policy concern. Even with these differences, the extent of Canadian coverage indicates that the invasion certainly was a significant news story. Indeed, it is hard to imagine any greater coverage for a story that did not involve Canadians directly.

Issue Coverage

The leading issues explored as a part of the news coverage of the invasion appear in Table 13.1. On this dimension, similarities between Canadian and American storyline decisions are dramatic. There are relatively few discrepancies in the rank order of importance accorded to issues, and for only one of the top twelve issues is there a statistically significant difference in the amount of coverage. That American coverage of casualties suffered by its own troops is higher than Canadian coverage is self-explanatory. Canadian government policy is of almost no interest to American networks, and even in Canada, where it was reported in 13% of stories, it barely placed on the list of top twelve issues covered by Canadian media.

In both countries, U.S. government policy and the capture of Noriega created the greatest interest by far. The purely military aspects of the invasion, while significant in coverage, were quickly replaced by the dramatic elements that swirled around the person of Noriega himself: First, would he be found? Second, once he was found, how would the United States get its hands on him? And third, what would be his fate at the hands of American justice? The future of Panama, both politically and economically, continued as a secondary focus throughout the entire period of coverage. Analysis of these issues, however, was not very sophisticated. For example, only one story dealt in any way with the racial/class divisions in Panamanian society that Noriega had been able to exploit, and while Panama's role in the international drug trade was a primary topic of coverage, Noriega's position was so central in the discussion that one might easily get the impression that his removal would solve the problem, which clearly was not the case. It was the events themselves, as they unfolded in Panama day-by-day, that tended to drive story coverage (Larson 1986).

Table 13.1

**Major Issues During the Invasion of Panama
(due to multi-coding, columns do not add to 100%)**

	Percentage of Stories in Which Issue Is Mentioned			
	Can	US	Total	X²Sig
	N=63	N=134	N=197	
U.S. Government Policy	67%	65%	66%	NS
Capture of Noriega	64	60	61	NS
Panamanian Government Policy	46	41	43	NS
Military Operations	33	39	37	NS
Vatican Policy	37	26	29	NS
Extradition of Noriega	27	30	29	NS
Panamanian Opinion	21	22	22	NS
Implication of Invasion	18	24	22	NS
Noriega's Links to Drug Trade	18	23	21	NS
Protection of American Citizens	19	22	21	NS
U.S. Casualties	10	23	19	.05
Damage to Panama	19	17	18	NS

Sources

Table 13.2 analyzes the major sources used by the U.S. and Canadian TV networks to construct their news stories on the invasion and its aftermath. Data here are indeed revealing. American spokespersons, whether they be President Bush, U.S. military in the field, the Pentagon, the administration or the State Department, dominated among the voices who supplied the information that was woven into news stories. Panamanians, whether government officials or private citizens, also featured prominently as news sources. Other than for the first five days of coverage, the Panamanian government meant the Endara government, which, while at times not entirely on side with U.S. policy, was certainly not about to "bite the hand" that had placed it and held it in office. Panamanians on the street who appeared in news film, in the majority, were supportive or at least neutral with respect to the invasion. Of the fifty-one Panamanians on the street who appeared among the first three sources in a newscast, only two were judged to be unfavorable to the U.S. military action that in many cases had destroyed their homes or businesses or in some cases had killed loved ones. The only other significant sources were American "experts" on Panama, on foreign policy in the region more generally and on military and legal questions.[8] While there was some critical commentary from these sources, for the most part they were either neutral or supportive of U.S. policy (Paletz and Entman 1981).

It is obvious from even a cursory examination of this data that the American government was able to get its relatively unopposed point of view across to the American people via TV news. While this source dominance on American TV is at least somewhat predictable, it is less obvious why a greater range of sources was not used by Canadian media.

Perhaps an answer to this question is that in the United States as well as in Canada, there was a virtual absence of organized opposition to the invasion. In the United States, Democratic senators and congressmen seemed reluctant to criticize the invasion, given its short time span, its early and relatively casualty-free military success and the seeming support it received among the Panamanian population. This eliminated traditional major rivals for media access (Kern et al. 1983). For probably the same reasons, traditional anti-war groups were unable to establish a presence in news coverage. It is somewhat ironic that the Vatican provided the only sustained source of negative views on American policy in Panama.

Data in Table 13.3 report the evaluative positions taken by the first three cited sources regarding U.S. decisions to initiate and carry out various policies involved in the invasion. Not surprisingly, given the sources that we have identified, this evaluation was skewed strongly in a favorable direction (51% to 62% of sources). Conversely, unfavorable evaluations, while given some air time, were much less in evidence (15% to 17% of sources). Neutral or ambiguous sources fluctuated a little more widely, from 22% to 34%. Again, the degree to which sources offered similar evaluations of U.S. policy in Canadian and American news is remarkable, and is no doubt a reflection of the fact that similar news sources tended to dominate access to the news in both countries.

Some stories utilized more than three sources. The favorable, neutral/ambiguous and unfavorable sources in each story were totaled

Table 13.2

Primary Sources About the Invasion of Panama

	Percentage of Stories Cited		
	Can	US	Total
First Source (based on 197 stories)			
President Bush (N=28)	18%	13%	14%
U.S. Military in the Field (N=27)	16	13	14
Pentagon (N=25)	11	14	13
Panamanians on Street (N=17)	5	10	9
Panamanian Government (N=11)	3	7	6
Vatican (N=11)	3	7	6
Second Source (based on 153 stories)			
Panamanian Government (N=26)	26	13	17
U.S. Military in the Field (N=21)	15	13	14
Panamanians on Street (N=19)	6	15	13
Pentagon (N=16)	4	13	8
U.S. Administration (N=12)	9	8	8
American Experts (N=10)	2	9	7
Third Source (based on 107 stories)			
Panamanians on Street (N=15)	18	13	14
President Bush (N=11)	15	9	11
Panamanian Government (N=10)	10	10	10
U.S. Military in the Field (N=9)	6	10	9
Pentagon (N=9)	12	7	9
American Experts (N=8)	0	11	8

Total number of times primary sources cited in leading positions:

U.S. Military in Field	57
Panamanians on Street	51
Pentagon	50
Panamanian Government	50
President Bush	39
U.S. Administration	29
American Experts	25
Vatican	15
U.S. State Department	15

Table 13.3

**Evaluative Direction of Three Leading Sources
Regarding American Foreign Policy in Panama**

	Can	US	Total
First Source	N=63	N=134	N=197
Favorable to U.S. Policy	57%	56%	56%
Neutral/Ambiguous	27	27	27
Unfavorable to U.S. Policy	16	17	17
X^2=.0533, DF=2, NS			
Second Source	N=47	N=106	N=153
Favorable to U.S. Policy	49%	52%	51%
Neutral/Ambiguous	32	35	34
Unfavorable to U.S. Policy	19	13	15
X^2=.9059, DF=2, NS			
Third Source	N=33	N=74	N=107
Favorable to U.S. Policy	55%	64%	62%
Neutral/Ambiguous	33	18	22
Unfavorable to U.S. Policy	12	18	16
X^2=3.3490, DF=2, NS			

for all stories. Leaving out the neutral/ambiguous category (27%), 78% of the remaining sources commented favorably on US policy, while 22% were unfavorable. In summary, the U.S. government generally received a very positive portrayal of its Panamanian military and foreign-policy initiatives by both U.S. and Canadian TV networks.

"Spin" Factors

Data in Tables 13.4 and 13.5 focus on textual and visual components of newscasts as they might influence a viewer to take a positive or negative view of the invasion. In the case of textual material, where the comparison is made by country, a pro-invasion orientation is evident for both Canadian and American reporting. The pattern varies only in the case of the CBC, where there were fewer stories with a pro-invasion slant (38%) as opposed to about 50% for all other networks including

Table   13.4

Evaluation of Text in Stories of the Invasion of Panama

	Can	US	Total
	N=63	N=134	N=197
Pro-Invasion	44%	51%	49%
Neutral/Ambiguous	46	40	42
Anti-Invasion	10	9	9
X^2=.69875, DF=2, NS			

Table   13.5

Evaluation of Visuals in U.S. Stories of the Invasion of Panama

	ABC	CBS	NBC	Total
	N=38	N=43	N=43	N=124
Pro-Invasion	29%	28%	37%	32%
Neutral/Ambiguous	68	70	61	66
Anti-Invasion	3	2	2	2
X^2=1.0358, DF=4, NS				

CTV. Anti-invasion textual material was found in less than 10% of stories, and in this case the CBC follows the pattern established by the other networks.

Only U.S. TV network data offered an opportunity to analyze positive or negative visual impact. While two-thirds of the visuals were coded as neutral and the percentage of pro-invasion visuals was smaller than was the case with text, there was again a decidedly pro-invasion bent, as there was a virtual absence of anti-invasion visual material.

Leader Images

Given the analogy of a morality play with which we introduced this discussion of findings, the manner in which main characters in the drama were portrayed is of major interest.

Table 13.6

Percentage of Descriptors Reflecting Positively or Negatively on Major Actors in the Invasion of Panama

	Can	US	Total
Manuel Noriega	N=120	N=158	N=278
Positive	8%	6%	6%
Negative	92	94	94
George Bush	N=7	N=22	N=29
Positive	29%	59%	52%
Negative	71	41	48
Guillermo Endara	N=8	N=11	N=19
Positive	62%	91%	79%
Negative	38	9	21

The chief villain of the piece is undoubtedly General Manuel Noriega. He received an extraordinary amount of press attention. Further, of the words and phrases used to describe him, which were coded either positive or negative by our panel, fully 94% were negative. This is about as close to "demonization" of an individual as one can get. As for President Bush, fewer than half the descriptors were valenced, and these were split about evenly between positive and negative. While the descriptor pattern in Canadian and American news stories was consistent with respect to Noriega, in the case of Bush, negative descriptors predominated in Canadian news stories, while positive descriptors were more likely to be used in American newscasts. Guillermo Endara was given considerably less attention than the other two leaders, but that attention was decidedly more positive than negative, especially in American newscasts.

Conclusion

While there is disagreement among analysts regarding whether the media are likely to be supportive or critical of U.S. military operations, there is virtual universal agreement among them that they are powerful shapers of our images of foreign events, through both the information they provide and the spin or interpretation that they place on that material (Smith 1980; Merrill 1983; Gitlin 1980).

The general finding that pervades the data collected for this chapter is that, with few exceptions, there was a consistency in the news coverage of the Panamanian invasion among the networks and the two countries in which these networks operated. Moreover, that coverage (given higher priority in the United States) tended to present a positive picture of the invasion in both text and visual material. A set of common news sources, which tended to be supportive of American initiatives, dominated access to the news media in both the United States and Canada. There was little organized opposition to the invasion, and the importance of what there was, certainly was not inflated by prominent media access. Manuel Noriega has to be seen as having the quintessence of a "bad press." Following the actual invasion on December 20, he was powerless to defend himself, as he lacked access to the media. File footage of him, as well as tours of his captured office, were presented in a way to inflame American public opinion against him. He truly became the man "Americans could love to hate."

The two questions investigated in this study can be answered with documented support. Television news coverage of the United States invasion of Panama cast events in a positive light. Canadian TV coverage revealed few differences compared with U.S. coverage, with most differences having to do with the prominence accorded the story rather than its substance or tone. With the exception of the negative image presented of President Bush in a relatively small number of Canadian news stories, and of the CBC not being quite as supportive as other networks, coverage of the invasion in the two countries is virtually indistinguishable.

It is now left to us to speculate why the coverage was as homogeneous and laudatory as it was. If news reporting on Panama had been managed, as it has been in other U.S. military operations (Grenada and the Gulf War, for example), the answer would be self-evident. But in the case of Panama, the military phase of the operation began and ended so swiftly that the "press pool" system, so effective in controlling news from the Gulf, did not arrive in Panama until after the major fighting had ended.[9] In any event, reporters and camera operators, plus local stringers, were on site at the time of the invasion and initially reported what they were hearing and seeing by telephone and satellite. Following the initial assault, TV crews seemingly had reasonable access to news venues, most of which were not military in nature. In contrast to the 1983 invasion of Grenada, never in the course of this study was the issue of military censorship discussed by TV anchors or reporters.[10]

Thus, a large part of the positive spin so evident in the coverage resulted from reporters' encounters with Panamanians who seemed genuinely happy with having been invaded. Beyond this, the new Panamanian government (the one denied its spring election victory) was anxious to legitimize the American initiative. Needless to say, those Panamanians who either supported Noriega or opposed the American invasion on the grounds that it violated Panamanian sovereignty, kept a low profile. Further, as was mentioned previously, there was virtually no opposition to the invasion on the part of the Democratic Congress, and traditional anti-war voices were unable to muster much of a challenge to the invasion, which almost immediately became a fait accompli. Thus, in addition to the prickly relationship with the Vatican over giving Noriega sanctuary, the only negative factor that emerged in TV coverage revolved around whether too much force had been used, causing needless economic destruction and loss of civilian life. In this regard, there is no evidence to suggest that the media generated positive reports because they were denied access to film areas such as El Chorillo where destruction had been most severe.

Other than the general predisposition of major U.S. networks to support American policy, at least while U.S. troops are committed to combat operations (Larson 1986, pp. 127–128), we have the added factor that the invasion was aimed at a truly unsavory antagonist, General Noriega. This set the stage for the personalization of the conflict in the classic "good guy" vs. "bad guy" scenario so dear to TV viewers. The file videos of Noriega brandishing a machete while speaking to his puppet legislature provided a caricature of fear for U.S. news watchers. Likewise, file footage of his "Dignity Battalions" beating vice-presidential candidate Guillermo "Billy" Ford during the 1989 election campaign, and descriptions of his involvement in the drug trade as a "poisoner of children," reinforced his negative image. In this climate of fear and hate, the legitimacy of conducting what some might consider a blatant violation of Panamanian sovereignty to carry out an international kidnapping, was hardly debated, either in Panama or the United States.

Why this should have been the case in Canada as well calls into play a number of factors peculiar to Canada and its media. One, of course, is the Canadian dependence on U.S. sources for international news (Scanlon 1974; Scanlon and Farrell 1983; Canada 1981). In this case, although the sources used tended to be American, over 90% of the reporters used by the Canadian networks worked for those Canadian networks; hence, we are not looking at American network material purchased for use on Canadian news programs. Nonetheless, even when the sources and reporters were Canadian, they were confronted with the reality of the Canadian government position on the invasion, which, while circumspect, was supportive. The unsavory nature of Noriega's character would have the same impact in Canada as it did in the United States.

While the Herman and Chomsky propaganda model certainly fits the pattern of American media coverage of the invasion, for a number of idiosyncratic reasons, it is unlikely that the Panamanian invasion will serve as a predictor of media reaction to future U.S. military operations. First, political opposition at home is likely to be more organized and vocal; second, the military combat phase is not likely to be as easy and quick as this one was (not every country wants to be invaded and has American troops already stationed within its borders); and third, not every international opponent is as devoid of redeeming traits and as isolated as was General Noriega.

However, even if a number of these factors are not in place, the research reported in this chapter has demonstrated the remarkable extent to which the American government, through a variety of news sources, can get its viewpoint expressed in the news. Should there be domestic opposition and should the international context be less favorable, it is likely that opposing points of view will be given greater media access. At the same time, it is also quite likely that government sources will continue to predominate as primary shapers of the media message.

Notes
1. This chapter is an edited version of "Cheerleader or Critic? Television News Coverage in Canada and the United States of the U.S. Invasion of Panama," which appeared in the *Canadian Journal of Political Science,*

Vol. 27, No. 3 (September 1994). It is published here with permission. The authors would like to express thanks to Stuart Surlin for sharpening a number of points in the analysis of the data.

2.   In news coverage of the Panama invasion, the five TV networks used Cold War language in only 6% of their stories. Even this total, however, overstates the salience of the Cold War, as some references were made to Soviet-made arms found in Panama and to Soviet-made tanks in Nicaragua. The invasion itself was not framed in the context of the Cold War.

     Why this is the case is not entirely clear, as Noriega's links to Cuba's Fidel Castro went back at least as far as 1984, and with the defection of José Blandón, Panamanian Consul General in New York in January 1988, United States intelligence knew in detail the extent to which Castro was involved in providing military hardware, training and advice to Noriega (Oppenheimer 1992, pp. 167-92). According to one argument, the Panamanian invasion consciously marks the end of the Cold War framework in favor of a "moral juridical" aterritorial international logic that now underlies the American "New World Order" (Sutley 1992).

3.   For an overview of U.S. relations with Panama see (Dinges 1990; Scranton 1991; Kempe 1990; Donnelly et al. 1991; Buckley 1991; McConnell 1991; and Conniff 1992).

4.   While the boundaries of the study could have been extended in either direction, these dates seem best to frame what were the actual military invasion and subsequent operations aimed at capturing Noriega. Thus, the findings cannot be taken as indicative of television coverage either with respect to pre-invasion U.S. policy toward Panama or to events subsequent to Noriega's removal from the country.

5.   Special thanks go to Dot Hamilton of the Television News Archive and to Lydia Miljan of the National Media Archive for their prompt and professional assistance in assembling the research materials. Neither organization of course is in any way responsible for coding decisions or interpretations of data that they furnished to us in raw form.

6.   Length of story is a special case. For U.S. stories, the running time was indicated on the video of the newscast. For Canadian material, running time was not indicated and was determined by reading the story transcript aloud and recording the elapsed time on a stopwatch. On a sample of eight stories read by the authors and a professional broadcast journalist, identical times were recorded on four stories, five-second differences were recorded on three stories and a ten-second difference was recorded on one story. We calculate that in 87% of cases, our cited running time is within five seconds of the actual time of the story as it was broadcast.

7.   All coding was done jointly by Professors Soderlund and Wagenberg working in a concentrated period of time of under a month. Each story was viewed or read at least three times, and any disagreements were

settled to the satisfaction of both coders prior to a final decision being made.
8. Not many "experts" were interviewed on Canadian news stories, and all experts were located in the United States.
9. The "press pool," which was created as a response to the lack of journalists' access to Grenada, was alerted at approximately 8:00 p.m. on December 19, left Washington at 11:20 p.m. and arrived in Panama at 4:55 a.m. on December 20. It witnessed combat at 10:00 a.m. and sent its first video to the U.S. at 5:20 p.m. on December 20. It was disbanded after four days (Jones 1989; Merida 1990).
10. Charges of denial of access were confined to treatment of the press pool and focused on two points: (1) It arrived after the majority of the fighting was over, and (2) helicopters were not available to transport it to combat sites around Panama. For an article on a Pentagon-commissioned report on problems of press coverage, see Gordon 1990.

Chapter 13 Descriptors

Manuel Noriega
Words/Phrases Judged to Be Positive
Honored guest in the Pentagon
Won high praise from all over Washington
Vigorous
In good shape
Calm
An innocent man
Did much to professionalize the armed forces
Man of power

Words/Phrases Judged to Be Negative
Narco-military Idi Amin of the Americas
Practiced voodoo/witchcraft
Used drugs
Counts on army to keep him in power
Poisoner of children
Irritant to U.S.
Made reckless threats and attacks upon Americans
$1 million reward for his capture
Indicted in U.S. on drug-trafficking charges/faced two American indictments for drug trafficking
Drug runner/drug dealer/drug trafficker
Thug/skilled thug/general who is a thug
Assassin
Through puppets, cronies, armed henchmen and rigged elections, ran Panama as though it was his own personal turf in a gang war
Heroes are Mao Tsetung and Genghis Khan

Greatest defender is Fidel Castro
Nobody wants him
Propelled by no ideology beyond simple pursuit of power/his ideology
    was self-interest
Schemed his way to the top
Man heading America's most-wanted list
Ousted military leader
Crook who should stand trial in the U.S.
Dictator/military dictator/criminal dictator/deposed dictator/disgraced
    dictator/ brutal dictator/former dictator/ousted dictator/tin pot dictator/
    ex-dictator
Cowering for his life
Old arch enemy/an old foe
A common criminal
Exile is too kind a fate for him
Should be punished/have him face justice/gonna face justice/must be
    brought to justice
May try to blindside the whole justice system
Will eventually face trial/will finally face justice
Made Panama a safe haven for the Medellin cocaine cartel
Cunning and unpredictable
A goddamn drug-smuggling rotten dictator
More cunning than intelligent
Federal prisoner 41586
Stripped of general's rank
Physical and mental condition is deteriorating
A thorn in the shoe
His time has run out/time is running out
Outlived his welcome
Murder charges await him/accused of murdering ten military officers
Is not a man, he's an animal, a beast
Has nowhere to go and no way to get there
Panama's most wanted man
Opulent lifestyle/fond of a flamboyant lifestyle
Spy
Very unsavory character
Very rough character
A man who loved his wine, weapons and women
Stole from his people
Sent his personal army to beat up on politicians
No electric chair here [Panama] big enough for him
Person of low principles and even lower morals
Kept a picture of Adolf Hitler in his closet
Kept a ready supply of pornography in his desk
A totally brutal person/brutal ruler
His picture will be in every post office in town
A guy who kills people

Unpopular in the U.S.
The man you love to hate
Villain
Evil man
Public enemy #1
Bad news for Panama, bad news for the region
Narco-terrorist
A pockmarked Jesse James Americans could love to hate
Rivals Qadaffi and the Ayatollah
America's favorite bad guy
Destroyer of his people and his own country
Arrived in manacles/handcuffed and in chains
Reluctant and defiant defendant
Corrupt
Cut the cards and came up with a deuce
Looked helpless and afraid
Once worth millions, a bible, comb and toothbrush is all he has left/man
   who lost it all
Began to cry/in tears
Took $5 million in bribes
Infamous defendant
Tyrant
Unwanted guest
Fugitive/fugitive former dictator
Facing possible criminal charges
Would cause turmoil, conflict and violence
A criminal, not a political refugee
Continued source of danger and threats
Bush's nemesis
Monster
Got $10 million in drug money/$10 million in drug money stashed in
   overseas accounts
Trying to save his own skin
Painted as devil

Words/Phrases Judged to Be Neutral or Ambiguous
Strongman
Used to be on very close terms with Washington
Just might pull it off
Working class
Liked to strut and stand up to the Americans
Knows how to play to Panamanian nationalism
Favorite of Omar Torrijos
Was on CIA payroll/CIA informant/CIA agent/ CIA operative
Ruled by proxy
No longer inspired fear
Rated a visit from VP Bush

Prisoner
Wrote to the Pope proclaiming his innocence
His strength was always his ability to threaten, his greatest weakness his [inability] to command loyalty
Remains [Panamanian] government's most pressing problem
Dressed in four-star general's uniform/wearing uniform of a Panamanian general
Captured illegally by American military
Immune from prosecution
Defendant
Former general
Supreme ruler/maximum ruler
Dismissed as commander of Panama's military
Former leader
Still dominates Panamanian politics, even as a fugitive
Secretly worked for the Americans for years/worked for the U.S. over a long period
Mr.
Safe and sound
Fate in the hands of lawyers and diplomats
Vulnerable
Main target/prime target/prime purpose of invasion
The man they cannot catch
Key man in the battle for Panama
Still a force to be reckoned with
Despondent/despondent and recluse
Feeling defeated
Former U.S. agent
Stumbled
In good frame of mind
Glad-handing with top U.S. military brass
Feared he might commit suicide
Impenetrable
Virtually a prisoner
Head of government/head of state
De facto ruler
Panamanian leader
Moody, alone and isolated
Proclaimed himself maximum leader
Had a very close working relationship with Oliver North and William Casey
The pineapple
The pineapple is in the can
Looking tired, thin and nervous
Joked with U.S. officers
Lost his composure, clutched a bible and cried
Has most to fear
Normal

Tired and depressed
Walking expressionless
Growing more isolated
Just beyond the U.S. military's reach
Ousted ruler
Man who was judge and jury
Saw handwriting on the wall
He's not gonna laugh at us
So exhausted he could hardly speak
Not acting like a captive
He's not out threatening lives of Americans
Former chief of state

George Bush

Words/Phrases Judged to Be Positive
Asserted leadership effectively
Cool and cautious
Triumphant
Won't bargain with drug dealers and terrorists
Emotional over loss of American lives/emotionally moved
Gets his man
Handled entire Panama problem correctly
Restored democracy in Panama
Is in a strong position
Looks like a commander and chief
The bold, visionary, outstanding, strong leader he's always been

Words/Phrases Judged to Be Negative
Weak and timid
Vulnerable on drugs and education
Was severely criticized for cozying up too much to repressive Chinese and
    Salvadoran regimes
Admitted that someone made the wrong call
Embarrassed
Gonna look awfully bad if he pulls out
Accused of attempting to destabilize Panama and its armed forces
Was called timid, now may becoming trigger-happy
Overreacted

Words/Phrases Judged to Be Neutral or Ambiguous
President/U.S. president
Ever mindful of the legal process
Has only won the battle of Panama, he still hasn't won the war with Manuel
    Noriega
Sure to be hounded by questions which he can duck with a good excuse
Head of CIA in 1970s/former director of CIA
Personally involved in Noriega operations

Suffered embarrassments of Iran-Contra and survived
Does not want a fight with the Vatican
Not too much of a wimp any more
Choking back tears
As VP, opposed to Noriega's going to Spain [in negotiated exile]
Personally involved in negotiations/diplomatic maneuvers re Vatican and
  Noriega

Guillermo Endara
Words/Phrases Judged to Be Positive
U.S.-backed leader
Rightful leader of the country
Started to govern
Won 74% of popular vote in last May's election
Popularly elected
Certified as victor [in election]
Opposition leader beaten by Noriega's soldiers

Words/Phrases Judged to Be Negative
Smug
Caught in a contradiction
Has no real power

Words/Phrases Judged to Be Neutral or Ambiguous
President/Panamanian president/new president/ newly sworn in president
Reveling in his own popularity
Confirmed in office
Hunted by Noriega
Head of state
Must convince the world he can rule without U.S. troops
A free man
At work

Chapter 14

The End of the Cold War?
Cuba as Seen on North American
TV Network News, 1988–1992[1]

WALTER C. SODERLUND, RONALD H. WAGENBERG
AND STUART H. SURLIN

Between 1988 and 1992, the international system experienced a series of profound changes. The fall of the Berlin Wall in late 1989 signaled the end of communism in Eastern Europe, while the failed coup in Russia in the summer of 1991 marked the end of communist control in that country as well. These events ended the Cold War, which had set the framework for international politics for over forty years, and, while scholars debated what it would look like and what forces would drive it, a "New World Order" was widely proclaimed (Huntington 1993; Sideri 1993; Cox 1994; Pfaltzgraff 1994). It is for those years (1988 to 1992) that the coverage of Cuba on Canadian and American television news is examined in this chapter.

From 1947 to 1992 the Cold War between the United States and the Soviet Union was waged on a global scale. While no Western Hemisphere country completely escaped the machinations of the Cold War, Guatemala, Guyana, the Dominican Republic, Chile, Nicaragua, El Salvador and Grenada were deeply affected. Cuba, however, was the preeminent flash point for U.S.-U.S.S.R. conflict in the hemisphere (Huberman and Sweezy 1969; Dominguez 1978; Geyer 1991; Oppenheimer 1992). Most analysts agree that the few weeks of the Cuban Missile Crisis of 1962 marked the closest point during the Cold War where a full-scale nuclear war between the U.S. and the U.S.S.R. could have begun (Blight, Nye and Welch 1987; Garthoff 1988). Thus, not discounting U.S. hostility to Fidel Castro's domestic policies and their impact on U.S. interests, it was Cuba's role as a military ally/

base/surrogate that allowed the U.S.S.R. to project its military power into not only the Western Hemisphere, but also Africa. And it was this role that magnified U.S. opposition to the Cuban Revolution (Bernell 1994).

Canada was a full partner of the United States in the Cold War, as evidenced by military alliances such as the North Atlantic Treaty Organization (NATO) and the North American Aerospace Defense Command (NORAD). Nonetheless, a desire to conduct an independent foreign policy as a middle power frequently led Canada to adopt postures different from their ally. None has turned out to be as significant as Canada's independent policy on Cuba. A historical detachment from Latin America had meant that few Canadian vital interests had developed in the area that were threatened by the Cuban Revolution. Thus, Canadian policy makers did not accord Cuba the same prominence as did their American counterparts. Indeed, as time passed, the maintenance of some degree of normalcy in relations with Cuba was viewed as a testament to a "made in Canada" foreign policy and a symbol of Canadian nationalism.

The contribution of mass media to understanding the world beyond one's range of personal experience is wide-ranging (Galtung and Holmboe Ruge 1965; Stevenson and Shaw 1984; Thompson 1988; Bennett 1988). We know that there is *reality* as well as multiple media portrayals of that reality (Tuchman 1978; Gans 1979; Chang, Shoemaker and Bredlinger 1987), and, as Todd Gitlin has summarized the relationship, the role of media "is to certify reality as reality" (1980, p. 2). The question is which "reality" is certified? That is to say, which of myriad events are reported and in what perspective are those events portrayed?

The momentous changes in the international system from 1988 to 1992 resulted in basic alterations in the structure of international conflict, which led to significant foreign policy changes on the part of both Russia and the United States. In such circumstances media were offered an opportunity to reassess the frameworks employed to explain international events. In this regard, Deutsch and Merritt argue that perceptions of international reality (in their word, "images"), once formed, act as filters or screens through which new information on the subject must pass (1965, pp. 133–137). For Cuba, to what extent did Cold War imagery outlive the Cold War?

The summary justice employed by the Castro government against officials of the Batista government in the immediate post-revolutionary period, the souring of relations between Cuba and the United States, followed by the abortive Bay of Pigs invasion in 1961 and the move by Cuba into the Soviet orbit culminating in the Missile Crisis of October 1962 established a powerful set of negative filters through which events involving Cuba and Castro, in subsequent years, were interpreted by U.S. media. In a study of Fidel Castro's image presented in *The New York Times* from 1953 to 1992, it was found that beginning in 1988, precisely when changes in the international system suggested a reduced threat emanating from Cuba, Castro was presented in a more negative manner. For the first time, including the hostility-filled years of the 1960s, there was a focus on the negative aspects of Castro the *person*, as opposed to Castro the *politician* (see chapter 2, this volume, as well as Lewis 1960; McCaughan and Platt 1988).

It appears that U.S. media would have four main framing or filter options available for dealing with Cuba in the post–Cold War era (Gamson 1989; Entman 1991; Iyengar 1991). First, they could retain the Cold War frame of conflict and confrontation toward both Cuba and Castro without noticeable change. Second, they could depart radically from the earlier frame, presenting a positive "forgive and forget" image, characterizing Cuba as an emerging nation and Castro as a misguided but nevertheless honorable leader. Third, they could separate the image of Cuba the nation from that of the man who has dominated its politics for the past forty years; Cuba could be presented in either a positive or negative fashion, while Castro could be presented in the opposite direction. Presenting Cuba and Cubans as a country and a people in need of liberation from a demented, power-hungry dictator who has lost touch with world developments is probably the most likely scenario for the third option. Fourth, as suggested by the change in *The New York Times* treatment of Castro beginning in 1988, we could see an increased coupling of Fidel Castro's leadership with the progressively severe problems faced by Cuba in the post–Cold War period. This frame would result in the image of the country and its leader in fact coming closer together. Each of these options offers a "reality" that U.S. media can choose, independent of the facts of the situation. Each version of reality could serve as a possible framework for presenting facts regarding Cuba as events occurred over the period of the study. Perhaps there is a fifth filter more relevant for Canadian media. This would frame Cuba as a relatively unimportant, small country that, having lost its Cold War status, is no longer considered to be particularly newsworthy; hence, coverage would drop off.

U.S.-Canadian Comparisons

This study compares U.S. and Canadian television news treatment of Cuba during a critical period of transition from one world order to another. As noted above, Canadian foreign policy toward Cuba had diverged considerably from that of the United States (Baranyi 1985; Haglund 1987; Rochlin 1988; Gorham 1992). Most notably, Canada never recognized the U.S.-imposed economic embargo of the island and continued to carry on diplomatic and trade relationships with Cuba. Pierre Trudeau, Canadian prime minister for most of the period 1968 to 1984, developed a warm personal relationship with Fidel Castro, and in 1976 the Trudeau family made a highly visible visit to Cuba. Canadian foreign policy differences with the United States made Canada wary of entry into the Organization of American States, which finally occurred in 1990, because successive Canadian governments feared that membership would either lead to conflict with the U.S. over Latin American policy (Cuba in particular) or could create circumstances in which Canada might be perceived as a foreign policy handmaiden to the United States. In any event, one would expect that coverage of Cuba in the Canadian mass media would have less of an ideological basis than would be the case in the United States. If a country's mass media broadly reflect government policy (Parenti 1986; Herman and Chomsky 1988), one would hypothesize a less negative image of Cuba and Castro on Canadian, as opposed to American, television news and predict further that this less negative image would become even more evident with the end of the Cold War. In the case of American TV networks, in addition to expecting a more negative portrayal of the island and its leader overall, it is debatable as to which reality filter U.S. television would follow when moving from a Cold War to a New World Order relationship with Cuba and Castro. Thus, there are two interrelated questions that guide our inquiry: (1) What differences were there in Canadian and American TV presentations and images of Cuba and Castro, and (2) how did the end of the Cold War affect TV coverage of Cuba in each country?

Methods

During the five-year period of this study, we chose to examine stories that focused primarily on events in Cuba, rather than those that dealt with essentially domestic American concerns, such as Cuban immigration or the power of the Cuban-American lobby in American politics—questions that had no Canadian counterparts. Nine issue clusters emerged:

1. Drug trafficking and Castro's relationship with Panama's Manuel Noriega;
2. Cuba's military withdrawal from Angola;
3. Mikhail Gorbachev's visit to Cuba and Cuban-U.S.S.R./ Russian relations;
4. The trial and execution of General Arnaldo Ochoa;
5. Cuba's economic crisis;
6. Cuban human rights abuses;
7. The Pan American Games;
8. Fidel Castro as ruler and personality;
9. New insights into the Cuban Missile Crisis as gleaned from a series of meetings between Cuban, Soviet and American participants.

The total data set is composed of 207 stories; 148 aired on the evening newscasts of the major American networks (ABC, CBS and NBC), and fifty-nine aired on similar newscasts of the two leading English-language Canadian networks (CBC and CTV).

Data for the American networks were supplied by the TV News Archive, Vanderbilt University in the form of video recordings of actual news stories, while Canadian data were transcripts of news story texts supplied by the National Media Archive of the Fraser Institute.[2] Unfortunately, the lack of Canadian video recordings made a comparison of visual dimensions of stories impossible. All coding was done by the authors, working both separately and together. Stories were examined on a number of variables such as placement in the newscast, running time, format, as well as race and gender of all anchors, reporters, experts and sources (Soderlund and Wagenberg 1995). Initial intercoder reliability on such items was 96% (Holsti 1969, p. 140), and in the relatively few cases where disagreements could not be resolved, missing data values were assigned. Intercoder reliability on dimensions such as thematic evaluation, source favoritism, text and visual bias were established at 88%, and on these dimensions, unresolved coding disagreements were settled by placing them in the neutral category.

Positive and negative images of Cuba and Castro were constructed in the following manner. First, all descriptive words and phrases used with respect to country and leader were recorded. These were then collated and sent to a panel of six experts in the areas of politics, communication and Latin American Studies, with instructions to adopt an American perspective and categorize each descriptor as to whether it reflected positively or negatively on the island or its leader. If unsure, the descriptor was to be judged neutral or ambiguous. If at least five of the six members on the panel (83%) categorized a particular descriptor as either positive or negative, it was so counted and used in our analysis. (See the full list of descriptors and how they were coded at the end of this chapter.) Neutral or ambiguous descriptors were omitted from the analysis.[3]

Findings

Cuban politics are a concern in the domestic politics of the United States, while in Canada they are not. Consequently, it is not surprising that over the five-year period, Canadian networks each averaged just under thirty Cuban stories, while the American networks averaged just under fifty each. This reflects an average of six stories per year for each Canadian network and ten Cuban stories for each U.S. network. In addition to the volume of coverage, the U.S. networks gave far more prominence to Cuban stories, whether by use of experts to put events into context (20% versus 5%), placement of stories in leading positions in the newscast (35% versus 10%) or time allotted to them (26% over three minutes versus 10% over three minutes). In short, Cuba was a far more important area of interest for American media gatekeepers than it was for their Canadian counterparts.

With respect to changes over the five-year period, media interest in Cuba was higher prior to the key events that marked the end of the Cold War rather than after. Cuban coverage was greatest in 1988 and 1989 (26% and 31% of the total, respectively) and decreased thereafter (15% in 1990, 17% in 1991 and 11% in 1992). Moreover, interviews with experts peaked in 1989 and 1990, while both assignment of Cuban stories to leading positions in newscasts and allocation of greater time also peaked in 1988 and 1989.

Table 14.1 shows the relative salience of the nine Cuban issue clusters in Canadian and U.S. television news reports. By a fairly wide

Table 14.1

Television Coverage of Cuban Issue Clusters*

	Percentage of Stories Focusing on Particular Issue Clusters		
	Can	US	Total
	N=59	N=148	N=207
Drugs/Panama Connection	0	14%	10%
Withdrawal from Angola	17%	14	15
Gorbachev's Visit/U.S.S.R. Relations	20	22	21
Ochoa Trial and Execution	5	7	7
Economic Crisis	46	18	26
Human Rights Abuses	3	5	5
Pan American Games	3	5	5
Fidel Castro	2	10	7
Missile Crisis	3	6	5
	99%	101%	101%

*Sample not large enough for statistical analysis

margin, the three most newsworthy issues in both Canada and the United States were (1) Cuba's economic crisis; (2) changing relations with the U.S.S.R./Russia, centered on Gorbachev's visit in the spring of 1989 (which brought the anchors of the three U.S. networks, but not the Canadian, to Havana); and (3) Cuba's military withdrawal from Angola, which ended a fifteen-year presence on the African continent.

American media interest in Cuba was spread more evenly across issue clusters than was the Canadian, with relations with the U.S.S.R./ Russia eliciting the greatest amount of American coverage. American networks also gave both Cuba's drug connection to Panama and Fidel Castro as person and leader, more coverage than these issues generated on Canadian TV news broadcasts. In contrast, Cuba's economic crisis was for Canadian television news by far the most compelling issue. In fact, despite the much greater American coverage of Cuban issues generally, there were exactly the same number of stories focusing on the state of the Cuban economy (twenty-seven) featured on the two

Canadian networks as there were on the three American networks. Perhaps this reflects Canadian interest in Cuba as a trade partner rather than as an ideological adversary.

Data in Table 14.2 allow us to identify which specific dimensions of Cuban domestic and international activity came under journalistic scrutiny and to interpret the attitudes portrayed with respect to these dimensions by the networks in the two countries. A statistically significant finding is evident only for the question of Cuba's role in international politics. This might reflect the fact that while Canadian and American journalists share a distaste for communism, dictatorships and the dictators that lead them, Canadian broadcasters seem significantly less worried about the impact of this particular communist dictatorship and its leader on hemispheric and world politics. That differences between the two countries are not evident on other dimensions indicates that a common interpretation of Cuba's domestic realities has not led to a shared interpretation of its external impact. This difference is reflected in neutral/ambiguous Canadian evaluations rather than negative ones.

Table 14.3 shows trends in the evaluation of Cuba from 1988 to 1992. Following the end of the Cold War, there was both a declining interest in Cuba's international role and, paradoxically, a more negative evaluation of that role. Reasons for this are not entirely clear; however, we suggest two possible explanations. First, 1988 and 1989 may represent a temporary upswing in interest in and positive evaluation of Cuba's international role, accompanying the military withdrawal from Angola. We have no prior benchmark from which to measure. Second, the increased negative evaluation, peaking in 1990, might reflect a bewilderment on the part of journalists regarding Castro's stubborn adherence to communism at a time when it was in worldwide retreat. Whatever the cause, Cuba's international role, although not the subject of as much press interest, was evaluated more negatively at the end of the study than it had been at the beginning. Further, while the trends are subtle, "the country in general" is presented more favorably and less negatively after the Cold War ended, while Fidel Castro's earlier modest amount of favorable coverage fell to zero in 1992 and his negative coverage peaked at 78%.

Data in Table 14.4 show the frequency with which sources appeared in newscasts. Cuban sources (citizens on the street, the Cuban government and Fidel Castro) contributed to Canadian news

𝒯𝑎𝑏𝑙𝑒 14.2

Percentage of Stories Containing Positive, Neutral/Ambiguous and Negative Evaluations of the Cuban Revolution, by Country

Dimension of Revolution	Can	US	Total
International Role	N=33	N=94	N=127
Positive	0	7%	5%
Neutral/Ambiguous	61%	39	45
Negative	39	53	50
X^2=5.85 DF=2, sig<.05			
Country in General	N=35	N=86	N=121
Positive	9%	13%	12%
Neutral/Ambiguous	31	19	22
Negative	60	69	66
X^2=2.49 DF=2, NS			
Fidel Castro	N=31	N=85	N=116
Positive	7%	6%	6%
Neutral/Ambiguous	42	34	36
Negative	52	60	58
X^2=.67 DF=2, NS			
Economy	N=23	N=47	N=70
Positive	0	2%	1%
Neutral/Ambiguous	4%	11	9
Negative	96	87	90
X^2=1.32 DF=2, NS			
Political System	N=18	N=43	N=61
Positive	0	0	0
Neutral/Ambiguous	11%	7%	8%
Negative	89	93	92
X^2=.28 DF=2, NS			
Social Programs*	N=4	N=14	N=18
Positive	100%	64%	72%
Neutral/Ambiguous	0	15	11
Negative	0	21	17

*Sample not large enough for statistical analysis

Table 14.3

Percentage of Stories Containing Positive, Neutral/Ambiguous and Negative Evaluations of the Cuban Revolution, by Year

Dimension of Revolution	1988	1989	1990	1991	1992	Total
International Role	N=51	N=43	N=18	N=12	N=3	N=127
Positive	6%	9%	0	0	0	5%
Neutral/Ambiguous	55	44	28%	33%	33%	45
Negative	39	47	72	67	67	50
Country in General	N=7	N=50	N=21	N=27	N=16	N=121
Positive	0	8%	10%	22%	13%	12%
Neutral/Ambiguous	14%	26	19	19	25	22
Negative	86	66	71	59	62	66
Fidel Castro	N=11	N=47	N=26	N=23	N=9	N=116
Positive	9%	4%	8%	9%	0	6%
Neutral/Ambiguous	36	36	31	48	22%	36
Negative	55	60	62	44	78	58
Economy	N=2	N=21	N=16	N=24	N=7	N=70
Positive	0	5%	0	0	0	1%
Neutral/Ambiguous	0	14	19%	0	0	9
Negative	100%	81	81	100%	100%	90
Political System	N=0	N=28	N=15	N=9	N=9	N=61
Positive	0	0	0	0	0	0
Neutral/Ambiguous	0	7%	13%	0	11%	8%
Negative	0	93	87	100%	89	92
Social Programs	N=1	N=6	N=3	N=5	N=3	N=18
Positive	100%	67%	67%	60%	100%	72%
Neutral/Ambiguous	0	0	33	20	0	11
Negative	0	3	0	20	0	17

stories to a far greater extent than was the case in the United States, where the U.S. administration, American experts, prominent Americans and members of Congress all made more frequent contributions to

Table 14.4

Number of Times Leading News Sources Used for Stories About Cuba (first four sources only[4])

	Can	US	Total
Cubans on the Street	30	43	73
Cuban Government	16	29	45
Fidel Castro	13	30	43
American Experts	9	27	36
U.S. Administration	7	29	36
Prominent Americans	4	24	28
Cuban Dissidents	6	14	20
Cuban Defectors	4	14	18
U.S. Congress	0	17	17
Soviet/Russian Government	3	13	16

newscasts. Noteworthy by their absence in Canadian newscasts are the contributions of Canadian experts and politicians. This, without doubt, reflects the lower place occupied by Cuban affairs on the Canadian as opposed to the American foreign policy agenda.

Despite the different mix of sources, the favorable to unfavorable balance in evaluation was exactly the same for both countries: 39% favorable to 61% unfavorable. Given the predominantly negative treatment of Cuba already noted, it is a testament to the goal of balanced reporting that the favorable/unfavorable ratio of sources is not more skewed than it is (data not shown in tabular form).

In terms of overall story text, while neither Canadian nor American reporting had a significant pro-Cuban bent, American reporting had a stronger anti-Cuban direction than did Canadian (56% negative as opposed to 39%). Visuals on the American networks, again, reflected a measure of balance, as the number of positive visuals almost equaled those that reflected negatively on Cuba (12% to 13%) (data not shown in tabular form).

Taken as a whole, these findings reflect some interesting Canadian-U.S. differences as well as similarities that may be related to either differences in the news gathering process, differing attitudes of news producers or a combination of the two. Working with an identical balance of positive and negative sources, U.S. networks were decidedly more anti-Cuban in their textual representation of Cuba than were Canadian networks. Interestingly, however, this negative thrust was not reflected in the visuals that accompanied the U.S. story texts.

Percentages of positive and negative descriptors used with respect to Cuba and Fidel Castro in the Cuban stories under study are reported in Table 14.5. For both Canadian and American networks, portrayals were overwhelmingly negative (90% for Cuba and 80% for Castro). It is interesting to note that although the percentage of positive and negative descriptors for both Cuba and Castro are basically the same in both countries, in terms of actual number of descriptors used, Canadian stories tended to focus more on the country than on its leader, while American stories tended to focus more on Fidel Castro than on Cuba.

Table 14.5

Percentage of Descriptors Reflecting Positively and Negatively on Cuba and Fidel Castro (neutral and ambiguous descriptors omitted)

	Can	US	Total
Cuba	N=118	N=203	N=321
Positive	9%	10%	10%
Negative	91	90	90
Fidel Castro	N=76	N=273	N=349
Positive	17%	21%	20%
Negative	83	79	80

Conclusion

Two questions were posed initially in this chapter: (1) Were there differences in Canadian and American TV news portrayals and evaluations of Cuba, and (2) how were these changes in coverage related to the end of the Cold War?

First, it has to be reemphasized that Cuba is simply not as important a story for Canada as it is for the United States. There are many reasons for this. There is no large Cuban émigré population in Canada, which could have the effect of domesticizing Cuban affairs as is the case in the United States. Beyond that, Canadian-Cuban relations have not been characterized by the hostility evident in U.S.-Cuban relations; trade and diplomatic relations have been maintained (there was even a modest Canadian foreign aid program for Cuba); and Cuba has become a popular tourist destination for a large number of Canadians. Thus, for Canada, Cuba is a somewhat interesting third world country with severe economic problems, rather than a hornet's nest of evil as seen by many in the United States. Also, over time, Cuba has represented, for at least some Canadians of a strongly nationalistic persuasion, an opportunity to underline the type of foreign policy choices that should differentiate Canada from its dominant neighbor.

Given this context, it is somewhat surprising that the coverage of Cuba on the Canadian networks is so similar to U.S. coverage. On only two evaluative dimensions does Canadian news coverage seem less anti-Cuban than American coverage: Cuba's international role seems less worrisome and text evaluations are not as negative. On other dimensions, coverage of Cuba in the two countries is virtually indistinguishable.

In making these assessments we must recognize that objective conditions in Cuba warrant negative appraisals: Cuba is a country with extremely serious economic problems and it is led by a communist dictator who has never tested his popularity at the polls. Such characteristics merit no more praise in Canadian newsrooms than in those of other democratic countries, including the United States.

One other factor bears mentioning as a reason for similarities in Cuban coverage. Thirty-seven of the fifty-nine Canadian news stories featured a reporter in the field. Twenty of these reporters were Canadian, fifteen were American, while two were from other countries. Thus, 25% of all Canadian stories on Cuba (all on the CTV network) had significant input from American reporters. This situation would lend credence to complaints from some Canadian nationalists regarding the excessive "American spin" put on foreign news reporting, were it not for the fact that CBC reporting, done exclusively by Canadian reporters, was not significantly different from that of CTV.[5]

The events marking the end of the Cold War in 1989 and 1990 appear to have heightened media interest in Cuban affairs, especially when Gorbachev visited the island and Cuban troops came home from

Angola. Interest in the misfortunes besetting the Cuban economy and
the enduring dictatorial behavior of the Cuban government continued
throughout the study period, but by 1992, media interest in Cuba had
declined to just over a third of the 1989 peak. It is also apparent that
the evaluations of Cuba and its leader were not altered in any
fundamental way by the demise of communism in its Soviet/Russian
military ally and economic benefactor. Cuba, its political system, its
economic system and its long-time leader were portrayed negatively at
the beginning, in the middle and at the end of this critical transition
period in world order. Even though Cuba no longer posed a strategic
threat, the communist political system was seen to remain a bane for
its people. Moreover, these findings hold true for TV news reportage in
both Canada and the United States, although Canadian media did not
choose to dwell on the subject to the extent the American media did. In
summary, while the Cold War may have ended, its demise is not
apparent from an examination of North American television news
coverage of Cuba. Thus, of the possible frames that we indicated might
be used by media in reporting on Cuban stories, the "conflict and
confrontation" frame is most evident, while there is no evidence of the
"forgive and forget" frame. Also, analysis of the positive descriptors
used with respect to Cuba reveals there is little language that suggests
an attempt to orchestrate a "good people/bad leader" scenario.

Clearly international diplomacy offers many instances where
changed circumstances have led to reinterpretations of leaders and
countries; China and Russia are notable recent examples. Such a
reinterpretation was certainly possible for Cuba during the period of
this study. A question that remains at the end of the study is why the
Cold War frame persisted in the absence of the Cold War. An equally
interesting question deals with how American and Canadian media
dealt with the shooting down of the two "Brothers to Rescue" aircraft
by the Cuban air force in February 1996 and the subsequent American
retaliation in the form of the Helms-Burton Bill, which had a direct
negative impact on Canadian business operations in Cuba.

Notes

1.   This chapter is an edited version of "The Impact of the End of the Cold
      War on Canadian and American TV News Coverage of Cuba: Image
      Consistency or Image Change?" which appeared in the *Canadian Journal
      of Communication*, Vol. 23, No. 2 (1998). It is published with permission.

The authors wish to thank Lisandro Pérez and Carmelo Mesa-Lago for constructive criticism on an earlier version of this paper.

2. Both the TV News Archive and the National Media Archive furnished us with stories in unedited form. Neither organization is in any way responsible for analysis or interpretations of the material.

3. We acknowledge with thanks the assistance of Sukhiminder Osahan in the computer analysis of data reported in this study.

4. The first four sources, either cited or actually appearing on the newscast, were coded.

5. There was no consistent difference in the pattern of evaluations between the two Canadian networks. For example, 69% of CTV sources were unfavorable to Cuba as opposed to 63% of CBC sources. However, the CBC was slightly more critical of Cuba's international role than was CTV (42% to 36%) and was far more critical of Cuba as a country than CTV (75% to 47%). On other evaluative items, differences were insignificant.

Chapter 14 Descriptors

Cuba
Words/Phrases Judged to Be Positive
Standard of living is better than in Central America or Caribbean

The revolution has given Cubans a better education system and better health facilities than anywhere in the third world/has healthy and well-educated youth/literary is at 97%/no lack of education

Loves sports

Proud/people are not ashamed of island or revolution

After thirty-one years the revolution is institutionalized

Has potential for tourism

Standard of medical care is very high/medical care is available to all Cubans/ health care is world class/no lack of health care/has state-of-the-art heart surgery/figures on infant mortality continue to be the best in Latin America/medical care is of high quality/no malnourishment

Cubans full of enthusiasm for Pan Am Games/Pan Am Games a source of pride at the worst of times

Signs Angolan Accord at the UN/to withdraw troops from Angola

Change is possible

Is now open for business/will welcome foreign investment and joint ventures

Island of sun and sea breezes/has most beautiful capital in the Caribbean/ picturesque

Model for development in the third world/model in the developing world

Words/Phrases Judged to Be Negative
Communist Cuba/still dedicated to communism/Marxist-Leninist state/ more Marxist-Leninist than ever/communist government/communist for

three decades/hard-line, repressive communist dictatorship/drab, bleak
communist dictatorship/dictatorship/only one party in Cuba, the
Communist Party/perfecting a single Leninist party/largest communist
nation in the Western Hemisphere/will remain staunchly communist/
communism in Cuba is still pretty solid/one of the last places on earth
where people say they believe in Marx and Lenin/one of the last bastions
of communism/only totalitarian-Marxist regime in the West/one of the
last bastions of the hard-line/so far has refused to back away from its
hard-line stance/stands as a government that doesn't change/more Soviet
than the Soviet Union/revolution brought thirty-seven years of strict
communist rule
Soviet military satellite ninety miles off the U.S. coast/important Soviet
outpost in the Cold War/client state of the U.S.S.R./U.S.S.R.'s most faithful
ally in the Americas/for thirty years, has been regarded by much of the
world as a puppet of the Russians/base for Soviet ships and electronic
surveillance/arms supplied by U.S.S.R.
Economy in shambles/economy shakier than usual/likely to suffer economic
collapse/headed for complete economic collapse/outright economic
disaster is near/facing hard economic times/economy is still a basket
case/economy is a maximum mess/economy is stagnating/economy is
in a mess/economy languishes/much underemployment/Marxist
economy doesn't break even/in an economic crisis/teetering on the brink
of economic disaster/economy is in a crisis/headed for complete economic
collapse/economy edged toward collapse/battle against economic
disaster/has big economic problems/economy is crumbling/economy
has been in a tailspin/no hope for the Cuban economy/in a tailspin/is
reeling/failed economic and political system/in a time of economic and
political crisis/only 15% of oil needed is produced/starving for oil/has
rationed tobacco/no meat, no poultry available/bread rationed/starving
for food/shortages of food/no food/lineups for food are longer/rationing
is tighter/prices are higher/shoppers can't find products/people are
fighting over food/egg prices raised/bread is rationed/Cubans know all
too well the trauma of bare shelves/forced to ration fuel, food, and most
basic consumer goods/food and fuel shortages are worsening/people
are facing acute shortages of everything from bread to shoes/ten million
people have to live with rationing and shortages/action taken to cut down
on the use of oil/a growing economic crisis means long lines/lack of fuel
has forced the widespread reintroduction of oxen/nutritional standards
are deteriorating/has implemented deep austerity measures/bracing for
electric power shortages/headed for hard times/facing a bleak future/
facing greatest crisis in thirty-year history/will return to a pre-industrial
society/hard times in Havana/zero option, a return to a kind of pre-
industrial society/facing grim prospects/we will have nothing – nothing/
people are suffering/the pressures of daily life for people are devastating/
all we can do is try to stay afloat/Cubans dreaming of an end to their
economic woes

Guilty of flagrant human rights violations/holds hundreds of political
prisoners/most repressive government in all the Latin American
continent/forty political dissidents arrested/crackdown growing on
dissent/opposition to be crushed/dissidents arrested by security forces/
characterized by human rights abuses/dissidents get thrown into jail/
government controls all demonstrations/repression is tightening/you feel
like you're in a cage/there's no freedom of expression, there's no freedom
there/one party police state that has stifled human rights/lack of freedom
and fear of arrest make life difficult/regime cracked down by arresting at
least two dozen opponents in the last two years/government announced
that it will crush all opposition/no civil liberties exist/no freedom of
speech/no freedom of the press/the neighborhood has ears/opponents
have had it too good for too long/few people dare to criticize the
government out loud/an awful lot here you can't do
Economic hardships are coupled to a rising crime rate
Soviet economic aid to be extended
People don't want to be there/1,600 have fled the island
Soviet aid reduction means hard times ahead/without five billion in Soviet
aid, Castro's revolution would go belly-up/without Soviet aid, cannot
maintain its military machine/economy kept afloat by Soviet goods/faces
a future of shrinking support from U.S.S.R./preparing to get less from
the Soviets/Soviet supply line is virtually cut off/is squeezed by turmoil
in U.S.S.R./Soviet military assistance coming to an end/economy is
dependent on Soviet aid/receives six billion a year in U.S.S.R. aid/receives
5.8 billion in Soviet subsidies/receives five billion in Soviet aid per year/
dependent on U.S.S.R./receives fifteen million per day in Soviet aid/
recipient of one-half of Soviet foreign aid budget/economy is kept afloat
by Soviet aid/recipient of Soviet military aid/for thirty-two years has
been getting trade and aid from the U.S.S.R.
Isolated/growing isolation/growing more isolated every day/even more
isolated/feeling more isolated than ever
Communism is in poor health/party may soon be over/not the best of
times for Cuba/Cubans are tired of being on the outside looking in/
revolution is getting old/little to celebrate in Cuba on the eve of thirty-
seventh anniversary of Moncada attack/after thirty-one years of lineups,
the Cuban revolution is fighting for its life/the party will be over
One of the first countries to go communist not under the heel of the Red
Army
Ruled out multiparty option/rejected multiparty democracy/sticking to
one-party communist rule
Interior ministry cooperated with drug smugglers/drug running is a serious
business/has a role in international drug smuggling/played a major role
in the drug trade/cocaine connection/major drug-trafficking station under
the full protection of Cuban officials/Cuban bases used to help Colombian
drug cartel
Beset by worst scandal since Castro came to power thirty years ago/shaken
by monumental scandal/scandal has hit Cuba hard/rocked by drug

scandal/drug smuggling and corruption is growing/growing drug scandal/drug smuggling and corruption

Defied the U.S. for one-third of a century

May Cuba soon be free/there is hope that 1991 could be the year of liberty

Like a voyage through a time machine/a place that got lost in time/sounds the same as ever/still prefers the old slogans

Cuban gun towers shoot possible Cuban refugees/Cuban version of the Berlin Wall

Shadows can't obscure the reality of Cuba

Standard of living dropped in the 1980s

Only country in the world with a policy of putting AIDS patients in quarantine/AIDS policy is harsh/AIDS policy puts the interests of the state ahead of those of the individual/those who suffer from AIDS treated as pawns in the protection of society

Has a long way to go in the competitive world of Caribbean tourism/hotel accommodations are just a step above seedy

Situation is almost a powder keg/if it continues like this, there's going to be an explosion/light a match and it will blow up/government is walking towards an abyss from which there is no way out/troubled island/we don't have a future/once a communist showpiece/beset by many problems/paradise lost

Perfectly capable of acting on its own in support of revolutionary movements in Latin America

Revolution is set in stone/a totally closed society

Picture postcard communist dictatorship

At 150,000, has the highest per capita number of people under arms/largest military in Latin America/island bristles with armaments

Infrastructure is in decline/run-down buildings/antique cars/compared to the U.S. doesn't look too good/shabby

Its stifling bureaucracy operates on orthodox Marxist thinking

In great debt to the U.S.S.R.

50,000 Cuban troops supported communist government in Angola since 1975/ally to the leftist government of Angola/supported Marxist government in Angola/supports leftist government in Nicaragua and rebels in El Salvador/Cuban troops were fighting anti-communist rebels supported by the U.S.

Rejected timetable for getting troops out of Angola

Profit is a dirty word

Supplying arms to Panama/three planeloads of Soviet weapons flown from Cuba to Noriega/Cuban troop buildup in Panama/one hundred Cuban advisors sent to Panama to help train and supervise Panama's security forces/infusion of Soviet-Cuban arms destabilizing Panama

Old socialist friends are rapidly disappearing/many of its friends are turning away

Police deployed around the Canadian Embassy/has accused Western diplomats of encouraging asylum seekers

An impoverished police state

Its future depends on its connection with the U.S.S.R.

We are back into a kind of besieged fortress mentality
Socialism will collapse unless there is more democracy

Words/Phrases Judged to Be Neutral or Ambiguous
Human rights record is better than it used to be
Not about to go the way of Eastern Europe
Sugar accounts for 75% of everything exported
There are no shortages for tourists
Cubans are anxious to talk but cautious
Model for socialism
Had 50,000 soldiers in Angola/supports Angola
Socialist paradise
Handing out thousands of guns to the people
Not imitators of the U.S.S.R.
Creators of a revolution
Hard to imagine a Cuba without Fidel Castro in power
People not going into the streets to overthrow Castro/most Cubans support
    Fidel Castro/absence of visible dissent
Motorcade carrying the symbol of glasnost passed them by
End of communism is in sight/if roots are gone, how can the rest of the tree
    survive
300 Cubans have AIDS
Vulnerable to the U.S.
People speaking openly of need for change/there is growing dissent/
    characterized by internal dissent
Its rigid system would not collapse overnight
The revolution can succeed Castro/can survive/can survive alone
Getting serious about curtailing drug smuggling
Ordered 750,000 bicycles from China/Havana has turned into a city of cyclists
Perfected baseball
Country of contradictions
Tiny island nation
Has not fulfilled its revolutionary promise
Convinced that the U.S. would invade
Did not become a model for the third world/no longer a model for
    development/no model for third world countries
Worst of times — best of times
Considering reforming its Communist Party system/must revitalize its
    party and institutions/planning to revitalize its system through internal
    change
Change will not mean giving up socialism
Would stick in America's throat
Tropical climate
Revolution is thirty-one years old
Less of a Soviet asset than in the past/an also ran in Russian military
    priorities/doesn't count much in the Soviet scheme of things/strategic
    importance to U.S.S.R. declining/less important as a Soviet base

Secretly warned not to interfere with U.S. troops landing in Grenada
Cuba will improve its system on Cuban terms rather than abandon it

Fidel Castro

Words/Phrases Judged to Be Positive

Has millions of supporters/still a popular figure/is still popular/enjoys
    genuine support/very popular
Viewed almost as a god/he is God
Consistently has shown he functions best when his back is against the wall/
    has always had a way of hanging tough
Wanted to eliminate nuclear weapons worldwide
Once a pretty good [baseball] pitcher
Has a passion for sports
Has built new trade contacts/built new trade contacts across the hemisphere
Has had a remarkable run since 1959
Opening up a little/a new, more moderate Castro/showing a new face
Best leader in the world
We love him
A practical man
A large number of Cubans have been willing to die for him
Determined as ever
Still a father figure who can do no wrong
Wants to work with the U.S. and the rest of Latin America on narcotics
    control/threatened to shoot down drug-running airplanes/had not
    cooperated with drug smugglers/wants to get to the bottom of the drug
    problem/offered the U.S. cooperation to halt drugs/has a new-found
    enthusiasm for attacking drug smuggling/fired a cabinet minister for
    failing to stop drug smuggling/denied Cuban involvement in drug
    trafficking/insisted that Cuba had not cooperated with drug traffickers
No mere supporting player
Proud of Cuban achievements
Powerful, experienced, strong-willed man
Rode in triumph into Havana
Trying hard to make an accommodation with the church/has reconciled
    with the church
Declared Cuba open to the world's capitalists/inviting more Canadian and
    European countries to do business here
Asking for public opinion on how to improve the system
Welcomed participants to Pan American Games
Urged Congress to wage all-out war against crime
Responsible regional leader
Had a good day
Man of impressive talent/his talent is undeniable/a leader like him comes
    along every generation or two
Led a revolution, survived an invasion and a U.S. economic blockade and
    dozens of assassination attempts/for most of his life he has defied the

odds/managed to stay in power during most of the Cold War despite assassination attempts, invasions and a series of economic disasters
Ousted a corrupt dictator
Hero/old guerrilla hero/heroic figure/remains Cuba's #1 hero
Passionate
An icon in the developing world
Will work for improved East-West relations
Delivered most to those who had least
Ready to pull forces out of Africa

Words/Phrases Judged to Be Negative

Communist/communist leader/hard-line communist/communist leader/ communist holdout/communist close to home/embraced hard-core communism/his communist rule/his communist government/communist of the first order/hard-line/vowing to take a harder line/holds a harder line/hard-liner who is not changing/old hard-liner/dug in and stuck in his revolutionary ways/has vowed never to reform hard-line communism/insisting on orthodoxy/vowed never to flirt with capitalism/ real believer in the need for old-fashioned tough communist system/ uncompromising/last of the true believers in old-time communism/last Marxist-Leninist/rigid Marxist
No longer has Soviets to lean on/if the Kremlin pulls the economic plug Castro goes down the drain/impact of cuts in Soviet aid will be severe not just on the economy, but on the government of Fidel Castro trying to survive without Mother Russia/feeling the Soviet economic squeeze/ beginning to talk about cuts in Soviet aid/is being forced to accept that his friendship is just too expensive for Moscow/can't get along without Soviet money/needs Soviet support
His regime is faltering/may be at the end of his rope/his time has come/his downfall predicted/on his way out/can his fall be far off/will be the next to be overthrown/cannot last much longer/just a matter of time/there is evidence that support for Castro is waning/how much longer can he swim against the tide/growing disillusionment with Fidel/opposition standing up to him/growing opposition to him/there is a growing challenge to his government/his government is shaken/the deep faith Cubans had in Castro has been shattered/his leadership is in question/ struggling in his sea of discontent/struggles on/facing greatest challenge yet/faced with challenges on all sides/confidence the Cuban people have in Fidel Castro is being severely tested/many hope he will step down/ more isolated and under greater pressure than ever before/showing signs of strain/must be sweating/has a lot to worry about/increasingly isolated in a changing world/signs of panic in the Castro regime as history leaves it behind/talk of change makes him nervous
Dictator/Cuban dictator/dictator of the old school
Wants capital without capitalism/walks a thin line between his passion for communism and hatred for capitalism and his need for cash

Khrushchev's client/Soviet surrogate around the world/allowed Soviet
missiles in Cuba/Soviet ally/eagerly sent troops to Africa to support
Soviet interests
Prevents change by prohibiting freedom/more likely to crack down than to
loosen up/would never tolerate opposition parties/has no intention of
changing one-party system/whether he will heed the message [need for
greater democracy] is at best doubtful/doesn't tolerate dissent/not
abandoning monopoly of power/his talk of reform little more than that/
his word is law/tough on his opposition/repressing dissent/has not gotten
around to giving his people a political choice/hardly tolerates any dissent/
has a poor record on human rights/has police state manners/most of his
critics have fled/struggling against reform/no sign he will adopt reforms/
man who will not be defied/is not buying democracy/called Western-
style democracy complete garbage/determined to hang on to power/
holds on defiantly/defiant as ever
Needs crisis to maintain his regime/can demonstrate to Cuban people that
they are victims of external aggression/played on innate hatred of
America to stop public opinion swinging against him/warning Cubans
about U.S. attack/used executions to send a message to his people: outside
aggressors are causing Cuba's problems. The system is not to blame
One of the few communists left standing in the world today/sticks out like
a sore thumb/as out of place on a beach on a hot day as he is in the world
community/isolated and alone/out of step/totally isolated from outside
reality/out of step with the new world of democratization/out of step
with world communism/tries to defy history/how much longer will the
applause [for him] last/aging comandante/aging/getting old/aging leader
who refuses to change/an older Castro/old revolutionary/aging hippie/
seemed mired in an old drama/once was leading the parade of events,
today he's at the tail end/there is a profound sadness about him
Admonishes the U.S./denounces the U.S./speech is full of anti-American
rhetoric/fiercely critical of the U.S./has flourished by taking on the U.S./
challenged the US. around the world/set to revolutionize the U.S.
backyard/his destiny is to spend his life in conflict with the U.S./seized
U.S. properties worth billions of dollars/his anger at the U.S. started a
long time ago and will last as long as Castro does/taunted eight American
presidents/an anathema to eight U.S. presidents/can still challenge the
U.S. and get away with it/doing everything he can to circumvent the U.S.
embargo
Refuses to match new economic opening with political freedom
If he doesn't change his ways soon, the country is likely to suffer complete
economic collapse/faces a battle against economic disaster
Assassin
Gangster
Ridiculed democratic reforms in Eastern Europe/has no use or time for
changes sweeping through Eastern Europe/changes in Eastern Europe
challenge everything he stands for/refuses to get caught in the whirlwind
of change sweeping through Eastern Europe/taking a divergent path

from Gorbachev/doesn't like Gorbachev's brand of communism/failed
to embrace perestroika and glasnost/no great supporter of Gorbachev's
reforms and more open brand of communism/thinks Gorbachev's
perestroika is a betrayal of communism/has complained about
perestroika/criticized perestroika/publicly criticized changes in the
U.S.S.R./perestroika won't work here/perestroika and glasnost no way/
rejects adopting glasnost /may turn a deaf ear to Gorbachev's demands/
thumbs nose at Gorbachev/not receptive to Gorbachev's thinking/differs
from Gorbachev as to where to go from here
Wanted a preemptive nuclear strike against the U.S./asked Khrushchev to
launch a nuclear strike against the U.S.
Warning Cuban people about a bleak future/trying to put fire in Cuban
bellies/has told his people to get ready for a drastic solution/warns people
to prepare for a special period of great difficulty/has only bad news/
taking the Cuban people back in time
Responsible for staggering levels of human suffering
One of Daniel Ortega's heroes
Rejects ideas that are not his own
Old fashioned
Grayish beard/beard is graying/graying and thinner than in recent past/
hair is starting to fall away
Trapped in a way
Eliminated Ochoa because Ochoa was a political rival/using Ochoa trial to
eliminate a popular rival/wanted to get rid of Ochoa
Is damaged goods/his image is blemished/his message is tarnished/in
trouble internationally/cracked down on drug smuggling to save his
image/suffered a public relations disaster
Some bum who calls himself a communist and won't shave
Facing the biggest scandal of his career
Draconian/practices severe and swift justice/ordered trials and executions
Long-time protector of the U.S. fugitive Robert Vesco
Insincere
Nothing happens in Cuba without Castro knowing about it/gets to decide
who says what and when/what happens here basically boils down to
Fidel/everything begins and ends with Fidel/I'm in charge and don't
think there's anyone else around/has final say in Cuba
Knew of drug smuggling all along/involved in drug smuggling/moving
drugs to U.S./mediated dispute over profits between Colombian drug
lords and Noriega/has not stopped drug smuggling/really wants to cover
up something
Castro took our future
His police take no chances
Supports communist insurgency in El Salvador
Does not respond to negotiations, only responds to pressure
Hasn't had too many victories since 1970
His wardrobe is from Hart, Shaftner and Karl Marx
Believes in Mao's adage that power comes from the barrel of a gun

Under increasing international pressure to allow greater freedom/Western leaders pressuring Soviets to cut him off
Afraid of holding a plebiscite
More on the defensive than usual
Practiced an expansionist foreign policy
Loaded up the Mariel boat lift with criminals and mentally ill
"Socialism or death" is still his battle cry/says it's his brand of socialism or death/"socialism or death"/"fatherland or death"/"patria o muerte"/"this island will remain Cuban as long as there is a Cuban with a loaded rifle still alive willing to fight for it"
Only radical that remains in power governing a communist state
Enjoys the diplomatic profile that association with Moscow gives him
Worked with Noriega to circumvent U.S. blockade/did business with Noriega/has close business dealings with Noriega/Latin America's odd couple (with Noriega)
Likened to Stalin and Mao
Replacing economic incentives with ideological ones/banned farmers markets in 1986/found profit unacceptable
Berated Spain and the U.S.
Vows Cuba and socialism will survive/hopes to save socialism, not abandon it/will stay on the road to communism/"capitalism will never come back to our country"/vision was and remains to create a socialist paradise/stayed true to his name, faithful to his own vision of Cuban socialism/believes in moral persuasion/determined to prevent Cuba from becoming that next communist domino/insists Cuba will never change/still fighting the revolution
Admitted Cuba's trade with some Eastern European countries had practically disappeared
Doing what he can to hang on to his Soviet friends
Cubans wonder whether his luck has run out/50-50 chance of a popular uprising against him
All the setbacks have failed to persuade Castro to introduce reforms

Words/Phrases Judged to Be Neutral or Ambiguous
Is center stage/is always the star of the show/loves the spotlight/genius for theatrics/theatrical communist leader/a dramatic and charismatic player who knows how to command the stage
President/el presidente/head of Council of State
Still has enough popular support to hang on for a few more years/it is not inevitable for him to fall
Denied any role in Kennedy assassination
Sixty-two to sixty-five [actual age]
Double-crossed by Krushchev/bound to feel sold out
Cuddling up with the capitalists
Cuban leader/leader of the revolution
Firmly in power/in control of the Party Congress and the country/very much in control/in command/not counted out yet/has a lot of lasting

power/has tight control of the country/very much in charge/his control
of the army is impressive/controls the army/Castro and his brother have
consolidated their positions/tightening central control/has consolidated
his position/shifting personnel to strengthen his regime/has disarmed
potential enemies/adversaries
Knows there are hard times ahead
Gave up his trademark cigars some years ago
Will transform Soviet Embassy into Museum of Socialist History
If decision to host Pan Am Games were made in today's economy, Cuba
would pass
Vintage Castro
In power for thirty years/more than thirty years/thirty-two years/came to
power in a revolution thirty-two years ago/third-longest-serving world
leader
No alternative to him
Disagrees with President Bush
Rarely talks to U.S. journalists
No movement to overthrow him
Calls Soviet policy shameful
Put his faith in the nation's youth
His dictatorship is alive and relatively well
Furious at his betrayal by the East Bloc/could not contain his fury
Gives off enormous energy while speaking
Soviets never liked him/Gorbachev doesn't like him
Unlikely he will go the way of Ceausescu or Honiker
Warned U.S. against Panama-style invasion
Important symbol of change
Risks people wanting to be just like the U.S.
Going around the country pressing the flesh as if nothing had happened
Trying to improve his image/cleaned up Cuba's image overseas/has
enhanced his image
Feels threatened by the strength of the military and Ministry of the Interior
Ochoa's fate is in his hands
Fought with Ochoa in the revolution/close friend of Ochoa/former comrade
in arms with Ochoa/closely linked to Ochoa
His criticisms of the Soviet Union will have no effect on relationships between
the two countries
Insistent guide
Cannot avoid change/can't resist currents of history
Upstaged Gorbachev
His rock-hard anti-Americanism is softening
A grandfather
A survivor
Claimed victory over AIDS
His interventions in the region coming to an end
In danger of becoming a tragic figure
Maximum leader

Kicked the capitalists out thirty years ago/put an end to capitalist decadence

Decided that beaches could be profitable

José Martí is one of his heroes/idolizes José Martí

Has a reputation for being a world-class talker/likes to make long-winded speeches/droned on

Rarely blamed for problems/so far he has suffered little damage

Expressed concern over Latin American debt

Dressed in fatigue uniform

Mr.

Pure revolutionary/as revolutionary as ever/real revolutionary/ revolutionary in the late 1950s/young revolutionary/maverick revolutionary/a revolutionary giant/still looks like a revolutionary

Has a special reputation in the communist world and Latin America as a heroic figure who stood up to the U.S.

Ignored past Soviet leaders

Was warned not to send troops to Grenada in 1983

Experimented with homegrown perestroika

Doesn't want lectures/wants Moscow's money, not its advice

Defiant/gesture of defiance

Seemed like an old friend of Gorbachev's/praised Gorbachev/downplayed his differences with Gorbachev

Praised Gorbachev as brilliant because he did not tell him what to do

Spoke out against too much change

Not charged with drug smuggling in indictment

Has been sticking to his own path/each country must choose its own path/ reserved Cuba's right to differ from Moscow on domestic policy

Defied the imperialists

Use of the blockade to ignite revolt and oust Fidel Castro may be backfiring, serving as a catalyst for unity and strengthening the country's resolve

Led a disastrous attack against the Batista government/led a disastrous guerrilla raid

Angry

Is closer to the people than any of the former communist leaders in Eastern Europe

Playing a card he's used successfully in the past, an appeal to national pride and independence

Putting on a display of confidence and resolution

Can do without American investment

Challenged Western nations to back up words about freedom with visas

Can no longer rely on pure socialist ideology to keep his country going/ increasingly relying on material incentives/adapting his economy bit by bit

Fiery

Calls upon the Cuban people to save the country, the revolution and socialism/using more than speeches to keep his socialist system alive

Chapter 15

Creation and Development of Media Image: Jean-Bertrand Aristide and Haiti on TV Network News, 1990–1993

WALTER C. SODERLUND AND RALPH C. NELSON

As early as the 1920s, Walter Lippman observed the importance of mass media to the construction of the "pictures in our heads" regarding the world around us (1965). While media's role in the development of public attitudes was recognized, the precise mechanisms by which their influences were exercised remained unclear. In the early 1960s, Cohen advanced Lippman's observation by pointing out that while media might not be successful in telling people "what to think," they were successful in telling them "what to think about" (1963, p. 13). Building on this observation, McCombs and Shaw in the early 1970s introduced the concept of *agenda setting*, arguing that mass media influence public opinion by the amount of coverage they give a particular issue or event (1972).

The McCombs-Shaw study set in train an impressive and extensive line of research that has added tremendously to our understanding of the role of media in attitude formation, both at mass and elite levels. Rogers and Dearing, in a 1988 review and critique of agenda-setting research, point out that in addition to confirming the public agenda-setting role of media, the policy agendas of government decision makers are also influenced by media coverage: "The public agenda seems to have direct, sometimes strong, influence upon the policy agenda of the elite decision-makers, and, in some cases, policy implementation" (1988, p. 579).

Further, it is now apparent that media do more than affect our "what to think about" agenda; they do indeed influence "what" we think — that is, our actual attitudes (Iyengar and Kinder 1987; Iyengar 1991; McCombs and Shaw 1993). And, as Parenti observed, the power of media to shape public attitudes is magnified in those situations where the audience has few if any prior attitudes and lacks alternative sources of information. Citing the example of the Sandinista revolution, he argues that "millions of Americans who have an unfavorable view of the Sandinista government in Nicaragua came to that opinion through exposure to press reports rather than from direct contact with the Nicaraguan revolution. Here then is an original implant; people are prepared to hate and fear a foreign government on the basis of what they read in the papers or hear on television and radio" (1986, p. 22).

It has been apparent since the mid-1970s that, of all media, television has emerged dominant in terms of where Americans go for information and what information they consider most believable (Alger 1989, pp. 22–23), and, as argued by Iyengar, the "latter half of the twentieth century may well go down as the age of television" (1991, p. 1). As a case study of media agenda setting through image making, the research reported in this chapter examines the way in which Jean-Bertrand Aristide, elected president of Haiti in 1990 and deposed in 1991, was presented to the American public on network television news between late 1990 and mid-1993. Aristide offers an excellent case study on the power of television, because prior to his entry into the presidential race in the fall of 1990 and his subsequent election in December, he was a virtual unknown in the chaotic Haitian political milieu in which few Americans could have identified any politician, save the Duvaliers, father and son. Hence, with respect to Aristide, the media were able to write on what was essentially a blank slate.

In this chapter we seek to answer the following questions: (1) What initial image of Aristide was presented to the American viewing audience in the context of his election to the Haitian presidency in 1990; and (2) did Aristide's image change significantly in news reporting on two succeeding crisis points — the coup d'etat that overthrew him in September 1991 and the negotiations to affect his restoration to power in July 1993? In examining TV news coverage of these three events, news stories presented on each of the major TV networks (ABC, CBS and NBC) were compared in detail with respect to salience (number, placement, type and length of items) as well as to anchors, reporters and news sources used. Singled out for special attention is the evaluative direction of coverage accorded to Aristide and his chief opponent following the coup, General Raoul Cédras.[1]

Data for the chapter were derived from videotapes of news stories dealing with Haitian politics on the major evening newscasts of the three major U.S. TV networks as collected by the TV News Archive at Vanderbilt University.[2] All stories dealing with the Haitian election of December 1990, the September 1991 coup, which ousted President Aristide, and the negotiations for his restoration, held in New York City in the summer of 1993 and known as the Governors Island Agreement, comprise the data set. While the actual number of stories is not great (N=39), they represent the universe of coverage of these three key events on American network TV news. Thus, to the extent that the American people had an image of President Aristide during the crucial years leading up to the American "intervasion" to restore him to power in October 1994, arguably these television news stories provided significant raw materials for their initial evaluation of the Haitian president in exile.

Background

The focus on U.S. television news coverage of Haiti and its charismatic political leader is important for at least two reasons. First, the United States plays a very important role in Haitian politics, and as we have stated, mass media play an important role in the formation of public opinion. This in turn becomes a factor in the decision-making elite's consideration of, for example, levels of foreign aid to be granted to a country (Rioux and Van Belle 2001).

Second, the focus on U.S. television coverage of Jean-Bertrand Aristide is especially important because, perhaps even to a greater extent than was the case with Fidel Castro in the early to mid-1950s (see chapter 2), Aristide was largely unknown outside of Haiti prior to his successful run for the presidency in late 1990 (see chapter 11). In this respect the observation of Gitlin that the media tend to "search for the dramatically personal" is crucial (1980, p. 149). "From the media point of view, news consists of events which can be recognized and interpreted as drama; and for the most part news is what is made by individuals who are certifiably newsworthy" (p. 146). Whatever one's assessment of Aristide, he certainly provided a unique, controversial and interesting personality on which the media could focus in their coverage of Haiti.

For better or worse, in the early 1990s democracy in Haiti came to be equated largely with the presidency of Jean-Bertrand Aristide. And when the United States debated the wisdom of the policy of seeking Aristide's return to power following the September 1991 military coup that deposed him, "restoration of democracy" to Haiti literally became synonymous with his return. There was a disastrous false start in October 1993 when an American naval ship was forced to retreat after being denied a docking facility in the Port-au-Prince harbor (Morely and McGillion 1997, Shacochis 1999). Finally, nearly a year later, when the time arrived to put American lives on the line in a military invasion of Haiti to accomplish his restoration, what the American people knew of Aristide and the judgments they made regarding his suitability to lead Haiti out of the dictatorial wilderness depended for the most part on what they had seen and heard about "the little priest" on televison news (Iorio and Huxman 1996). It is these media images of Aristide, generated in the context of TV coverage of three events in Haiti, that this chapter seeks to discover and analyze.

The democratic election of Jean-Bertrand Aristide to the presidency of Haiti was not allowed to stand. Aristide's presidency was marked by controversy,[3] and a little over seven months after taking office, Aristide was overthrown on September 30, 1991 in a military coup carried out by the Haitian army, led by Lt. General Raul Cédras, an Aristide appointee. During and shortly after the coup, an estimated 1,500 supporters of Aristide were killed. In addition, the coup initiated a period of systematic terror and killing directed against the grass roots groups that had supported the deposed president (Constable 1992–93; Packer 1993; Farmer 1994).

The United States, while calling for the restoration of Aristide to the presidency, decided not to intervene militarily to accomplish it.[4] After it became clear that the Haitian army had no intention of surrendering power, the U.S. adopted a policy of forcing the junta to give up power by means of a commercial embargo implemented by the Organization of American States. Despite widespread recognition that the Bush Administration had developed severe misgivings regarding President Aristide (Doyle 1994), the rhetorical policy of seeking his restoration through non-violent means continued to be official U.S. policy.

Haiti, specifically the flow of refugees from the island to U.S. shores and American policy to dealt with it, became an issue in the 1992 presidential election. The Bush Administration began interdicting

Haitian refugees at sea and either returning them directly to Haiti or interning them at the U.S. naval base at Guantanamo Bay, Cuba. During the campaign, Democratic candidate Bill Clinton criticized this treatment of Haitians. However, when he assumed the presidency and was forced to deal with the unpleasant political repercussions of thousands of Haitian refugees landing in Florida, "he tumbled from the high moral ground of the election campaign and announced that the existing policy would remain in place" (Morely and McGillion 1997, p. 367).

Faced with the ongoing problem of refugees and prodded by the Congressional Black Caucus, in the spring of 1993 President Clinton attempted to deal with the Haitian problem by turning up the heat: on the one hand on the Haitian generals to leave, and on the other on President Aristide to accept amnesty for the generals for their involvement in the coup and their subsequent misdeeds. A mutually acceptable resolution, brokered by the UN (the Governors Island Agreement), appeared to have been achieved in the summer of 1993. The agreement set in motion the return of Aristide by October 30, 1993, his return to be preceded by the removal of sanctions, provision of international development assistance, and amnesty and retirement for the generals (Martin 1995, p. 80). This agreement unraveled in early October 1993, in part due to the intransigence of the generals and in part because of a lack of resolve by the U.S. Administration to press for its implementation at a point when a show of force probably would have forced the generals' hand. It was not until September 1994, when faced with an immanent American military invasion, that the Haitian generals decided to cut and run, clearing the way for Aristide's return to the presidency.

Findings

The 1990 election that resulted in Aristide's presidential victory was covered in eight news stories on the major TV networks, the coup that overthrew him generated twenty stories, while the negotiation of the Governors Island Agreement to enable his return to power produced eleven stories. With a total of thirty-nine stories (eleven on ABC, fifteen on CBS and thirteen on NBC), as of the summer of 1993, we see that events in Haiti were definitely not perceived to be of particularly high interest to those producing network TV news in the United States.

Table 15.1

Network Story Characteristics About Events in Haiti

	Percentage of Stories			
	ABC	CBS	NBC	Total
	N=11	N=15	N=13	N=39
Lead Story	0	6%	0	3%
First Three Stories	9%	33	23%	23
One Minute and Under	82	60	54	64
Just Anchor	82	60	54	64
Reporter in Haiti	9	33	0	15
Film	64	87	69	74
Text Violence	55	73	46	59
Visual Violence	18	53	15	31
Dead Bodies	9	13	15	13
Anchor Gender — Male	100	73	100	90
Reporter Gender — Male	100	100	83	93
News Source Gender — Male	100	94	87	93
Anchor Race — White	100	86	100	95
Reporter Race — White	50	14	100	50
News Source Race — White	43	47	50	48

Further, when we look at story characteristics as shown in Table 15.1, we see that only one Haiti story garnered lead status, and less than 25% of Haiti stories were shown in the first three positions in the newscast. Anchors alone reported 64% of stories, which correlates exactly with the 64% of stories that were a minute or less in length. Only 15% of stories featured a reporter actually in Haiti. Stories tended to be brief; nevertheless, 74% were accompanied by film. Violence featured more prominently in coverage than the actual level of violence associated with these particular Haitian events would seem to have dictated, being mentioned in 59% of story texts and shown visually in 31% of stories. Photos or film of dead Haitians appeared in 13% of stories, some of these from files depicting past violent events. Anchors, reporters and news sources used on Haitian stories were at least 90%

male. With respect to race, 95% of story anchors, 50% of reporters and 48% of news sources were white.

Data in Table 15.2 show the major news sources used in the news stories on Haiti. The list is very conventional, with Aristide himself by far the most important news source, followed by spokespeople for the OAS, George Bush and spokespeople for the UN—all involved in attempts to restore Aristide to power. Raoul Cédras was used as a source only three times (all in the context of the Governors Island negotiations), and interestingly, foreigners living in Haiti appeared more often than Haitians themselves as news sources. Given the mix of sources used, it is not surprising that, overall, 92% were coded as expressing opinions favorable toward Aristide (data not shown in tabular form).

Data in Tables 15.3, 15.4 and 15.5 compare the way in which Aristide and Cédras were evaluated on U.S. network TV. Three dimensions were considered: overall text evaluation, overall visual evaluation and the balance between positive and negative descriptors (actual words and phrases) used with respect to the two Haitian leaders.[5] With respect to text and visual portrayals, Aristide came off extraordinarily well, and only on CBS did any story (and on that network only one) reflect negatively overall on the Haitian president. With the exception of the one CBS story, negative information on

Table 15.2

Actual Number of Times Leading News Sources Used for Stories About Events in Haiti, by Network (first four sources in each newscast were coded)

	ABC	CBS	NBC	Total
Jean-Bertrand Aristide	3	6	5	14
OAS	3	3	3	9
George Bush	1	3	2	6
UN	3	0	2	5
Haitian Government	1	3	0	4
Raoul Cédras	0	1	2	3
Foreigners in Haiti	0	3	0	3

Table 15.3

Evaluation of Jean-Bertrand Aristide

| | Percentage of Stories Favorable and Unfavorable | | | |
	ABC	CBS	NBC	Total
	N=11	N=15	N=13	N=39
Text Material				
Favorable	55%	40%	46%	46%
Unfavorable	0	7	0	3
Visual Material				
Favorable	27%	27%	23%	26%
Unfavorable	0	7	0	3

Table 15.4

Evaluation of Raoul Cédras

| | Percentage of Stories Favorable and Unfavorable | | | |
	ABC	CBS	NBC	Total
	N=11	N=15	N=13	N=39
Text Material				
Favorable	0	7%	0	3%
Unfavorable	9%	40%	31%	28%
Visual Material				
Favorable	0	0	0	0
Unfavorable	0	33%	8%	15%

Aristide did not appear significantly in TV news coverage of Haiti. In contrast, nearly 50% of story texts and just over 25% of visual material accompanying stories reflected positively on Aristide. Such was not the case for Aristide's chief political opponent following the September 1991 coup, Raoul Cédras, who was evaluated very negatively. In no story was there a positive visual portrayal of the leader of the military

Table 15.5

Percentage of Descriptors Reflecting Positively and Negatively on Aristide and Cédras

	ABC	CBS	NBC	Total
Aristide	N=15	N=21	N=12	N=48
Positive	80%	57%	83%	71%
Negative	20	43	17	29
Cédras	N=5	N=10	N=10	N=25
Positive	40%	20%	20%	24%
Negative	60	80	80	76

government, and only one story (on CBS) presented a sustained positive verbal portrait of him. On the opposite side, 28% of stories contained negative verbal information, while 15% presented him in a negative visual light. Thus the big picture in the heads of American viewers in the summer of 1993 was "Aristide=Good/Cédras=Bad."

The final table above shows the evaluations of Aristide and Cédras on American TV news based on the actual balance of positive and negative descriptors used with respect to the two leaders. (See the full list of descriptors and how they were coded at the end of this chapter.) It is here where we see the only evidence of more than the most cursory and stereotyped presentations of the two leaders. Negative features of Aristide's character and performance are indeed mentioned, accounting for nearly 30% of total valenced descriptors. This is seen especially in CBS coverage, where 43% of Aristide descriptors are negative. One must bear in mind, however, that these negative references were largely contained in one story, which detailed abuses of power on the part of Aristide while serving as president. Mostly, however, on CBS as well as on the other networks, negative references, while certainly present in the news stories, were simply attributed to Aristide by his opponents and not legitimized by reporters or anchors. Whatever the case, at this micro level he was presented as somewhat less saint-like than was conveyed by overall story evaluations.

In contrast to Aristide, Cédras comes across a good deal less villainous when the actual language used to describe him is examined:

Approximately three-quarters of valenced Cédras descriptors are negative, while one-quarter are positive. It should be noted, however, that Cédras was described with evaluative words or phrases only about half as often as Aristide.

Conclusion

The establishment of democratic governance in Haiti has been a priority policy for the United States at least since 1986 when the Reagan Administration played a key role in getting Jean-Claude Duvalier to leave the island. While some progress toward this end clearly has been made, given the various misadventures along the way (aborted elections, rigged elections, successful and unsuccessful coups and societal violence), it is obviously too early to proclaim that the goal is even near to being achieved. American television news, as of the summer of 1993, had without doubt failed to adequately prepare the American public for the virtually certain difficulties that lay ahead.[6]

Looking at TV news reporting of Haiti, we have to conclude that overall coverage was thin, neglected any in-depth treatment of Haitian society and the roots of problems besetting it, and was inordinately focused on personalities (Aristide in particular) and on violence. With respect to Aristide, with the exception of CBS, coverage was unidimensional, presenting a far more simplistic and positive image of him than his record both prior to and after his election to the presidency would seem to have warranted. Network TV news presented to the American public a largely sanitized image of Aristide, highlighting his democratic credentials and omitting his less than reassuring verbal and behavioral record. Thus, to the degree that television is important in attitude formation, the American public was primed to accept the notion that Haiti's problems were personal rather than systemic and centered on removing an illegal military government and restoring the democratically elected Aristide to power.

This indeed formed the basis for Clinton's policy initiatives toward Haiti, culminating in the fall 1994 invasion that turned at the last minute into an intervention. Haitian problems are so pervasive, deep and multifaceted, however, that any nation wishing to help in their resolution has to be prepared to be involved in the country for the long haul. The style of American TV news reporting on Haiti did not give the American people this message, and was in fact congruous with the early American military withdrawal from Haiti in favor of the UN.

Notes

1. All coding for this chapter was completed by the authors. Intercoder reliability on characteristics of news stories was 96%, while on overall text and visual evaluation it was 89% (Holsti 1969, p. 140).
2. We wish to thank the Vanderbilt TV Archive for providing us with videotapes of news stories; however, the Archive bears no responsibility for the coding or the interpretation of the data reported here.
3. Without doubt the most contentious practice seen under Aristide's presidency was the "necklacing"of supporters of the old Duvalier regime with a gasoline-filled tire. While there is mixed evidence regarding Aristide's stance on this, he did give a speech shortly before the coup that appears not only to condone the practice, but to encourage it. (See Evans-Pritchard 1993.)
4. Bush appears to have reassessed Aristide's suitability to serve as president within days of the coup. The gap between U.S. rhetorical and operational policies became apparent very quickly and no doubt was a factor in the failure of the sanctions policy to oust the generals. (See Doyle 1994; Ives 1995; and Morley and McGillion 1997.)
5. All words and phrases used to describe Aristide and Cédras in the news stories, either by news sources or reporters and anchors, were recorded. These were then collated and sent to a six-member panel of academics in political science and communication studies, who were instructed to adopt an American perspective and judge whether each word or phrase applied to the two leaders would be seen as positive or negative. At least five of the six panel members had to agree on a positive or negative designation in order for it to be so counted. Thus, intercoder reliability on data in Table 15.5 is at least 83%.
6. In ongoing work on the October 1993 attempted restoration of Aristide, we can report that a far more critical portrait of Aristide emerged on American network TV news. Sadly, as the final revisions to this book are being made (summer 2001), Haiti has still not established a political consensus that could form the basis for needed social and economic reforms.

Chapter 15 Descriptors

Jean-Bertrand Aristide

Words/Phrases Judged to Be Positive

Popular/enjoys strong support/enjoys support of poor
Champion of the poor
Widely regarded as front-runner

Brother who wants peace for everybody, who wants justice for everybody, respect for everybody
Apparent winner in Haiti's first truly free election/appears to have been elected president in Haiti's first democratic election/winner in free election
Elected president/legitimate president
First democratically elected president/first freely elected president/took office in February as Haiti's first freely elected president
Promised to return to power
Got help from OAS
Willing to give his life for democracy
Rallying point for fighting back
Powerful lobbyist for his own cause
Walking, talking accusation against the military who overthrew him
Assured of American support/got warm words from Bush
Considered a hero
Pleased with American policy

Words/Phrases Judged to Be Negative
Communist
Leftist/left wing
Man elected as a democrat was becoming a demagogue
Distributed hatred
Promoted social warfare
Employed thugs to murder opponents
Covered up atrocities
Incited mob justice against opponents
Delivered a chilling speech condoning summary executions by placing a burning tire around the victim's neck
Backtracked

Words/Phrases Judged to Be Neutral or Ambiguous
Father/priest/Roman Catholic priest
President
Deposed president/ousted president/exiled president
Thirty-eight years old
Apparent winner
Scheduled to be sworn in next month
Arrested/reported arrested
Served just seven months
Fled to Venezuela
Flew into exile in Venezuela/exiled in Venezuela/forced into exile
Warned of possible new blood bath
Delivered a call to arms
Reported to have signed a letter of resignation
Took his appeal to the White House
Refused to meet General Cédras

Will sign Governors Island Agreement
At first rejected the [Governors Island] Agreement

Raoul Cédras

Words/Phrases Judged to Be Positive
Took over the country to rescue it from horrors of uncertainty
Indicated Aristide's return might be negotiable
Intelligent man
Agreed to step down/agreed to resign by October 30 [1993]

Words/Phrases Judged to Be Negative
Criminal
Pariah
Working as marauders
In disarray
Not clear who is in control/will be some time before military government
    can consolidate power
Isolated politically, diplomatically and economically/needs to be isolated
He wants to shoot us down
Will never accept the restoration of Aristide
Came to New York to buy time, not to find a solution
Wants to test the resolve of the U.S. and UN
Cannot be trusted to give up power
No evident sign of public support

Words/Phrases Judged to Be Neutral or Ambiguous
General/Lt. General
Army chief/army commander/military leader/leader of Haitian military
Still in control

Conclusion[1]

Although this book has not dealt primarily with policy outcomes, we can say with some assurance that what the media cover and how they cover it does get reflected in public policy, albeit in sometimes circuitous ways. While the analysis below was written in the context of post–Cold War humanitarian interventions, arguably the processes involved in gatekeeping, agenda setting, and framing that have underpinned our studies were no less important with respect to the forty-year history of the Cold War in the Caribbean Basin, when the issue was clear (anti-communism) and the enemies of the United States were more readily identifiable.

> How well the forces of the media transmit information about overseas crises greatly influences policy-making. Whether directly by beaming facts and interpretations into the offices of the president of the United States and his principal aids, or indirectly, by affecting the thinking of members of Congress, opinion-makers, or the American public, the way that the media shape and package news from foreign parts is obviously critical. (Rotberg and Weiss 1996, p. 1)

In assessing conclusions that span the discrete studies of this book, it should come as no surprise to readers that we find that a society's mainstream mass media share the dominant values of that society and that these values tend to be reflected in their reporting on world events. After all, journalists are exposed to the same agents of political socialization as are politicians, bureaucrats, business executives, educators and at least those military officers who did not attend one of the nation's service academies. Since anti-communism was a chief concern of the United States in the forty-five years following World War II, it would be strange in the extreme to find American mainstream mass media taking positions systematically opposed to their government's policy. It is also clear that the sources used by reporters in constructing news stories are an important factor in determining their content and slant. On this point it is well established that policy makers in Washington (not to mention U.S. military forces in the field) tend to be primary sources of information (Larson 1984; Bennett 1990; Mermin 1997). One question, then, deserves investigation in light of this general predisposition to support government policies aimed at containing communism: How balanced was media coverage in terms of giving readers an appreciation of alternative perspectives on particular Cold War crises or key events?

In reviewing the findings pertinent to this question two conclusions stand out. First, there is tremendous variation in the extent to which American mass media played what Herman and Chomsky (1988) have termed a "propaganda conduit" role in support of American foreign policy objectives. Strongest evidence for such a role is seen in coverage of the Cold War events in British Guiana and Guatemala in the early 1950s, where an anti-communist stance was adopted uncritically. It is also seen in informational and evaluative aspects of coverage of elections in El Salvador, Nicaragua and Grenada in the mid-1980s; in a failure to explore alternative frames for reporting on Cuba and Fidel Castro following the collapse of communism in the early 1990s; and in the cheerleader style coverage of the U.S. invasion of Panama in late 1989. It must be pointed out, however, that in the latter case, while mass media support for U.S. policy was strong, anti-communism was not an important justification for U.S. action.

On the other hand, there is also evidence of media opposition to government policy and active resistance to the Washington media line. Coverage of the intervention in the Dominican Republic in 1965, the invasion of Grenada in 1983, and aid to the Nicaraguan Contras in 1986 — all cases where the American government justified its actions primarily on the grounds of anti-communism — demonstrated considerable media suspicion of, if not outright hostility toward administration explanations of conflict dynamics. Further, in almost every case investigated, even those demonstrating the greatest congruence between government policy and media coverage, at least some dissenting media voices questioned government policy explanations.

In presenting their "propaganda model," Herman and Chomsky argue that

> the "societal purpose" of the media is to inculcate and defend the economic, social, and political agenda of the privileged groups that dominate the domestic society and the state. The media serve this purpose in many ways: through selection of topics, distribution of concerns, framing of issues, filtering of information, emphasis and tone, and by keeping debates within bounds of acceptable standards. (1988, p. 298)

While we can characterize *some* media coverage of at least *some* Cold War conflicts as coming close to fitting within the above description, clearly *most* coverage of *most* Cold War conflicts reflects far more sophistication and balance. What is demonstrably clear is that even at the height of the Cold War, mass media did not speak with one voice.

A second conclusion, evident from most of the studies, is a confirmation of the episodic nature of media coverage, perhaps most dramatically seen in the 1979 Nicaraguan Revolution and the 1983 U.S. invasion of Grenada. Crises tend to literally pop up on media radar screens, dominate for a brief period of time and then disappear (Rotberg and Weiss 1996). Background and continuity with respect to a single crisis or event are in short supply, as are linkages between different crises and events. Encapsulation, isolation and personalization are key characteristics of media coverage, none of which lead to especially well-founded or coherent patterns of public opinion regarding causes and outcomes of crises nor to possible implications of U.S. policy toward those crises.

In order to substantiate the earlier stated conclusion that a country's mass media are generally in touch with mainstream societal values, let us examine more closely the various data on leader evaluations presented in the chapters. While there are some idiosyncratic cases (which are identified), we believe that evidence for such a conclusion is found in a comparative examination of media portrayals of the various leaders based on actual language used to describe them. In the analysis that follows, we have also included data on some leaders who were profiled in other studies but not included in the book.[2] In all, we examined U.S. media profiles of thirty-four leaders, using data collected on them at forty-six different points in time between 1953 and 1993, as shown in Table C.1.

At the time that the actual reporting on these leaders was done, ten were generally perceived to be on the "left" of the political spectrum, twelve were seen generally to be occupying the political "center," while another twelve tended to be placed to the "right" of political center.[3]

For purposes of comparative analysis, percentage differences (PD) between positive and negative descriptors ranging between +/-10 are considered *neutral*; those ranging between +/-12 and +/-40 are considered *moderately positive* or *moderately negative*; those ranging between +/- 42 and +/-70 are considered *strongly positive* or *strongly negative*; while those ranging between +/-72 and 100 indicate *extremely positive* or *extremely negative* evaluations (Ma and Hildebrandt 1993).

Table C.2 shows clear trends with respect to which groups of leaders are portrayed positively or negatively. On the whole, "centrist" leaders did very well in terms of their media portrayals. For twelve leaders so identified, as measured at 17 data points, only two—Juan Bosch (PD = +4) and Fidel Chavez Meña (PD = -26)—did not receive a clear positive image, with only the latter actually falling on the negative side of the ledger. Four leaders received extremely positive images: Edward Seaga, Marc Bazin (in both 1987 and 1988), Arturo Cruz and Guillermo Endara. Three leaders received strongly positive images: Fidel Castro (from 1953 to 1958), Herbert Blaize and Marc Bazin (in 1990). The remainder—Joaquin Balaguer, José Napoléon Duarte (in 1982, 1984 and 1989), Francisco Guerrero, Leslie Manigat and Violetta Chamorro—received moderately positive images.

It is also clear that "leftist" leaders did not fare very well with respect to their media images. For ten leftist leaders, measured at 14 data points, only one—Jean-Bertrand Aristide (on TV from 1990 to mid-1993 with a PD = +42)—received a score that was on the positive side of the ledger. Three leaders—Cheddi Jagan, his wife Janet Jagan and Fidel Castro (in 1961 and 1962)—received extremely negative

Table C.1

Examined U.S. Media Profiles of Caribbean Leaders

Leader	Country	Time Period(s)
Cheddi Jagan	British Guiana	1953
Janet Jagan	British Guiana	1953
Fidel Castro	Cuba	1953-58; 1961-62; 1988-92 1988-92*
Jacobo Arbenz Guzmán	Guatemala	1954
Carlos Castillo Armas	Guatemala	1954
Rafael Trujillo Molina	Dominican Republic	1961
François Duvalier	Haiti	1964
Joaquin Balaguer	Dominican Republic	1965
Juan Bosch	Dominican Republic	1965
Francisco Caamaño Deño	Dominican Republic	1965
Elias Wesin y Wesin	Dominican Republic	1965
Antonio Imbert Barerra	Dominican Republic	1965
Anastasio Somoza Debayle	Nicaragua	1978-80
Michael Manley	Jamaica	1980
Edward Seaga	Jamaica	1980
José Napoléon Duarte	El Salvador	1982; 1984; 1989
Roberto D'Aubuisson	El Salvador	1982; 1984; 1989
Maurice Bishop	Grenada	1983
Daniel Ortega	Nicaragua	1984; 1990
Arturo Cruz	Nicaragua	1984
Francisco Gurrero	El Salvador	1984
Sir Eric Gairy	Grenada	1984
Herbert Blaize	Grenada	1984
Marc Bazin	Haiti	1987; 1988; 1990
Henri Namphy	Haiti	1987; 1988
Leslie Manigat	Haiti	1988
Alfredo Cristiani	El Salvador	1989
Fidel Chavez Meña	El Salvador	1989

Table C.1 *(continued)*

Leader	Country	Time Period(s)
Guillermo Ungo	El Salvador	1989
Manuel Noriega	Panama	1989–90*
Guillermo Endara	Panama	1989–90*
Violeta Barrios de Chamorro	Nicaragua	1990
Jean Bertrand Aristide	Haiti	1990; 1990–93*
Raoul Cédras	Haiti	1990–93*

*Television coverage; all others based on newspaper coverage

images; while three others—Jacobo Arbenz, Fidel Castro (in both newspaper and TV reporting from 1988 to 1992) and Guillermo Ungo— received strongly negative images. Michael Manley, Maurice Bishop, Daniel Ortega (in both 1984 and 1990) and Jean-Bertrand (in newspaper coverage in 1990) received moderately negative images, while the portrayal of Francisco Caamaño Deño (PD = -8) was considered neutral.

While American media were not favorably impressed with leaders on the left, it is evident that they were even less impressed with leaders on the right of the political spectrum: Of twelve rightist leaders measured at 15 data points, nine received negative images. In fact, for fully half of the rightist leaders—Rafael Trujillo, François Duvalier, Anastasio Somoza, Roberto D'Aubuisson (in 1989), Henri Namphy (in 1988) and Manuel Noriega—media images in the extremely negative category were recorded. Of the remainder, three had strongly negative images—Roberto D'Aubuisson (in 1984), Henri Namphy (in 1987) and Raoul Cédras—while Antonio Imbert Barerra recorded a moderately negative image. Imbert's fellow general, Elias Wesin y Wesin, was portrayed in a neutral fashion (PD = +6). Only two leaders perceived to be on the right—Carlos Castillo Armas (PD = +26)[4] and Alfredo Cristiani (PD = +18)—were portrayed in what was scored a moderately positive manner.

In order to gauge the uniqueness of the pattern of American media evaluation, Table C.3 shows data on media images presented by Canadian mass media for roughly half of the above leaders—seventeen

Table C.2

U.S. Media Profiles of Caribbean Basin Leaders

Centrist/Democratic Leaders	Years	%+	%–	Dif
Fidel Castro	1953–58	73	27	+46
Joaquin Balaguer	1965	63	36	+27
Juan Bosh	1965	52	48	+4
Edward Seaga	1980	90	10	+80
José Napoléon Duarte	1982	59	41	+18
	1984	70	30	40
	1989	61	39	22
Arturo Cruz	1984	100	0	+100
Francisco Guerrero	1984	65	35	+30
Herbert Blaize	1984	78	22	+56
Marc Bazin	1987	98	2	+96
	1988	97	3	+94
	1990	82	18	+64
Leslie Manigat	1988	66	34	+32
Fidel Chavez Meña	1989	38	62	–24
Guillermo Endara	1989–90*	91	9	+82
Violeta Barrios de Chamorro	1990	68	32	+36
Leftist Leaders	**Year**	**%+**	**%–**	**Dif**
Cheddi Jagan	1953	6	94	–88
Janet Jagan	1953	13	87	–74
Jacobo Arbenz Guzmán	1954	19	81	–62
Fidel Castro	1961–62	13	87	–74
	1988–92	16	84	–68
	1988–92*	21	79	–58
Francisco Caamaño Deño	1965	46	54	–8
Michael Manley	1980	30	70	–40
Maurice Bishop	1983	40	60	–20
Daniel Ortega	1984	36	64	–28
	1990	41	59	–18
Guillermo Ungo	1989	20	80	–60
Jean-Bertrand Aristide	1990	44	56	–12
	1990–93*	71	29	+42

Table C.2 *(continued)*

Rightist Leaders	Year	%+	%-	Dif
Carlos Castillo Armas	1954	63	37	+26
Rafael Trujillo	1961	12	88	-76
François Duvalier	1964	9	91	-82
Elias Wesin y Wesin	1965	53	47	+6
Antonio Imbert Barerra	1965	32	68	-36
Anastasio Somoza Debayle	1978-80	3	97	-94
Roberto D'Aubuisson	1982	32	68	-36
	1984	17	83	-66
	1989	12	88	-76
Sir Eric Gairy	1984	39	61	-22
Henri Namphy	1987	26	74	-48
	1988	14	86	-72
Alfredo Cristiani	1989	59	41	+18
Manuel Noriega	1989-90*	6	94	-88
Raoul Cédras	1991-93*	24	76	-52

*Television coverage; all others based on newspaper coverage

leaders measured at twenty-four different points in time. Overall, a comparison of the two tables points to considerable congruence in leader evaluation between media in the two countries. As was the case with the United States, Canadian media generally portrayed centrist leaders positively (six of nine): José Napoléon Duarte (in 1982 and 1984), Francisco Guerrero, Herbert Balize, Marc Bazin (in 1987, 1988, and 1990), Leslie Manigat and Guillermo Endara. Two others — Duarte (in 1989) and Violeta Chamorro — fell into the neutral category, while another two — Arturo Cruz and Fidel Chavez Meña — had negative media profiles. Perhaps because Canadian data on some of the more high-profile leftist and rightist leaders were not collected, these leaders appear not to have been as negatively evaluated as was the case in the United States. Among leaders on the left, Jean-Bertrand Aristide garnered a moderately positive evaluation (in newspaper coverage of the 1990 election), and Daniel Ortega was the recipient of neutral evaluations (in both 1984 and 1989). Guillermo Ungo and Fidel Castro

Table C.3

Canadian Media Profiles of Caribbean Basin Leaders

Centrist/Democratic Leaders	Years	%+	%-	Dif
José Napoléon Duarte	1982	57	43	+14
	1984	63	37	+26
	1989	50	50	0
Arturo Cruz	1984	27	73	-46
Francisco Guerrero	1984	82	18	+64
Herbert Blaize	1984	78	22	+48
Marc Bazin	1987	91	9	+82
	1988	100	0	+100
	1990	79	21	+58
Leslie Manigat	1988	56	44	+12
Fidel Chavez Meña	1989	40	60	-20
Guillermo Endara	1989-90*	62	38	+24
Violetta Barrios de Chamorro	1990	55	45	+10
Leftist Leaders	Years	%+	%-	Dif
Daniel Ortega	1984	47	53	-6
	1990	50	50	0
Guillermo Ungo	1989	33	67	-34
Fidel Castro	1988-92*	17	83	-26
Jean-Bertrand Aristide	1990	63	37	+26
Rightist Leaders	Years	%+	%-	Dif
Sir Eric Gairy	1984	55	45	+10
Roberto D'Aubuisson	1982	37	63	-26
	1984	16	84	-68
	1989	7	93	-86
Alfredo Cristiani	1989	50	50	0
Manuel Noriega	1989-90*	8	92	-84

*Television coverage; all others based on newspaper coverage

(on television between 1988 and 1992) were evaluated moderately negatively. Among leaders on the right, Roberto D'Aubuisson received negative evaluations (moderate in 1982, strong in 1984 and extreme in 1989), as did Manuel Noreiga (PD=-84 in 1989). Sir Eric Gairy and Alfredo Crisitiani were evaluated neutrally, while not a single rightist

Table C.4

Press Reporting of Centrist, Leftist and Rightist Leaders

	Centrist	Leftist	Rightist
United States	+47	-41	-43
Canada	+29	-8	-42

leader received a positive evaluation. Only three leaders on which comparative U.S.-Canadian data are available — Arturo Cruz, Sir Eric Gairy and Jean-Bertrand Aristide (in newspaper coverage of the 1990 election) — received a positive evaluation in one country and a negative one in the other.

Based on the assumption that language used by journalists is the raw material out of which they create meaning (Crocoran 1984), if we sum the percentage difference scores for centrist, leftist and rightist leaders as revealed in both American and Canadian press reporting and then divide by the number of observation points, we arrive at the scores shown in Table C.4 above.

This analysis, showing a decided "tilt toward the center" in terms of leader evaluation by mass media in both countries, is congruent with the widely held belief that in terms of societal values Canada and the United States are quite similar and that neither is characterized by a political culture that holds extremism in high regard. The less negative portrayal of leftist leaders in Canada is also congruent with that country's foreign policy, which was more tolerant of left-wing governments in the Caribbean Basin than that pursued by the United States. It is significant that the press of neither country had much in the positive vein to say about leaders of the right.

In pursuing these conclusions, one must be mindful of the controversy regarding the extent to which mass media can affect the direction of public attitudes as opposed to merely raising the salience of issues in public consciousness. The conclusion that emerges from the literature examined in detail in this book is that for knowledge of complex events occurring far from the nation's shore, in a world characterized by modern mass communication (subsumed under the term the "CNN factor"), media probably play a greater role in attitude formation than research done even a decade ago would have led us to believe. However, even if we adopt the more conservative assessment that limits press influence largely to an "agenda setting" role, the way in which mass media portray events and leaders is still important. What we see from the preceding analysis is that during the Cold War both American and Canadian mass media did in fact reflect mainstream societal values, and provided little in the way of support for either leftist or rightist alternatives.

The overall conclusion that emerges from this over-time study of coverage of Cold War events in the Caribbean Basis is that, while far from perfect, American mass media did a reasonable and competent job of reporting. While in some instances one can see a lack of objectivity, in most, a sensitivity to alternative explanations is evident. As well, press criticism — especially of the Johnson and Reagan Administrations' policies toward the Dominican Republic, Grenada and Nicaragua — was strongly stated, if not dominant in reporting.

Due to the centrality of the Cold War, perhaps the unintended result of forty years of media coverage of the Caribbean Basin by American mass media has been to intensify the perception that it is international politics, rather than factors indigenous to the countries themselves, that drives development in the region. Given the importance of such factors as trade, investment and drug trafficking to the region, such a perception is of course not altogether misplaced. It does, however, cause citizens who are interested in understanding the dynamics of U.S. foreign policy to give the United States too high a profile and to place too great an emphasis on what United States policy is capable of achieving in other societies. In the final analysis, it is a lack of understanding of the internal problems faced by developing societies that will cause confusion in public support for American policy toward the region in the post–Cold War era.

Notes

1. Material in the conclusion appeared previously in "Left, Right and Center: Cold War Press Portrayals of Caribbean and Central American Leaders," co-authored with E. D. Briggs and appearing in *International Communication Bulletin, 30* (Spring 1995), pp. 18–23. It is used here with permission.
2. Leader evaluations on Michael Manley and Edward Seaga are derived from an M.A. thesis, "'UnManley Persuasion': Coverage of the Manley Government in Jamaica by *The New York Times, Time* and *Newsweek*

between *1972–1980*," written by Lauriston Johanson (Communication Studies, University of Windsor) in 1984. All other studies were done by the author.

3. Fidel Castro is the only leader who shifted from one category to another. From 1953 through 1958 he was seen basically as opposing the dictator Fulgencio Batista and, to the extent that his policies were commented on, as a democratic reformer. Once he assumed power in 1959 his image began to tarnish; first with the executions of Batista officials and later with his conflicts with the United States and his ultimate shift to an ally of the Soviet Union.

4. Given his well-deserved reputation as a repressive, right-wing dictator, Carlos Castillo Armas presents a difficult case. In 1954 these dictatorial tendencies were not apparent to the press reporting on the exile invasion. For example, he was criticized for "lack of decisiveness" and for being "dilatory." He was also judged as "perhaps too moderate a figure to control the government for long." This misperception perhaps accounts for his relatively positive media profile.

References

Abbott, E. (1988). *Haiti: An Insider's History of the Rise and Fall of the Duvaliers.* New York: Simon and Schuster.

Adkin, M. (1989). *Urgent Fury: The Battle for Grenada.* Lexington, MA: Lexington Books.

Alexander, R. (1957). *Communism in Latin America.* New Brunswick, NJ: Rutgers University Press.

— — —. (1954). "The Guatemalan Communists." *The Canadian Forum, 17,* pp. 81–83.

Alger, D. (1989). *The Media and Politics.* Englewood Cliffs, NJ: Prentice-Hall.

Ali, M. (1983a, June 1). "Grenada leader in Washington to improve links." *The Times,* p. 7.

— — —. (1983b, June 2). "Grenada's leader seeks to reassure Reagan." *The Times,* p. 6.

— — —. (1983c, June 6). "Reagan rebuff fails to deter Grenada Premier." *The Times,* p. 6.

Altheide, D. (1982). "Three-in-One News: Network Coverage of Iran." *Journalism Quarterly, 59,* pp. 482–486.

Anderson, T. (1971). *Matanza: El Salvador's Communist Revolt of 1932.* Lincoln, NE: University of Nebraska Press.

Aristide, J-B. (1991). "The Church in Haiti: Land of Resistance." *Caribbean Quarterly, 37,* pp. 108–113.

Aybar de Soto, J. (1978). *Dependency and Intervention: The Case of Guatemala in 1954.* Boulder, CO: Westview Press.

Baranyi, S. (1985). "Canadian Foreign Policy Towards Central America, 1980–1984: Independence, Limited Public Influence and State Leadership." *Canadian Journal of Latin American and Caribbean Studies, 10,* pp. 21–57.

Barney, R., and D. Nelson. (1983). "North America." In J. Merrill (Ed.), *Global Journalism: A Survey of the World's Mass Media.* New York: Longmans.

Bell, C. (1982). *Crises and Policy-makers.* Canberra: The Australian National University.

Bellegarde-Smith, P. (1990). *Haiti: The Breached Citadel.* Boulder, CO: Westview.

Bennett, W. L. (1983). *News: The Politics of Illusion.* New York: Longman.

— — —. (1988). *News: The Politics of Illusion.* 2nd ed. New York: Longman.

— — —. (1990). "Toward a Theory of Press-State Relations in the United States." *Journal of Communication, 40,* pp. 103–125.

Bennett, W. L., L. Gressett, and W. Haltom. (1985). "Repairing the News: A Case Study of the News Paradigm." *Journal of Communication, 35,* pp. 50–68.

Bernell, D. (1994). "The Curious Case of Cuba in American Foreign Policy." *Journal of Interamerican Studies and World Affairs, 36,* pp. 65–103.

Biancalana, F., and C. O'Leary. (1988). "Profile of U.S. Press Coverage of Cuba." *Social Justice, 15,* pp. 63–71.

Blight, J., and P. Kornbluh (Eds.). (1998). *The Politics of Illusion: The Bay of Pigs Invasion Reexamined.* Boulder, CO: Lynne Rienner.

Blight, J., J. Nye, Jr., and D. Welch. (1987). "The Cuban Missile Crisis Revisited." *Foreign Affairs, 66,* pp. 170–188.

Bohning, D. (1997, December 25). "An opposition threat in Guyana." *The Miami Herald,* p. 17A.

Booth, J., and M. Seligson (Eds.). (1989). *Elections and Democracy in Central America.* Chapel Hill, NC: University of North Carolina Press.

Bradley, C. (1963). "Party Politics in British Guiana." *The Western Political Quarterly, 16,* pp. 353–370.

Braestrup, P. (1985). *Battle Lines: Report of the Twentieth Century Fund Task Force on the Military and the Media.* New York: Priority Press.

Brecher, M. (1977). "Towards a Theory of International Crisis Behavior: A Preliminary Report." *International Studies Quarterly, 21,* pp. 39–74.

Brecher, M., B. Steinberg, and J. Stein. (1969). "A Framework for Research on Foreign Policy Behavior." *Journal of Conflict Resolution, 8,* pp. 75–101.

Brown, A. (1985). "The West Indies and the New International Information Order: The Case of Jamaica." In W. Soderlund and S. Surlin, (Eds.), *Media in Latin America and the Caribbean: Domestic and International Perspectives.* Windsor, Ontario: Ontario Cooperative Program in Latin American and Caribbean Studies.

Brumberg, A. (1985). "'Sham' and 'Farce' in Nicaragua? Documentary Evidence on the Nicaraguan Election." *Dissent, 32,* pp. 226–236.

Buckley, K. (1991). *Panama: The Whole Story.* New York: Simon and Shuster.

Bulmer-Thomas, V. (1987). *The Political Economy of Central America since 1920.* Cambridge: Cambridge University Press.

Canada, Minister of Supply and Services. (1981). *Report, Royal Commission on Newspapers*. Ottawa: Minister of Supply and Services.

Canada, Senate. (1970). *The Uncertain Mirror: Report of the Special Senate Committee on Mass Media*. Ottawa: Queen's Printer.

Center for Strategic Studies. (1966). *Dominican Action-1965: Intervention or Cooperation?* Washington, DC: Georgetown University Press.

Chang, T-K., P. Shoemaker, and N. Brendlinger. (1987). "Determinants of International News Coverage in the U.S. Media." *Communication Research, 14*, pp. 396–414.

Charnley, M. (1966). *Reporting*. New York: Holt, Rinehart and Winston.

Christian, S. (1986). *Nicaragua: Revolution in the Family*. New York: Vintage Books.

The Citizen (Ottawa). (1988, January 17). "Majority find media fair in reporting on politics: poll," p. A11.

Cohen, B. (1963). *The Press and Foreign Policy*. Princeton: Princeton University Press.

Cohen, E. (1984). "Constraints on America's Conduct of Small Wars." *International Security, 9*, pp. 151–181.

Conniff, M. (1992). *Panama and the United States: The Forced Alliance*. Athens, GA: University of Georgia Press.

Constable, P. (1992-93). "Dateline Haiti: Caribbean Stalemate." *Foreign Policy, 89*, pp. 175–190.

Corcoran, F. (1984). "Consciousness: A Missing Link in the Coupling of Technology and Communication." *Canadian Journal of Communication, 10*, pp. 41–73.

Cox, R. (1994). "Global Restructuring: Making Sense of the Changing International Political Economy." In R. Stubbs and G. Underhill (Eds.), *Political Economy and the Changing Global Order*. Toronto: McClelland and Stewart.

Crassweller, R. (1971). "Darkness in Haiti." *Foreign Affairs, 49*, pp. 315–329.

— — —. (1966). *Trujillo: The Life and Times of a Caribbean Dictator*. New York: Macmillan.

Crossette, B. (1983, August 7). "Grenadians anxious over new influence of Soviet and Cuba." *The New York Times*, p. A1.

Crowley, E. (1979). *Dictators Never Die: A Portrait of Nicaragua and the Somoza Dynasty*. New York: St. Martin's Press.

Cumming, C., M. Cardinal, and P. Johanson. (1981). *Canadian News Services. Research Studies on the Newspaper Industry*. Ottawa: Minister of Supply and Services.

Cuthbert, M. (1990). "Ideological Differences in Press Coverage of the Grenada Crisis." In S. Surlin and W. Soderlund (Eds.), *Mass Media and the Caribbean*. New York: Gordon and Breach.

— — —. (1985). *Journalistic Perspectives on the Grenada Crisis*. Kingston, Jamaica: Press Association of Jamaica.

Cuthbert, M., and S. Surlin. (1985). "Canadian and Caribbean Press Coverage of the Grenada Crisis." In W. Soderlund and S. Surlin, (Eds.), *Media in Latin America and the Caribbean: Domestic and International Perspectives.* Windsor, Ontario: Ontario Cooperative Program in Latin American and Caribbean Studies.

DaBreo. D. S. (1979). *The Grenadian Revolution.* Castries, St. Lucia: M.A.P.S. Publishing.

Dahl, R. (1984, April 2). "The Democratic Mystique," *The New Republic*, pp. 17–19.

— — —. (1971). *Polyarchy: Participation and Opposition.* New Haven, CT: Yale University Press.

Danner, M. (1991, August 11). "To Haiti, with love and squalor." Review of Herbert Gold's Best Nightmare on Earth. *New York Times Book Review*, pp. 18–19.

Despres, L. (1967). *Cultural Pluralism and Nationalist Policies in British Guyana.* Chicago: Rand McNally.

Deutsch, K., and R. Merritt. (1965). "Effects of Events on National and International Images." In H. Kelman, (Ed.), *International Behavior: A Social-Psychological Analysis.* New York: Holt, Rinehart and Winston.

Dewitt, D., and J. Kirton. (1983). "Media and Foreign Policy Towards the Middle East: Lebanon 1982." Paper presented at the Media and Foreign Policy Conference, University of Windsor.

Diamond, L., J. Linz, and S. Lipset (Eds.). (1989). *Democracy in Developing Countries: Latin America*, Vol. 4. Boulder, CO: Lynne Rienner.

Dickson, S. (1992). "Press and U.S. Policy Toward Nicaragua, 1983–1987: A Study of *The New York Times* and *Washington Post*." *Journalism Quarterly, 69*, pp. 562–571.

Diederich, B. (1981). *Somoza and the Legacy of U.S. Involvement in Central America.* New York: Dutton.

Dinges, J. (1990). *Our Man in Panama: How General Noriega Used the United States and Made Millions in Drugs and Arms.* New York: Random House.

Dominguez, J. (1978). *Cuba: Order and Revolution.* Cambridge: Harvard University Press.

Donnelly, T., M. Roth, and C. Baker. (1991). *Operation Just Cause: The Storming of Panama.* New York: Lexington Books.

Donohew, L., and P. Palmgren. (1971). "A Reappraisal of Dissonance and the Selective Exposure Hypothesis." *Journalism Quarterly, 48*, pp. 412–420.

Doyle, K. (1994). "Hollow Diplomacy in Haiti." *World Policy Journal, 6*, pp. 50–59.

Draimin, T., and L. North. (1990). "Canada and Central America." In M. Molot and F. Osler Hampson (Eds.), *Canada Among Nations, 1989: The Challenge of Change.* Ottawa, Ontario: Carleton University Press.

Draper, T. (1968). *The Dominican Revolt: A Case Study in American Policy.* New York: Commentary.

— — —. (1965). "The Roots of the Dominican Crisis." *The New Leader, 68,* pp. 3–18.

Dunkerley, J. (1982). *The Long War: Dictatorship and Revolution in El Salvador.* London: Junction Books.

Edelstein, A. (1982). *Comparative Communication Research.* Beverly Hills, CA: Sage.

Entman, R. (1993). "Framing: Towards Clarification of a Fractured Paradigm." *Journal of Communication, 43,* pp. 51–58.

— — —. (1991). "Framing U.S. Coverage of International News." *Journal of Communication, 41,* pp. 5–28.

Erbring, L., E. Goldenberg, and A. Miller. (1980). "Front Page News and Real World Cues: A New Look at Agenda-Setting by the Media." *American Journal of Political Science, 24,* pp. 16–49.

Etheredge, L. (1985). *Can Governments Learn? American Foreign Policy and Central American Revolutions.* Glenview, IL: Scott, Foresman/Little Brown.

Evans-Pritchard, A. (1993, November, 29). "Getting to Know the General." *National Review, 45,* pp. 24–26.

Fagen, R. (1966). *Politics and Communication.* Boston: Little Brown and Co.

Falk, R. 1992. "Recycling Interventionism." *Journal of Peace Research, 29,* pp. 129–134.

Farmer, P. (1994). *The Uses of Haiti.* Monroe, ME: Common Courage Press.

Fauriol, G. (1988). "The Duvaliers and Haiti." *Orbis, 32,* pp. 587–607.

Feldman, S. (Ed.). (1966). *Cognitive Consistency: Motivational Antecedents and Behavioral Consequences.* New York: Academic Press.

Fenwick, C. (1954). "Judicial Questions Involved in the Guatemalan Revolution." *The American Journal of International Law, 48,* pp. 597–602.

Fishlock, T. (1983, November 7). "Conflicting views on early poll." *The Times,* p. 5.

Flather, P. (1983a, April 29). "Learning a little to get ahead." *The Times Higher Education Supplement,* p. 6.

— — —. (1983b, June 3). "Planning ahead for a bumper harvest." *The Times Higher Education Supplement,* p. 17.

Forsythe, D. (1992). "Democracy, War, and Covert Action." *Journal of Peace Research, 20,* pp. 385–395.

Frederick, H. (1985). "Communication, Ideology and Democracy in Cuba." In W. Soderlund and S. Surlin (Eds.), *Media in Latin America and the Caribbean: Domestic and International Perspectives.* Windsor, Ontario: Ontario Cooperative Program in Latin American and Caribbean Studies.

Gabriel, R. (1962). "No Light in the Tunnel: Can U.S. Unconventional Forces Meet the Future." *Foreign Affairs, 40,* pp. 566–575.

Galtung, J., and M. Holmboe Ruge. (1965). "The Structure of Foreign News: The Presentation of the Congo, Cuba and Cyprus Crises in Four Norwegian Newspapers." *Journal of Peace Research, 2*, pp. 65–91.

Gamson, W. (1989). "News as Framing." *American Behavioral Scientist, 33*, pp. 157–161.

Gans, H. (1979). *Deciding What's News: A Study of CBS Evening News, NBC Nightly News, Newsweek and Time.* New York: Pantheon.

Garcia-Zamor, J-C. (1989). "Obstacles to Institutional Development in Haiti." *The Indian Journal of Political Science, 50*, pp. 409–437.

Garthoff, R. (1988). "Cuban Missile Crisis: The Soviet Story." *Foreign Policy, 72*, pp. 61–80.

Geyer, G. (1991). *Guerrilla Prince: The Untold Story of Fidel Castro.* Boston: Little, Brown and Co.

Gill, F. (1971). *Latin American–United States Relations.* New York: Harcourt, Brace, Jovanovich.

Gitlin, T. (1980). *The Whole World Is Watching: Mass Media in the Making and Unmaking of the New Left.* Berkeley: University of California Press.

Glasgow, A, (1970). *Guyana: Race and Politics Among Africans and East Indians.* The Hague: Martius Nijhoff.

Gleijeses, P. (1991). *Shattered Hope: The Guatemalan Revolution and the United States.* Princeton: Princeton University Press.

Goodsell. J. (1984, December 14). "Grenada's new moderate leaders are depending on U.S. to revive their island." *Christian Science Monitor*, pp. 13–14.

Gordon, M. (1983). "A Case History of U.S. Subversion: Guatemala, 1954." In J. Fried, M. Gettleman, D. Levenson, and N. Peckenham (Eds.), *Guatemala in Rebellion: Unfinished History.* New York: Grove Press.

– – –. (1990, March 20). "Cheney blamed for press problems in Panama." *The New York Times*, p. A8.

Gorham, R. (1992). "Canada-Cuba Relations: A Brief Overview." In M. Erisman and J. Kirk (Eds.), *Cuban Foreign Policy Confronts a New International Order.* Boulder, CO: Lynne Rienner.

Grant, D. (1955). "Guatemala Policy and United States Foreign Policy." *Journal of International Affairs, 9*, pp. 64–72.

Griffith, I. (1997a). *Drugs and Security in the Caribbean: Sovereignty Under Seige.* University Park, PA: Pennsylvania State University Press.

– – –. (1991). "The Military and the Politics of Change in Guyana." *Journal of Interamerican Studies and World Affairs, 33*, pp. 141–173.

– – –. (1997b). "Political Change, Democracy, and Human Rights in Guyana." *The Third World Quarterly, 18*, pp. 267–285.

Haberman, P. (1985). "Development in the Caribbean and Media Coverage of Grenada." In W. Soderlund and S. Surlin, (Eds.), *Media in Latin America and the Caribbean.* Windsor, Ontario: Ontario Cooperative Program in Latin American and Caribbean Studies.

Haglund, D. (1987). "The Missing Link: Canada's Security Interests and the Central American Crisis." *International Journal, 42*, pp. 789–820.

Haiti. (1987). *Constitution de la République d'Haiti*. Port-au-Prince: Ministère de L'Information et de la Coordination.

Halberstam, D. (1979). *The Powers That Be*. New York: Knopf.

Halperin, E. (1965). "Racism and Communism in British Guiana." *Journal of Interamerican Studies, 7*, pp. 95–131.

Handy, J. (1984). *Gift of the Devil: A History of Guatemala*. Toronto: Between the Lines.

Hector, C. (1988). "Haiti: A Nation in Crisis." *Peace and Security, 3*, pp. 6–7.

Hegstrom, E. (1998, April 24). "Church finds higher toll of victims in Guatemalan war." *The Miami Herald*, 26A.

Henfrey, C. (1972). "Foreign Influence in Guyana: the Struggle for Independence." In E. De Kadt (Ed.), *Patterns of Foreign Influence in the Caribbean*. London: Oxford University Press.

Herman, C. (1969). *Crises in Foreign Policy Decision-Making: A Simulation Analysis*. Indianapolis: Bobbs-Merrill Co.

Herman, E. (1985). "Diversity of the News: 'Marginalizing' the Opposition." *Journal of Communication, 35*, pp. 135–146.

Herman, E., and F. Brodhead. (1984). *Demonstration Elections: U.S.-Staged Elections in the Dominican Republic, Vietnam, and El Salvador*. Boston: South End Press.

Herman, E., and N. Chomsky. (1988). *Manufacturing Consent: The Political Economy of the Mass Media*. New York: Pantheon Books.

Hinden, R. (1954). "The Case of British Guiana." *Encounter, 2*, pp. 18–22.

Holsti, O. (1969). *Content Analysis for the Social Sciences and Humanities*. Reading, MA: Addison-Wesley.

Hoogendoorn, R. (1985). "The Cubanification of the Image of Grenada: The Media and the Unmaking of the Grenadian Revolution." In W. Soderlund and S. Surlin, (Eds.), *Media in Latin America and the Caribbean*. Windsor, Ontario: Ontario Cooperative Program in Latin American and Caribbean Studies.

Hope, K. (1985). "Electoral Politics and Political Development in Post-Independence Guyana." *Electoral Studies, 4*, pp. 58–60.

Huberman, L., and P. Sweezy. (1969). *Socialism in Cuba*. New York: Monthly Review Press.

Hughes, C. (1954). "The British Guiana Election, 1953." *Parliamentary Affairs, 7*, pp. 213–220.

— — —. (1953). "Semi-Responsible Government in the British West Indies." *Political Science Quarterly, 67*, pp. 338–353.

Huntington, S. (1993). "The Clash of Civilizations?" *Foreign Affairs, 72*, pp. 22–49.

Hvistendahl, J. K. (1979). "The Effect of Placement of Biasing Information," *Journalism Quarterly, 56*, pp. 863–865.

Immerman, R. (1982). *The CIA in Guatemala: The Foreign Policy of Intervention.* Austin: University of Texas Press.

Ince, B. (1974). *Decolonization and Conflict in the United Nations: Guyana's Struggle for Independence.* Cambridge, MA: Schenkman Publishing Co.

Iorio, S., and S. Huxman. (1996). "Media Coverage of Political Issues and the Framing of Personal Concerns." *Journal of Communication, 46,* pp. 97–115.

Ives, K. (1955). "Unmaking of a President." In D. McFadyen and P. LaRamée (Eds.), *Haiti: Dangerous Crossroads.* Boston, MA: South End Press.

Iyengar, S. (1991). *Is Anyone Responsible? How Television Frames Political Issues.* Chicago: University of Chicago Press.

Iyengar, S., and D. Kinder. (1987). *News That Matters: Agenda-Setting and Priming in a Television Age.* Chicago: University of Chicago Press.

James, D. (1954). *Red Design for the Americas: Guatemalan Prelude.* New York: John Day.

Jeffrey H., and C. Barber. (1986). *Guyana: Politics, Economics and Society: Beyond the Burnham Era.* London: Frances Pinter Publishers.

Johanson, L. (1984). "'UnManley Persuasion': Coverage of the Manley Government in Jamaica by The New York Times, Time and Newsweek between 1972–1980." M.A. thesis, Department of Communication Studies. Windsor, Ontario: University of Windsor.

Jonas, S., and D. Tobis (Eds.). (1974). *Guatemala.* Berkeley, CA: North American Congress on Latin America.

Jones, A. (1989, December 22). "Editors say journalists were kept from action." *The New York Times,* p. A19.

Karl, T., and P. Schmitter. (1991). "Modes of Transition in Latin America, Southern and Eastern Europe." *International Social Science Journal, 43,* pp. 269–284.

Kegley, C., and E. Wittkopf. (1987). *American Foreign Policy: Pattern and Process.* 3rd ed. New York: St. Martin's Press.

Kempe, F. (1990). *Divorcing the Dictator: America's Bungled Affair with Noriega.* New York: Putnam.

Kenworthy, E. (1984). "Grenada as Theater." *World Policy Journal, 1,* pp. 635–651.

Kern, M., P. Levering, and R. Levering. (1983). *The Kennedy Crises: The Press, the Presidency and Foreign Policy.* Chapel Hill, NC: University of North Carolina Press.

Krehm, W. (1954). "A Victory for the West in Guatemala." *International Journal, 9,* pp. 295–302.

Kriesberg, M. (1946). "Soviet News in *The New York Times*." *Public Opinion Quarterly, 10,* pp. 540–544.

Kumar, M, and M. Grossman. (1986). "Political Communication from the White House: The Interest Group Connection." *Presidential Studies Quarterly, 16,* pp. 92–102.

Kurzman, D. (1965). *Santo Domingo: Revolt of the Damned.* New York: Putnam.

LaFeber, W. (1983). *Inevitable Revolutions: The United States in Central America.* New York: W. W. Norton.

Lambert, J. (1967). *Latin America: Social Structures and Political Institutions.* Berkeley, CA: University of California Press.

Larson, J. (1982). "International Affairs Coverage on U.S. Evening Network News, 1972-1979." In W. Adams (Ed.), *Television Coverage of International Affairs.* Norwood, NJ: Ablex Publishing.

— — —. (1986). "Television and U.S. Foreign Policy: The Case of the Iran Hostage Crisis." *Journal of Communication, 36,* pp. 108-130.

— — —. (1984). *Television's Window of the World: International Affairs Coverage of the U.S. Networks.* Norwood, NJ: Ablex Publishing Corp.

Lemco, J. (1986a). "Canada and Central America: A Review of Current Issues." *Behind the Headlines,* pp. 1-19.

— — —. (1986b). "Canadian Foreign Policy Interests in Central America: Some Current Issues." *International Affairs, 28,* pp. 119-146.

Lewis, H. (1960). "The Cuban Revolt Story: AP, UPI and Three Papers." *Journalism Quarterly, 37,* pp. 573-578.

Lippman, W. (1965). *Public Opinion.* New York: The Free Press.

Lowenthal, A. (1987). *Partners in Conflict: The United States and Latin America.* Baltimore: Johns Hopkins University Press.

Lundahl, M. (1989). "History as an Obstacle to Change: The Case of Haiti." *Journal of Interamerican Studies and World Affairs, 31,* pp. 1-21.

— — —. (1991). "Underdevelopment in Haiti: Some Recent Contributions." *Journal of Latin American Studies, 23,* pp. 411-429.

Ma, J., and K. Hildebrandt. (1993). "Canadian Press Coverage of the Ethnic Chinese Community: A Content Analysis of the Toronto Star and the Vancouver Sun." *Canadian Journal of Communication, 40,* pp. 479-496.

MacLeod, M. (1973). *Spanish Central America: A Socioeconomic History, 1550-1720.* Berkeley, CA: University of California Press.

Maguire, R. (1997). "Democracy and Human Rights in Haiti." In I. Griffith and B. Sedoc-Dahlberg, (Eds.), *Democracy and Human Rights in the Caribbean.* Boulder, CO: Westview Press.

Maingot, A. (1986-87). "Haiti: Problems of a Transition to Democracy in an Authoritarian Soft State." *Journal of Interamerican Studies and World Affairs, 28,* pp. 75-102.

— — —. (1994). *The United States and the Caribbean.* London: Macmillan.

Manley, R. (1979). *Guyana Emergent: The Post-Independence Struggle for Nondependent Development.* Cambridge, MA: Schenkman Publishing Co.

Martin, I. (1995). "Haiti: Mangled Multilateralism." *Foreign Policy, 95,* pp. 72-89.

Martin. J. (1966). *Overtaken by Events: The Dominican Crisis from the Fall of Trujillo to the Civil War.* Garden City, NY: Doubleday.

Martin, L. J., and A. Chaudhary (Eds.). (1983). *Comparative Mass Media Systems.* New York: Longman.

Martz, J. (1988). *United States Policy in Latin America: A Quarter Century of Crisis and Challenge.* Lincoln, NE: University of Nebraska Press.

Matthews, H. (1969). *Fidel Castro.* New York: Simon and Schuster.

McCann, T. (1976). *An American Company: The Tragedy of American Fruit.* New York: Crown Publishers.

McCaughan, E., and T. Platt. (1988)."Tropical Gulag: Media Images of Cuba." *Social Justice, 15*, pp. 72–104.

McCombs, M., and D. Shaw. (1972). "The Agenda-Setting Function of Mass Media." *Public Opinion Quarterly, 36*, pp. 174–187.

— — —. (1993). "The Evolution of Agenda-Setting Research: Twenty-Five Years in the Marketplace of Ideas." *Journal of Communication, 43*, pp. 58–67.

McConnell, M. (1991). *Just Cause: The Real Story of America's High-Tech Invasion of Panama.* New York: St. Martin's Press.

McKitterick, T. (1962). "The End of a Colony: British Guiana 1962." *The Political Quarterly, 33*, pp. 30–40.

McSherry, J. (1992). "Military Power, Impunity and State-Society Change in Latin America." *Canadian Journal of Political Science, 25*, pp. 463–488.

Melville, T., and M. Melville. (1971). *Guatemala: Another Vietnam?* Middlesex, England: Penguin Books.

Merida, K. (1990, January 7). "The Panama press pool fiasco." *The Washington Post*, p. B2.

Mermin, J. (1997). "Television News and American Intervention in Somalia: The Myth of a Media-Driven Foreign Policy." *Political Science Quarterly, 112*, pp. 395–403.

Merrill, J. (1968). *The Elite Press: The Great Newspapers of the World.* New York: Pitman Publishing.

— — —. (Ed.). (1995). *Global Journalism: A Survey of International Communication.* 3rd ed. New York: Longman Publishers.

— — —. (1983). *Global Journalism: A Survey of the World's Mass Media.* New York: Longman.

— — —. (1965). "How *Time* Stereotyped Three U.S. Presidents." *Journalism Quarterly, 42*, pp. 563–570.

— — —. (1962). "The Image of the United States in Ten Mexican Dailies," *Journalism Quarterly, 39*, pp. 203–209.

Merrill, J., and H. Fisher. (1980). *The World's Great Dailies: Profiles of Fifty Newspapers.* New York: Hastings House.

Millett, R. (1977). *Guardians of the Dynasty.* Marymount, NY: Orbis Books.

Montgomery, T. (1993, April–May). "El Salvador from Civil War to 'Negotiated Revolution.'" *North-South*, pp. 22–25.

— — —. (1988). *Revolution in El Salvador: Origins and Evolution.* Boulder, CO: Westview Press.

Morales, C. (1985, January/February). "A Canadian Role in Central America." *International Perspectives,* pp. 12–15.

Moreira Alvez, M. (1988). *State and Opposition in Military Brazil.* Austin: University of Texas Press.

Morley, M., and C. McGillion. (1997). "'Disobedient' Generals and the Politics of Redemocratization: The Clinton Administration and Haiti." *Political Science Quarterly, 112,* pp. 363–384.

Munton, D. (1983–84). "Public Opinion and the Media in Canada from the Cold War to Détente to New Cold War." *International Journal, 39,* pp. 171–213.

Newman, P. (1964). *British Guiana: Problems of Cohesion in an Immigrant Society.* London: Oxford University Press.

The New York Times. (1983a, June 1). "Caribbean left-wing leader received coolly in Washington," p. 12.

— — —. (1983b, August 27). "Fund backs Grenada loan," p. 36.

— — —. (1983c, June 2). "Grenada leader renews plea on U.S. ties," p. 5.

— — —. (1983d, April 5). "Grenada official says force trains in Miami for invasion," p. 3.

— — —. (1983e, August 7). "Interview excerpts," p. 12.

— — —. (1986, January 16). "Poll finds 'no credibility crisis' for news media," p. 18.

Nicholls, D. (1996) *From Dessalines to Duvalier: Race, Colour and National Independence in Haiti.* New Brunswick, NJ: Rutgers University Press.

Nogee, J., and J. Spanier. (1988). *Peace Impossible – War Unlikely: The Cold War Between the United States and the Soviet Union.* Glenview, IL: Scott, Foresman/Little Brown.

North, L. (1981). *Bitter Grounds: Roots of Revolt in El Salvador.* Toronto: Between the Lines.

North, O. (1991). *Under Fire: An American Story.* New York: HarperCollins.

Nossiter, B. (1983a, June 10). "Grenada Premier establishes 'some sort' of U.S. rapport." *The New York Times,* p. 8.

— — —. (1983b, June 5). "Grenada's leader concedes jailing up to 40 foes." *The New York Times,* p. 6.

Nylen, W. (1988). *U.S.-Grenada Relations, 1979–1983: American Foreign Policy Towards a "Backyard" Revolution.* Pittsburgh, PA: Graduate School of Public and International Affairs, University of Pittsburgh.

O'Donnell, G. (1973). *Modernization and Bureaucratic Authoritarianism: Studies in South American Politics.* Berkeley, CA: University of California Press.

O'Donnell, G., P. Schmitter, and L. Whitehead. (Eds.), (1986). *Transitions from Authoritarian Rule: Comparative Perspectives.* Baltimore, MD: Johns Hopkins Press.

Oppenheimer, A. (1992). *Castro's Final Hour: The Secret Story Behind the Coming Downfall of Communist Cuba.* New York: Simon and Shuster.

O'Shaughnessy, H. (1984). *Grenada: An Eyewitness Account of the U.S. Invasion and the Caribbean History That Provoked It*. New York: Dodd Mead and Co.

Packer, G. (1993, Summer). "Choke Hold on Haiti." *Dissent, 40*, pp. 297–308.

Paletz, D., and R. Entman. (1981). *Media, Power, Politics*. New York: Free Press.

Parenti, M. (1986). *Inventing Reality: The Politics of the Mass Media*. New York: St. Martin's Press.

Parkinson, F. (1974). *Latin America, the Cold War, and the World Powers*. Beverly Hills, CA: Sage Publications.

Pastor, R. (1990). "The United States and the Grenada Revolution: Who Pushed First and Why?" In J. Heine, (Ed.), *A Revolution Aborted: The Lessons of Grenada*. Pittsburgh, PA: University of Pittsburgh Press.

Payne, A. (1990). "The Foreign Policy of the People's Revolutionary Government." In J. Heine, (Ed.), *A Revolution Aborted: The Lessons of Grenada*. Pittsburgh, PA: University of Pittsburgh Press.

Peterson, S. (1980). "A Case Study of Third World News Coverage by Western News Agencies and The Times (London)." *Studies in Comparative International Development, 15*, pp. 62–98.

Pfaltzgraff, R. (1994). "Dimensions of the Post–Cold War World." In R. Pfaltzgraff and R. Shultz (Eds.), *Ethnic Conflict and Regional Instability: Implications for U.S. Policy and Army Roles and Missions*. Washington: U.S. Government Printing Office.

Pike, F. (1955). "Guatemala, the United States, and Communism in the Americas." *The Review of Politics, 17*, pp. 232–261.

Premdas, R. (1986). "Politics of Preference in the Caribbean: The Case of Guyana." In N. Nevitte and C. Kennedy (Eds.), *Ethnic Preference and Public Policy in Developing States*. Boulder, CO: Lynne Rienner.

Ratliff, W. (Ed.). (1987). *The Selling of Fidel Castro: The Media and the Cuban Revolution*. New Brunswick, NJ: Transaction Books.

Riffe, D., and E. Shaw. (1982). "Conflict and Consonance: Coverage of the Third World in Two U.S. Papers." *Journalism Quarterly, 59*, pp. 617–626.

Rioux, J-S., and D. Van Belle. (2001). "L'influence des médias sur l'allocation d'aide bilatérale française, 1986–1995." Paper presented at the Annual Meeting of the Canadian Political Science Association, Quebec City.

Rivas-Gallont, E. (1992, junio–julio). "Es posible la paz social en El Salvador?" *Notre-Sur*, pp. 24–27.

Rochlin, J. (1988). "The Political Economy of Canada's Relations with Central America." *Canadian Journal of Latin American and Caribbean Studies, 12*, pp. 45–70.

Rockman, B. (1987). " Mobilizing Political Support for National Security." *Armed Forces and Society, 14*, pp. 17–42.

Rodriguez, M. (1965). *Central America*. Englewood Cliffs, NJ: Prentice-Hall.

Rogers, E., and J. Dearing. (1988). "Agenda-Setting Research: Where Has It Been, Where Is It Going?" In J. Anderson (Ed.), *Communication Yearbook*, Vol. 11. Beverly Hills, CA: Sage Publications.

Rosengren, K. (1970). "International News: Intra and Extra Media Data." *Acta Sociologica, 13*, pp. 96–109.

Rositzke, H. (1977). *The CIA's Secret Operations: Espionage, Counterespionage and Covert Action*. New York: The Reader's Digest Press.

Rotberg, R. (1988). "Haiti's Past Mortgages Its Future." *Foreign Affairs, 67*, pp. 93–109.

Rotberg, R., and T. Weiss. (1996). *From Massacres to Genocide: The Media, Public Policy, and Humanitarian Crises*. Washington, DC: The Brookings Institution.

Sarkesian, S. (1976). "Revolution and the Limits of Military Power: The Haunting Specter of Vietnam." *Social Science Quarterly, 56*, pp. 673–688.

Scanlon, T. J. (1974). "Canada Sees the World Through U.S. Eyes: One Case in Cultural Imperialism." *Canadian Forum, 54*, pp. 34–39.

— — —. (1967). *The Sources of Foreign News in Canadian Newspapers*. Ottawa: Report prepared for the Press and Liaison Division, Department of External Affairs.

Scanlon, T. J., and A. Farrell. (1983). "No Matter How it Sounds or Looks, It's Probably Not Canadian." Paper presented at the Media and Foreign Policy Conference, University of Windsor.

Scanlon, T. J., R. Luukko, and G. Morton. (1978). "Media Coverage of Crises: Better Than Reported, Worse Than Necessary." *Journalism Quarterly, 55*, pp. 68–72.

Schlesinger, A. (1965). *A Thousand Days: John F. Kennedy in the White House*. New York: Houghton Miflin Co.

Schlesinger, S., and S. Kinzer. (1983). *Bitter Fruit: The Untold Story of the American Coup in Guatemala*. Garden City, NY: Anchor Press/Doubleday.

Schneider, R. (1959). *Communism in Guatemala, 1944–1954*. New York: Praeger.

Scranton, M. (1991). *The Noriega Years: U.S.-Panamanian Relations, 1981–1990*. Boulder, CO: Lynne Rienner.

Semmel, A. (1979). "The Elite Press, Foreign News, and Public Opinion." Paper presented at the Annual Meeting of the International Studies Association, Toronto.

Serafino, N. (1992, August–September). "Nicaragua's Rocky Road to the 1989 Election." *North-South*, pp. 11–15.

Shacochis, B. (1999). *The Immaculate Invasion*. New York: Viking Press.

Shaw, D., and M. McCombs. (1977). *The Emergence of Political Issues: The Agenda-Setting Function of the Press*. St. Paul, MN: West Publishing.

Shoemaker, P. (1983). "Bias and Source Attribution." *Newspaper Research Journal, 5*, pp. 25–31.

Sideri, S. (1993). "Restructuring the Post-Cold War World Economy: Perspectives and a Prognosis." *Development and Change, 24,* pp. 7–27.

Sigal, L. (1973). *Reporters and Officials: The Organization and Politics of Newsmaking.* Lexington, MA: D.C. Heath and Co.

Simmons, D. (1985). "Militarization of the Caribbean: Concerns for National and Regional Security." *International Journal, 40,* p. 348–376.

Simms, P. (1966). *Trouble in Guyana: An Account of People, Personalities and Politics as They Were in British Guiana.* London: George Allen and Unwin Ltd.

Singh, C. (1988). *Guyana: Politics in a Plantation Society.* New York: Praeger.

Sires, R. (1954). "British Guiana: The Suspension of the Constitution." *The Western Political Quarterly, 7,* pp. 554–564.

Slater, J. (1964). "The United States, the Organization of American States, and the Dominican Republic." *International Organization, 188,* pp. 268–291.

Smith, A. (1980). *The Geopolitics of Information: How Western Culture Dominates the World.* New York: Oxford University Press.

Soderlund, W. (1994). "The Impact of the Aquino Assassination on the Press Image of Ferdinand Marcos: Transformation or Amplification?" *Communication Reports, 7,* pp. 36–42.

— — —. (1985). "Reporting Events in Central America by Canadian and American Newspapers." In W. Soderlund and S. Surlin (Eds.), *Media in Latin America and the Caribbean: Domestic and International Perspectives.* Windsor, Ontario: Ontario Cooperative Program in Latin American and Caribbean Studies.

Soderlund, W., and R. Nelson. (1990). "Canadian and American Press Coverage of the Haitian Election Crisis." In S. Surlin and W. Soderlund (Eds.), *Mass Media and the Caribbean.* New York: Gordon and Breach.

Soderlund, W., R. Price, and R. Krause. (1991). "Canadian Newspaper Editors' Evaluation of International Reporting." *Canadian Journal of Communication, 16,* pp. 5–18.

Soderlund, W., and C. Schmitt. (1986). "El Salvador's Civil War as Seen in North and South American Press." *Journalism Quarterly, 63,* pp. 268–274.

Soderlund, W., and S. Surlin. (1985). *Media in Latin America and the Caribbean: Domestic and International Perspectives.* Windsor, Ontario: Ontario Cooperative Program in Latin American and Caribbean Studies.

Soderlund, W., and R. Wagenberg. (1995). "Race and Gender in TV News Coverage of Cuba, 1988–1992." *International Journal of Race and Ethnic Studies, 2,* pp. 72–85.

Spinner, T. (1984). *A Political and Social History of Guyana, 1945–1988.* Boulder, CO: Westview Press.

Sprout, H., and M. Sprout. (1957). "Environmental Factors in the Study of International Politics." *Journal of Conflict Resolution, 1,* pp. 309–328.

Stepan, A. (1988). *Rethinking Military Politics*. Princeton, NJ: Princeton University Press.

Stevens, J. (1970). "Conflict-Cooperation Content in 14 Black Newspapers." *Journalism Quarterly, 47*, pp. 566–568.

Stevenson, R., and D. Shaw. (1984). *Foreign News and the New World Information Order*. Ames, IA: Iowa State University Press.

Stohl, M., and G. Lopez (Eds.). (1986). *Government Violence and Repression*. New York: Greenwood Press.

Stokes, W. (1952). "Violence as a Power Factor in Latin American Politics." *Western Political Quarterly, 3*, pp. 445–468.

Sunshine, K. (1988). "The U.S. and Haiti: Democracy's Image." *Christianity and Culture, 48*, pp. 55–56.

Surlin, S., and W. Romanow. (1985). "Heritage Language Newspapers Readers: Mass Communication Usage and Attitudes." Paper presented at the Annual Meeting of the Canadian Communication Association, Montreal.

Sutley, S. (1992). "The Revitalization of the United States, A Territorial International Logic: The World Before and After the 1989 Invasion of Panama." *Canadian Journal of Political Science, 25*, pp. 435–462.

Szulc, T. (1965). *Dominican Diary*. New York: Dell.

— — —. (1959). *Twilight of the Tyrants*. New York: Henry Holt.

Tan, A. (1975). "Exposure to Discrepant Information and Effect of Three Coping Models." *Journalism Quarterly, 52*, pp. 678–684.

— — —. (1973). "A Role Theory: Dissonance Analysis of Message Content Preferences." *Journalism Quarterly, 50*, pp. 278–284.

Taras, D., and D. Gotlieb Taras. (1987). "The Canadian Media, Domestic Interest Groups, and Middle East Reporting: The Effects of Structural Bias." *International Journal, 42*, pp. 536–558.

Taylor, P. (1956). "The Guatemalan Affair: A Critique of United States Foreign Policy." *The American Political Science Review, 50*, pp. 787–806.

Thompson, A. (1988). "The News Media and International Relations: Experience and the Media Reality." *Canadian Journal of Communication, 13*, pp. 39–54.

The Times. (1983, June 9). "Grenada talks," p. 6.

Tomasek, R. (1959). "British Guiana: A Case Study of British Colonial Policy." *Political Science Quarterly, 74*, pp. 393–411.

Treaster, J. (1984a, December 9). "Grenadians get new leaders and a pipeline to U.S. aid." *The New York Times*, p. E6.

— — —. (1984b, December 3). "Voters in Grenada cast ballots today: First time since '76." *The New York Times*, p. A1.

Tuchman, G. (1978). *Making News: A Study in the Construction of Reality*. New York: Free Press.

Underwood, P. (1983). "Europe and the Middle East." In J. Merrill (Ed.), *Global Journalism: A Survey of the World's Mass Media*. New York: Longman.

United States, Senate, Committee on Foreign Relations. (1965). *Background Information Relating to the Dominican Republic.* Washington, DC: Government Printing Office.

Weaver, D. (1984). "Media Agenda-Setting and Public Opinion: Is There a Link?" In R. Bostrom, (Ed.), *Communication Yearbook,* Vol. 8. Beverly Hills, CA: Sage.

Weiner, M., and E. Ozbudan (Eds.). (1987). *Competitive Elections in Developing Countries.* Washington, DC: American Enterprise Institute.

Weinstein, M. (1988). *Uruguay: Democracy at the Crossroads.* Boulder, CO: Westview Press.

Wells, H. (1963). "The OAS and the Dominican Elections." *Orbis, 7,* pp. 131–137.

Wesson, R. (Ed.). (1982). *Communism in Central America and the Caribbean.* Stanford, CA: Hoover Institution Press.

Wiarda, H. (1965). "The Politics of Civil-Military Relations in the Dominican Republic." *Journal of Interamerican Studies, 7,* pp. 465–484.

Wilentz, A. (1989). *The Rainy Season: Haiti Since Duvalier.* New York: Simon and Schuster.

Wilson, L. (1966). "The Monroe Doctrine, Cold War Anachronism: Cuba and the Dominican Republic." *The Journal of Politics, 28,* pp. 322–346.

Wise, D., and T. Ross. (1964). *The Invisible Government.* New York: Random House.

Wissan, J. (1965). *Cuban Crisis as Reflected in the New York Press, 1895–1898.* New York: Octagon Books.

Woodward, R. (1985). *Central America: A Nation Divided.* 2nd ed. New York: Oxford University Press.

Young, O. 1967. *The Intermediaries: Third Parties in International Crises.* Princeton: Princeton University Press.

Zajonc, R. (1960). "The Concepts of Balance: Congruity and Dissonance." *Public Opinion Quarterly, 24,* pp. 280–296.

Zwerling, P., and C. Martin. (1985). *A New Kind of Revolution.* Westport, CT: Lawrence Hill & Co.